IN SICKNESS, IN HEALTH...AND IN JAIL

T0323202

Mel Jacob's work has appeared in the *Good Weekend*, *Sunday Life*, *Sydney Morning Herald*, *Brisbane Times* and *Kidspot*, and has been performed on Radio National and at the Museum of Contemporary Art and the Australian Museum. Her manuscript *The Mothers' Group* was shortlisted for the HarperCollins manuscript award and her short film, *Mischief*, was a finalist for the Riverina Short Festival (Comedy). She lives in the Blue Mountains with her husband and two kids. This is her debut book. Read more about Mel at www.meljacob.com.

IN SICKNESS, IN HEALTH... AND IN JAIL

WHAT HAPPENED WHEN MY HUSBAND UNEXPECTEDLY WENT TO PRISON FOR TWO YEARS

MEL JACOB

ALLEN&UNWIN

SYDNEY • MELBOURNE • AUCKLAND • LONDON

Certain names and details have been changed to protect the innocent and guilty alike.

Allen & Unwin
83 Alexander Street
Crows Nest NSW 2065
Australia
Phone: (61 2) 8425 0100
Email: info@allenandunwin.com
Web: www.allenandunwin.com

Cataloguing-in-Publication details are available
from the National Library of Australia
www.trove.nla.gov.au

ISBN 978 1 92526 731 0

Set in 11.25/17 pt Sabon Pro by Bookhouse, Sydney
Printed and bound in Australia by Griffin Press

10 9 8 7 6 5 4 3 2 1

For Patrick

And for our children

AUTHOR'S NOTE

Dear reader, though we may not yet had the privilege of meeting, thank you for taking the time to read my book. I believe that reading allows people to connect in a most holy union and perhaps learn a smidgen more about the wonder and absurdity of being human.

To write this account, I leaned on my journals, recollections, notes, court transcripts, research and conversations. Patrick's letters, as they appear in the book, have been used as a device to include the details he shared with me via written correspondence, phone calls and prison visitations. Names and identifying features of many people who appear in the book have been changed for legal reasons and to afford certain individuals their privacy. Any similarities to names that have been changed is purely coincidental.

PROLOGUE

'There was a lot of swearing at the table next to us today,' my son Nick said, tapping a rhythm on the car door.

'Quiet. You'll wake up your sister.' We were halfway home on our now regular six-hour journey from the middle of nowhere. Our lives had taken a disastrous detour and I felt sad, fragile and exhausted. Solitude was scarce, but it was rare for Nick to strike up a conversation.

'Yes, there was a lot of swearing,' I agreed. It was true; the family seated next to us possessed a more colourful vocabulary than Tony Soprano.

'It was mainly the F word.'

'You know that word?'

'Yeah, I've known it . . . like, for ages. Haven't heard it that much though. It was like, eff this, eff that, like they were having a festival of the F word—an F parade.'

Nick was right. The F bomb *had* been the most prominent expletive in the family's conversation. But there was also the C bomb and the S bomb. Collectively, this family detonated more bombs than the IRA.

Maybe the father had a perfectly good reason for calling his pre-teen daughter a 'stupid bitch', and maybe she had an even better reason for calling him a 'fucking motherfucker'? Maybe they were being ironic. Until I had walked a mile in their fluorescent sneakers, who was I to judge?

So I said to Nick, 'Well, I don't want you having any parades like that, or even saying that word, for that matter. You're seven.'

'I know,' he said wearily. 'They were using it so much that if they were on TV and they had to beep out the swearing, every second word would be beep.'

We laughed and then he went quiet. Very quiet.

'Can I ask you something? I don't want to get in trouble, I just want to know,' Nick said.

'Of course you can. You can ask me anything,' I said, delighted that, when faced with life's tough questions, he chose to come to me. I was his anchor as he navigated the storms of life.

'We've been doing the "ck" sound at school and I was wondering if you spell the F word F-U-C-K?'

I paused. What does a good parent do in this situation? Frown with disapproval, or be all calm and Zen and open-minded?

'Yes, that's how you spell it.' I said.

'Yes!' he said, triumphant.

I glanced back at him in the rear-view mirror. 'Anything else you want to know?' I asked tentatively, wanting to keep the doors of communication open.

'Is "bitch" B-I-T-C-H, like a witch with a broom or is it like "Which one is that?"'

'Witch with a broom.'

'Thought so.'

There followed a spelling bee, of sorts, as he spelled every expletive from *arse* to *shit*. Though I can't call it a definitive Mother of the Year moment, I took comfort in the fact that, with the exception of 'bastard', he spelled everything correctly.

My kids are enrolled in an alternative-education institution that prides itself on extending childhood by immersing students in nature, creativity and tie-dye. Their verbal skills were outstanding and, while I relished the thought of them casting aside electronic devices, rediscovering the joys of skipping and playing with toys fashioned out of wood, sometimes I wondered if they would ever learn to read and write.

'Maybe Martin should use swear words for your spelling list?' I suggested.

'Really?' Nick asked, excited.

'No.'

'Sarcasm,' he said. 'It would be funny, though. Imagine him standing out the front of the class, strumming his guitar: 'Year Two, the first spelling word is—'

'Don't!' I noticed that Lexie, my five year old, had woken up.

'I wasn't going to. Jeez!'

'I'm sorry you had to hear those words today,' I said, making eye contact with her.

'I don't mind,' she said, desperate to be recognised as a big girl.

'You wouldn't,' Nick said, poking her in the side.

'Mum, Nick's poking me.'

'Am not.'

'But we went to see Dad because . . . he's your dad and . . . when you love someone . . .' My voice trailed off. I didn't know if I still loved my husband or if I even knew what love was anymore. I was stuck. The same old question of why played over in my mind, like a broken record.

'Mum, I'm talking to you!' Lexie said.

'Sorry—'

'Tell us the story of how you and Dad met,' she said.

'You know the story,' I reminded her.

It was New Year's Eve 1996, a lifetime ago, and though I have no recollection of our first introduction, Patrick insists he saw me across a crowded room and knew I was the woman he was going to marry.

'At a party. Dad said he knew I was the one.'

'Did you think he was the one?' Lexie asked.

'No.'

'Why not?' asked Nick.

'I thought he was immature—'

'What's immature?' Lexie asked.

'Childish.'

'Like you, in other words,' Nick said to Lexie.

'Or you,' I countered.

'So why did you marry Dad?' Nick asked.

An excellent question. Indeed, one that I had been asking myself in the past couple of gruelling years. In the beginning, it had been a case of opposites attract, and I had embraced his differences with the curiosity and fascination of exploring a foreign country. I used to think we were a perfect fit. Like two pieces of a puzzle.

'Well, over time I got to know him and he made me laugh, and ... and I knew deep down that, that ... even though we were really different ... he was a *good* person.'

Without skipping a beat, Lexie said, 'He's not that good, he's in jail!'

PART I

'THE COURSE OF TRUE LOVE NEVER DID RUN SMOOTH.'

William Shakespeare, *A Midsummer Night's Dream*

ONE

'Muuuum, it's the police!' Nick yelled down the hall, in a tone that suggested this was a regular occurrence. But it was not. The police had never knocked on our front door. We lived in a nice house in a good neighbourhood in the Blue Mountains. We had a white picket fence. We had roses.

I'd seen enough late-night TV to know how this kind of scenario plays out. Two disparate detectives exchange witty banter and they argue, to add complexity and tension to the scene, but mostly because of mounting pressure to solve the case. They knock on doors. They ask questions. The people who have nothing to hide answer those questions, and the guilty ones either lawyer up or try to make a quick getaway over the neighbour's fence.

But there were not two detectives at my door—there were eight. Nick, who was five years old at the time, gave me no indication of this. Having answered the door, he simply returned to watching *SpongeBob SquarePants* with Lexie.

'Mrs Jacob?' the tallest non-uniformed police officer asked.

'Yes, I'm Mrs Jacob.' No one, not even my children's friends, calls me Mrs Jacob. I am always Mel, or Melissa.

'I'm Detective Cartwright and this is Officer Newman. We have a warrant to search the premises,' he said, brandishing a piece of paper.

'What is this regarding?'

'It is in relation to your husband, Patrick John Jacob.'

'Where is he? Is he okay?' A montage of car-accident footage flashed through my mind.

'He has been detained,' the detective said, as though that somehow clarified the situation.

'What does that mean?'

'It *means*,' condescended Detective Cartwright, who I quickly decided was the Bad Cop, 'he has been arrested.'

'Arrested? What's going on?' I could no more imagine him being arrested than I could imagine him being dressed as a woman.

'I'm afraid we are not at liberty to say.'

Now, call me gullible, but in the fourteen years I'd been married to Patrick, certain incidents had given me the impression he was not the slightest bit interested in criminal activity. These included, but were not limited to: refusing to copy a yoga DVD for my mother because doing so would be in clear breach of the Copyright Act; regularly giving our clothing and blankets away to the homeless; and demonstrating an intolerably self-righteous attitude towards people who have either broken the law or expressed a modicum of interest in breaking it.

Shocked as I was it did at least explain where Patrick was. He ran an online archery and camping store, and usually worked from home and sometimes from our warehouse in Penrith. He'd popped down there to tie up some loose ends before we left to go on our beach holiday. I cringed at the thought of the increasingly angry voicemail messages I had left for him, which the police had, no doubt, intercepted.

10.03: Hi Paddy. Not sure where you are. Give me a call. Love you.

10.27: Everything okay? Call me back. Love you.

10.58: Paddy, it's me. Can you get some lettuce? We may as well have lunch here now.

11.02: What are you doing? I thought you only had to label a few boxes for the courier? Call me.

11.23: Paddy, where ARE you? Lexie keeps pulling the clothes out of the suitcases. Are you couriering the things yourself? Call me, PLEASE?

11.49: Okay, I'm officially angry. If you were going to take this long you should have told me so I could have planned to do something more fun like STAB MYSELF IN THE EYE WITH A PENCIL!

12.19: WE'VE BEEN WAITING HERE FOR OVER FOUR HOURS!!!! Is this your idea of a joke? And THERE'S NO LETTUCE!!!

12.31: Just giving you the heads up, there's a high probability I will kill you when you do eventually decide to come home.

12.33: Are you okay?

'Would you mind using the side entrance?' I asked. Bad Cop and the shorter, friendlier of the two men—hereafter Good Cop—exchanged glances, as if trying to decide whether I was going to make a run for it.

'It's just that the kids are here . . . and they're young . . .'

The men were unresponsive and I was unsure if they were being deliberately obtuse.

'Could just you two come in the front, then?'

Good Cop agreed but then, as though our conversation had

not taken place, the entire group followed me past the children, who were still glued to the TV, and into the kitchen/dining room.

The policemen towered above and around me. Bad Cop began a spiel about various protocols and about whatever I said being used in a court of law, but I swatted his words away because all I could think about was the kids.

'I'm willing to cooperate but I'd like someone to pick up my kids,' I said meekly.

'We need to get the search underway and then there'll be plenty of time for that,' Bad Cop said and I noticed the rest of the men looking around the house. Taking it in. Looking for clues. Trying, I imagined, to figure out what sort of people we are. What made us tick? I wondered what they made of the pile of dirty dishes in the sink, or the fancy red kitchen appliances.

After what seemed like forever, but may have only been fifteen minutes, I asked about the kids and, once again, Bad Cop dismissed my request with a wave. The same request and hand-waving dismissal occurred several more times until I heard my, usually very unassertive, self say, '*I need someone to pick up my kids now!*'

Good Cop and Bad Cop shared another look, this time clearly saying, *She's not going to shut up about those kids,* and authorised me to use the phone. I called my brother-in-law Karl who only lived a few minutes away.

'Why are they still here?' Nick asked, suddenly furrow-browed and pensive. I had switched the TV off, so I had his undivided attention.

'The police just need to have a look around.'

'Are we still going to the beach?' Nick asked hopefully just as Karl walked in the front door.

'No, darling, you and Lex are going to Uncle Karl's place to play,' I said.

'Can't I stay here?' Nick asked as Lexie wrapped clothes from our open suitcases around her body.

'It's going to take them a while, so I'm going help them,' I said, trying to make it sound fun. Nick seemed to accept this. Karl ruffled Nick's hair and scooped Lexie into his arms and walked out the front door.

As he left, Nick turned back to me and, as if it was the most important thing in the world, said, 'Mum, do you think you can ask them to find my Sensei Wu sword?'

The search commenced downstairs in the converted garage/ Bermuda Triangle. Things vanished there, perhaps because of our messy/non-existent storage method, or because Patrick had unwisely labelled all our moving boxes 'Bric-a-brac'. Items of interest, mainly army memorabilia as Patrick was in the Army Reserves, were tagged and laid out on the driveway; neighbours were suddenly compelled to stand on front verandahs and check letterboxes to get a better vantage point for quite possibly the most exciting event that had ever occurred on our leafy suburban street.

The police videotaped the search. In front of the camera, they made clear, reasonable and professional statements. Away from the camera, some of them sidled up to me and in hushed, accusatory tones asked: 'Where is the stash?' 'Where are the containers of machine guns?'

Machine guns? Patrick was a registered gun owner, and hunted foxes and boars. He didn't have a machine gun. He did have an online archery and camping store and, in the past, there'd been miscommunications with customs about permits and the like. I assumed it had something to do with that.

Too shocked to speak, and with nothing to tell the police anyway, I stayed silent.

So they changed tack: 'Do you know what sort of man you're married to? Do you have any idea about his secret life? What he gets up to in that little warehouse of his?' As far as I knew, any spare time he had was spent with the kids or watching TV.

I'd always empathised with detectives in those late night-crime shows, understanding how, in the pursuit of justice, they might get a little hot-headed or heavy handed. How they would need to stretch the truth to see what response doing so elicits. But this felt different. I was outnumbered and they were so big and convinced that Patrick was some kind of criminal mastermind.

As the afternoon wore on and the search continued, dark and disturbing thoughts began to creep in. Did I really know my husband? *Was* he living a secret life? Earlier that day, I had thought he was Paddy: homebody, introvert, business owner, father. Sure, he had taken calculated risks to start his own business. But aside from that, Paddy had the most conservative and predictable sensibilities of anyone I'd ever met. It just didn't add up. And that was precisely when I began to descend into panic. The aforementioned qualities are always cited when neighbours of accused criminals are interviewed on TV. 'He was a quiet man, a great father,' they say, before the reporter reveals exclusive details of an underground meth lab or trophies from long-term missing persons.

'I need to go upstairs . . . to get the yellow pages . . .' I said to Bad Cop, in the hope I could find a solicitor or arrange to see Patrick at the police station. I was also dying to go to the toilet.

'I need to accompany you at *all* times,' Bad Cop said and so I held off going to the bathroom.

Once upstairs, I was outraged at the state of our bedroom. Clothes were spilling out of drawers. Stationery was strewn all over the desk, and books and magazines lay in various states of abandon. It looked like someone had given it a really good going-over. Only, the police hadn't been in there yet. This was the way we left our bedroom most mornings since we had children.

Out of the corner of my eye, I spied a negligee. Although it was partially camouflaged by the abundance of other clothing that hung from the end of our bed, I was mortified. Under the guise of making the bed, I slipped it under the quilt.

But Bad Cop saw me. 'And what do we have here?' he said, whipping back the quilt to reveal a black gossamer-thin slip. The swirled lace on the bustier seemed to stare up at us with bulging eyes. Bad Cop blushed.

I called the police station. I called my sister-in-law, Cathy—a former legal costings consultant. My phone calls didn't clarify anything. The police weren't able to disclose the nature of the charges because a search was being conducted, and I was informed that Patrick had sent away the lawyer his sister had arranged for him to see.

Nothing about the events of the day made any sense. It all felt like a hoax. And the mood of what was turning out to be the single worst day of my life was not sombre. It was farcical. No more so than when a group of teenagers in a passing car slowed to a stop and shouted, 'Here, Piggy, Piggy, Piggy!'

It was dark when the policemen left, and I fell onto the couch in a stupor. A loud knock followed.

'Have you seen any sunglasses?' Good Cop asked when I answered the door.

'Is this some sort of code? Are you trying to tell me something?'

'Yes, that I've lost my sunglasses. Can I come in?' he asked.

'What for?'

'To look for them.'

'Um, okay.' After a quick search, he left me with his card so I could contact him if I found them.

'Where's Dad?' Nick asked later that night, snuggled in our bed. I went to great lengths to explain that he was still helping the police with their investigation.

'What time are we going to the beach?' he asked, and I smiled at the non sequitur, explaining that our relaxing beach holiday would have to wait.

'Is it because of paperwork?' he then asked. At five, Nick was a delightful blend of innocence and insight. Like me, he still thought this situation was a simple misunderstanding.

'I think so. Tomorrow I'll meet Dad at court and we can explain it all to the judge—'

'"Tell it to the judge, Pinky,"' Lexie said, quoting a line from their favourite show, *SpongeBob SquarePants*, which, coincidentally, referred to a pink starfish named Patrick.

'It's not funny, Lexie,' Nick said.

'"Tell it to the judge, tell it to the judge."' At two and a half, Lexie had no idea what was going on.

'She's only little,' I reminded him.

'What will the judge do if Dad didn't do the right paperwork?' Nick asked, concerned. The kids were both familiar with this term and they played a game that involved scribbling on paper and passing it back and forth.

'"Tell it to the judge, tell it to the judge".'

'Lexie!' yelled Nick.

'I don't know, it's probably just a mistake. But whatever happens, we'll work it out,' I said, stroking Nick's beautiful little face.

He smiled and began chanting with Lexie. I knew if there was one thing I could count on, it was our kids' fervent love of chanting. I couldn't allow myself to think about what might happen in court the following day. I had to hold it together. So, to lighten the mood, I joined them: '"Tell it to the judge, tell it to the judge".'

When the kids had finally settled down and drifted off to sleep in our bed, I lay there thinking *what has he done?*

TWO

The next morning, as I waited outside the local courthouse in Western Sydney, I smoked half a packet of passive cigarettes, courtesy of one heavily pregnant woman and several tattooed men (one with a mohawk and two missing teeth).

'Do you know what time the courthouse opens?' I asked a woman on the periphery of the motley crew.

'You a lawyer?' she asked accusingly.

'No, no . . . my husband was . . . is . . . locked up,' I found myself whispering conspiratorially, and her demeanour softened.

'Nine, but they don't start until nine-thirty.'

'First time?' asked an older man in a shiny polyester suit and white sneakers.

I nodded.

'Thought so, you look like a dove in shit. First time's the hardest. Here, have one of these,' he said warmly, proffering a cigarette.

'I don't smoke,' I said. And if I sounded judgemental, it wasn't because I was a stranger to chain-smoking, tattooed hooligans. I'd grown up in a neighbourhood in the Hunter Valley filled with them. All my life choices had been so careful and considered because I was determined not to end up in that sort of environment. And yet there I was, outside the courthouse, with just about the roughest looking group of people you could imagine.

'I don't smoke . . . *anymore*, but thank you,' I added, forcing a smile.

When the courthouse opened, I joined the long queue that led to the airport-style security checkpoint.

'Place all your personal items, including the contents of your pockets, in a clear plastic box,' the guard repeated to each person, as though his voice were looped. And as the items moved along the conveyor belt, each person walked one by one through the doorframe-shaped metal detector, before a hand-held wand was waved over them.

Up until this point, I had responded to everything the way I usually do. I'd internalised it all, burying it deep down inside me. And every time a thought bubbled to the surface, I would squash it back down. Over the years I'd worked hard on denial. Prided myself on my ability to stay in control. To keep it together. But standing there it was increasingly hard to deny the truth. I was thirty-eight years old. I had left my job to care for our two children. And my husband was locked up.

Inside the courthouse, denial was the order of the day. Many people were dressed in tracksuits, cut-off T-shirts or leggings. Surprisingly, most of them were wearing bright, expensive sneakers. From the ankles down (with the exception of a few people who were not wearing any shoes), it looked like a commercial for Foot Locker. I'd have thought that if you had to go to court, either to defend yourself or to show your support for someone you care about, you might want to rethink the anarchy singlet or try to conceal the bare-breasted lady tattoo. I had spent the best part of the morning trying to find an outfit that looked conservative enough and I was beginning to feel overdressed.

The corridor of the local courthouse is L-shaped, acting as both a meeting place and an entrance for each courtroom. Dilapidated chairs lined the corridor. I slumped into one of them opposite a small reception area. A large woman approached.

'Are you in danger? Do you have an AVO or DVO out against anyone?' she asked.

'No,' I said, unconvincingly. She looked dubious but went away. Several minutes later, another large woman appeared. 'Do you have any concerns for your safety?' she asked.

I imagined for a moment how nice it would feel to be comforted by her voluminous flesh. 'No, I'm fine,' I said, rising to find a seat at the other end of the corridor.

At twenty past nine, a smattering of suited individuals emerged through the sea of leisurewear. Some of them had manila folders, and others, for reasons that escaped me, were pulling wheeled suitcases. The youngest of the group peeled off and headed straight for me. He had honey-coloured hair, a designer suit (extra-fancy with exposed stitching on the lapels) and pointed black shoes that were so shiny they looked like polished stone. He oozed charisma. This was Patrick's junior solicitor, Mark, the only available lawyer I had been able to find on the phone that morning at short notice.

I greeted him with a series of rapid-fire questions. He placed his hand on my shoulder, told me to relax.

'Your husband is *not* going to prison. Not for something like this,' he said and gave me a winning smile. 'We have a barrister who's very experienced in bail applications who'll be here a little later, so let's all calm down and find a meeting room and then we can talk.'

There was only one meeting room available. It was tiny, and furnished with a single chair and a collapsible graffiti-covered school desk. At his insistence I took the chair but after a few minutes we both realised it was not really working out. He was trying to take notes and my head was level with his crotch. So we switched. Mark could take notes with greater ease but his head was now level with my chest, and on the desk separating us there was a very large black-permanent-marker drawing of a penis.

'Does your husband have a criminal record?' Mark asked.

I was distracted by the drawing. It was so out of place in a room designed for lawyers to meet with clients. 'No, nothing . . . a parking ticket.' I remembered this because, despite my own numerous traffic infringements, I had yelled at Patrick for not being more careful.

Mark asked about our relationship, and I explained that there had been the requisite conflicts about raising children and finances but assured him that we have a good marriage.

'Do you own your own home?'

'No.'

He looked worried. 'So you're renting?'

'No, we haven't paid off our house yet.'

'So you have a mortgage?'

I nodded.

'This is good . . . this is good.'

Mark asked more questions about our children and where we lived and our occupations and I told him everything I could think of. Then it was my turn to ask the questions about the charges. Mark began with the good news. My fears of him being a drug baron or a serial killer were way off the mark. The bad news was that Patrick had been charged with a number of offences: possession of a slingshot, two crossbows (one assembled, one unassembled), one unregistered rifle, and three metallic objects that look like miniature crossbows. The truth hit me like a sharp, stinging slap. I felt bewildered. I felt confused.

'Are you sitting down?' Mark quipped, given there was no chair for me to sit on. He went on to explain that possession was not the only aspect of the charges. Patrick sold, or, in the case of the unregistered rifle, agreed to sell (which under state law is the same thing), the items to an undercover police officer.

I had no idea what to say, what to think. I was frozen, except for my hand which fell onto the desk for support, landing right next to the words 'This is fucked', which had been carved into the surface. I couldn't have put it better myself.

Midmorning, Susan, the barrister, arrived. Her raven-coloured hair was slicked back into a ponytail and her manner was alarmingly brusque. Unlike Mark, Susan's responses to my questions were measured. Without an in-depth study of the laws pertaining to the case, she could not and would not give me any definite answers. 'What I can do now is my very best to get him out on bail. Mounting a case while someone is in custody can be a very difficult and costly exercise.'

Susan instructed me to secure seats in the courtroom, along with Patrick's six siblings and various in-laws who had arrived to show their support, while she went downstairs to meet with Patrick.

In the courtroom another matter, involving a boy hitting his stepfather in the cranium with a broken bottle, was underway. As the magistrate discussed the feasibility of future cohabitation, two guards escorted Patrick into the courtroom. They motioned for him to sit in the dock, a small area surrounded by bulletproof glass.

I'd been with Patrick for so many years, I assumed I'd already seen him in every possible light. I'd seen him tongue-tied and nervous when he first asked me out. I'd experienced his raw vulnerability when he asked me to marry him. I had seen the way he held our newborn children, with such tenderness my heart ached. I had shared his sense of loss when he was retrenched. I'd seen him naked. I had seen him sick. I'd seen him on the toilet. And once, while holidaying in Vietnam, I had seen a combination of all three. But I had never seen him like this. Dressed in yesterday's work clothes. Unkempt. Unshaven. Handcuffed. Completely and utterly demoralised.

After the broken-bottle-to-the-cranium matter, the magistrate asked Patrick to stand as his charges were read out.

The prosecution opposed bail and my heart sank. I began to panic about how I was going to look after the kids, and run an importing business when multiplying single digits without a calculator presents a challenge for me.

But I needn't have worried. Susan was incredible, both her presence and rhetoric. For the sake of brevity I will not include the transcript, but her argument was as follows: Her client is thirty-six years old with an unblemished record. He is aware of both the seriousness and the magnitude of the charges brought before the court but does not pose a flight risk or danger to the community for the following reasons: he is a homeowner with a successful and legitimate business specialising in furniture, camping and archery, a sport recognised in the Olympic Games. Her client has been happily married for fourteen years (after the previous twenty-four hours I felt the compulsion to object but managed to restrain myself), and has two children aged five and two, about to start primary school and preschool respectively. And he is deeply entrenched in the community, both through his large family, who are present for the proceedings, and through his patronage of a large number of charities.

After a brief deliberation, the magistrate granted Patrick bail and explained that he was to report to Penrith Police Station three times a week.

Patrick's handcuffs were removed and he was released from custody. I was flooded with relief. I exhaled so deeply, it felt like I had been holding my breath the whole time, afraid that our life—our simple, ordinary life—would be torn apart.

But he was out. He was free. In the corridor, I hugged him urgently, unable to believe that I could now talk to him and touch him. And as quickly as the relief had arrived, it was replaced by such an acute spasm of anger I wanted to hit him. Why? Why? Why did he do this? What was he thinking?

Patrick walked to the reception counter at the far end of the courthouse in order to sign the bail paperwork. I didn't accompany him. I needed some breathing space. Some time to process what had happened. So I lingered in the corridor, wrestling with the relief and the fury.

'Are you in any danger?' a welfare woman asked.

'No,' I replied.

But when we get home, my husband will be.

THREE

'So, how are you?' Steph asked, pen poised. She was the psychologist I had started seeing the year before, when a dark cloud of depression had lingered a little too long. I'd always been able to manage my bouts of melancholy until I had children.

'Not so great, actually . . . my husband got arrested.' I watched as Steph, normally the epitome of professionalism, physically recoiled.

In the short time since the arrest, I had experienced a myriad of reactions. Patrick's best mate Simon had laughed hysterically before saying, 'You're shitting me right?' And Nick's kindergarten teacher fell into a tiny classroom chair, reeling from shock.

'Okay,' Steph said, drawing it out. 'What happened?'

'It was just an ordinary day . . .' I began. I'd read somewhere that it is common for people to begin their account of a trauma that way. It's not that what came before was so ordinary, it's that what followed was so unexpected and so extraordinary that I was grappling for a way to distinguish between the before and the after.

I went through the whole police raid, courthouse shebang, and Steph took notes. Unlike the hairy-upper-lipped, orthopaedic-shod variety of psychologist I'd seen in the past, Steph was decidedly stylish. She wore figure-hugging dresses and stiletto heels, and a lot of expensive jewellery. Sometimes her impeccable appearance accentuated the tangled mess that was my life.

'And how are *you*?' Steph asked in her penetrating, unnerving way.

'I'm okay, still shell-shocked . . . I know it probably sounds clichéd but I just never thought . . . I didn't think that's who he was.'

'Who did you think he was?' Steph asked, smoothing the bottom of her charcoal dress.

'Someone who doesn't sell crossbows to undercover police officers,' I said, imagining Steph's perfect, professional, husband.

She looked up and off to one side, as if trying to recall what I had previously told her about my husband of fourteen years. 'Tell me about . . . Patrick.'

'Apparently, we look alike. When we got married, friends joked that we only took up one side of the church.'

Steph laughed. I liked that she got me. Other psychologists I had seen acted like their sense of humour had been extracted at graduation.

'So, you look alike. Are you the same in other ways?' Steph straightened her long legs, crossing them at the ankles.

'We have the same sense of humour, and the same taste in films and TV shows . . . except for shoot'em-up movies . . . but we're different, very different,' I said.

'How so?'

'He's currently on bail,' I said, joking, but mainly to buy myself some time. It's hard to sum up someone in a few short sentences. I believe that all of us are creatures of contradiction, and I had spent the past fifteen years getting to know all the nuances, depths and facets of Patrick, and now I felt like I didn't know the first thing about him. While Steph appreciated my sense of humour, she was astute enough to know when I trying to use it as a defence mechanism.

'And?'

'He's decisive and logical, and I come at things on a more emotional and intuitive level. He's neat. I'm messy. I love words, he's more a numbers person—' But it all sounded so general, so *Men Are from Mars, Women Are from Venus* and didn't come close to explaining who we really are.

I couldn't think of what else to say and Steph let me sit there in silence. I'm not sure if it was a strategy of hers but it was agony. She could see that I was struggling, and just when it got to the point I couldn't bear it anymore, she said, 'What was he like when you first met?'

I took a long sip of tea.

We met sixteen years ago. Unlike Patrick's version, I have no recollection of us meeting at that New Year's party in Balmain, but I distinctly recall the first time I noticed him, because I was mortified. I'd been invited by mutual friends from church to a barbecue in Centennial Park. I arrived to find, right next to the picnic blankets, a writhing mass of flailing limbs. A group of consenting male adults were wrestling. In public. When all the groaning and pleas for mercy finally ended, I noticed one man stand up. His previously arctic-white T-shirt was now covered in grass stains and had a large rip on the front. He walked towards me, having collected his water bottle from the rug and then promptly pouring it over his head. It did not escape my attention that his very-well-defined abdominal muscles were visible through his shirt. Not to mention his dark brown hair and eyes, and his unblemished olive skin. He was damn sexy.

But I was not the slightest bit interested in grown men who wrestled in parks. Now far from my hometown, I had tried to cultivate an air of sophistication. As such, my main hobbies were being pretentious, talking about pretentious things and reading pretentious books. I knew that I was going to end up with a charming, bookish intellectual. I hadn't met him yet but I imagined him to have black horn-rimmed glasses, a worn leather satchel and a delightful English accent. Our relationship would have all the hallmarks of other romances: the electric first kiss, the candlelit dinners, the walks on the beach during which he could explain to me the works of James Joyce and Gertrude Stein, and other writers that I only pretended to understand.

After the barbecue some friends I was with were going to see a movie. 'The book will be much better,' I interjected. And this man in a grass-stained, ripped T-shirt—whose name I'd since learned was Patrick—said 'Bring the book along.' The large group laughed and I joined in, even though I felt the slightest bit humiliated. His gaze lingered a little too long, and then he softly brushed my wrist, which caused the teensiest stir in me.

'Sorry, but it was worth it,' he said.

'Worth it?'

'To see you smile.'

'I smile,' I said defensively. But I'd been told from a number of reliable sources that I rarely ever did. I was far too earnest.

'You are now,' and he held my gaze.

There is no question that when I first met Patrick, I thought he was handsome. He had defined cheekbones and full lips, and energy, charisma. But, again, he was definitely not my type.

I didn't go to the movies that afternoon but I did see him over the course of the summer at events and parties when our different social groups collided. Patrick rarely ever drinks alcohol, but after hearing me bragging at a swanky party in Woollahra about the characteristics of a particular wine, he swilled some of it in a glass, sniffed ostentatiously and said, 'I can detect grapes, fermentation, alcohol . . . it's unoaked but with an oak-barrel flavour, bland but spicy . . .' On another occasion, he switched some very expensive wine with cheap vino, and I was forced to concede that I didn't actually know the first thing about wine. When it came to wine—or most other things, for that matter—I liked, bought and did what everybody else told me to.

Patrick, on the other hand, was refreshingly different. He treated everyone, regardless of wealth or status, in exactly the same way. Mind you, it was with a callous disregard for social etiquette but still . . . he was himself and he made no apologies for that. He was creative. A lateral thinker with a sharp mind for business. And even though he preferred movies to books, and didn't particularly like going to the theatre, or drinking fancy-pants wine, there was something about him that I found completely irresistible. He made me laugh, more than anyone I had ever met. With him I was lighter, sunnier, more effervescent, than I was on my own.

And somehow we fell deeply, inexplicably, in love.

In that warm glow of new love, I remember, every new fact felt like a rare archaeological discovery. He loves Johnny Cash. Hates coriander. This was when mobile phones were a rarity, and I literally sat by the phone waiting for him to call, just so I could hear his voice.

There in Steph's office, as I sipped my peppermint tea and thought about the beginnings of my relationship with Patrick, I remembered how romantic he used to be. He bought flowers, penned rhyming poems, and once, knowing that every time I opened a Turkish Delight chocolate bar I wished for a Willy Wonka golden ticket, he colluded with a newsagent and planted one inside said bar. The prize: a dinner date with him.

But that was a lifetime ago. When we were in the throes of young love. When we could stay up late without being tired, before the problems of real life began to seep in. Before financial struggles, and one heartbreaking miscarriage, and before Patrick decided that he wanted to live hand-to-mouth with a Papuan tribe, and I wanted to buy an enormous house filled with designer couches and decorative cushions.

It was hard to believe that our relationship had once been so romantic and so spontaneous. And I longed for the spontaneity. No sooner did the thought enter my mind than I realised that our busy-parent lives were, in fact, very spontaneous. But it was the cleaning-up-vomit, looking-for-escaped-guinea-pig form of spontaneity, not the romantic kind.

I thought of my life with Patrick as being fairly predictable. I thought I knew everything about him. I knew that he woke most mornings at a quarter past seven. And that he had cornflakes with three heaped spoonfuls of sugar for breakfast. And that he preferred baths and liked to drip dry in front of the heater. And that his saddest memories were to do with his father leaving his mother. And that he genuinely loved playing games with the kids, primarily because he was a big kid himself. And then he went and got himself arrested, and it felt as if a giant fissure had formed in our relationship.

'How did Patrick explain himself to you?' Steph asked, elegantly sipping her water with lemon.

'He tried . . . he said he'd purchased slingshots from a couple of different toy and fishing stores. He'd played with them as a child and assumed they were legal provided they were called bait throwers.'

'And the crossbows . . . ? Because they're not legal, are they?' Steph asked, jotting something down in her notebook.

'In New South Wales they're legal if unassembled,' I said.

'That doesn't make a lot of sense,' she replied, writing this point down in her diary.

'When Patrick told me I didn't believe him, so I looked it up myself, and he also showed me emails to that effect from Customs.' It was not surprising that Steph found it confusing, because so did I.

'And he sold one unassembled one and one assembled?' Steph clarified.

'Yes.'

'And the unregistered rifle?' she asked.

'It was a gift from an old school friend, Clogs. He found it in a container on his uncle's farm, and left it in the warehouse as a gift because he owed Patrick some money, knew he'd always wanted that model. Patrick said it was old and rusty, didn't know if it even worked. And then it became his problem. I know that's not an excuse . . .'

'Did he explain why he did it?' Steph asked.

'That's the first thing I asked him, "Why?" He'd told me he said no at first, but the undercover cop, Alex, kept calling. Said he was from Adelaide, where crossbows are legal, and that he was a licensed gun owner. After Patrick was released on bail we sat in the car in the car park across from the court and I said, "How could you do this?" And his head fell onto the dashboard. "I don't know. I don't know."'

My sessions with Steph didn't usually follow a Vesuvian format. And as I sat there in her office, I felt patches of emotion: a flash of anger here, a pang of a sadness there and a feeling of heavy disappointment in my chest. Mainly, I just felt numb. It felt as though most of my emotions had been gouged out of me and I watched everything around me with a detached and distant awareness.

FOUR

When I think back to the period following Patrick's arrest to his eventual incarceration, I think of a documentary about nuclear explosions I once saw. There's the direct impact of the blast, the obvious and immediate damage caused by thermal radiation. And then there's the fallout—the tiny particles projected into the atmosphere and carried by the elements. On a micro level, on an emotional level, that's what it felt like to me—a nuclear explosion.

There was the initial shock of the arrest, followed by the demanding conditions of bail and the exorbitant legal costs. Then there was the emotional fallout of living with the charges. The uncertainty that contaminated our life in ways we could never have imagined. But first we had to deal with the impact of the blast.

'I was told that you were belligerent and refused representation,' said Amar, a short, stocky man with thick, bushy eyebrows. After several meetings with Mark, it became clear that while his charm alleviated our worst fears, his knowledge of the law was sketchy. Amar was the solicitor Patrick's sister Cathy had sent to the police station following his one phone call.

'I told the detectives I wanted a solicitor, you can check the transcript,' Patrick insisted.

'I don't doubt you,' Amar said. 'The police are well versed in these kind of tactics.' I was shocked. 'If I represent you, if I agree to represent you, you do not, under any circumstances, talk to the police. If they ask you the time, if they ask what the weather is like outside, you do not say a single word. Am I clear?'

Patrick nodded, and I looked over at a stack of manila folders leaning precariously against the wall.

'Now, I need to know exactly what happened,' Amar said.

Patrick repeated the whole story. That Alex, a customer who purported to be a licensed gun owner from South Australia, purchased a slingshot and ball bearings. After that, he contacted Patrick numerous times and, in January, Patrick sold him an unassembled crossbow and, shortly afterwards, an assembled one.

'Told me he was from Adelaide, where they're legal . . . and I knew unassembled crossbows were legal because I had emails from Customs. When he wanted an assembled one I told him no, and then . . . then . . . I just . . .' Patrick trailed off, sounding defeated.

'It's entrapment,' Amar said and I felt a sprig of hope that finally there was a logical explanation for everything. 'But that's not a legal defense,' he continued. 'The police are allowed to do that, for weapons and drugs and prostitution. We don't have to worry about those, do we?'

'No,' said Patrick, perched awkwardly on the edge of his chair.

My husband, not me, had committed the crime but sitting next to him under Amar's scrutiny, I also felt the shame of his confession. The lawyer's office was on the second floor of a high rise overlooking a park. Through a window I could see small brown birds on a branch outside and I wished that I could fly out of the room and join them.

Amar tapped a pencil on the desk, bringing my attention back to the room.

'I knew it was wrong . . . to sell, or even to have, the rifle. A mate had left it there for me. In fact, it had been hidden for weeks there, so he says, and I made an appointment to register it, and I had to cancel . . . So this man, Alex, says he's licensed and I figured that he could register it but I was in two minds, so I said, "A thousand dollars," thinking he wouldn't go for it. But he did, he just had to go to the ATM to get more money.'

I felt a tightening in my stomach.

'It was only after he left,' Patrick continued, 'that I realised it didn't make sense that a licensed owner would pay way above market value for a rusty piece of junk. So I called him and reneged, and told him not to come back.'

'That is irrelevant, Mr Jacob,' Amar said sternly. 'You agreed to the sale, it was recorded on a wire and that's all they need for a conviction.'

I felt so conflicted. On the one hand, I was, and am, so glad Australia has tough gun laws. The low gun-crime statistics reflected their efficacy. On the other, Patrick was my husband and the father of my children, and I worried about what the laws would mean for him. For us.

'Now, the metallic items . . . what are they?' Amar asked.

'Movie props. A friend of a friend was working on an independent film and thought I might like to display them in the archery shop,' Patrick said.

'Do they work?'

'I dunno, I wouldn't have thought so. They're tiny, only about twenty centimetres.'

Amar moved the pencil up to his lips and twisted it around, thinking.

'What I don't understand,' Patrick said, and my ears pricked up because it rare for him to admit he didn't know something, 'is why an undercover cop was investigating me in the first place?'

Amar used the pencil to push his glasses frames closer to his eyes. 'That is a very good question, and it wasn't just one undercover cop, there was an entire task force devoted to you. Is there something you are not telling me, Mr Jacob, or anyone who has a gripe against you?'

'There's this guy whose archery shop closed down shortly after I launched my online shop. He started leaving me all these abusive emails and voicemails and I heard from other suppliers he was telling everyone I was selling illegal stuff.'

'You do realise that slingshots are illegal?' Amar asked, leaning back in his chair which let out a small hiss.

'I do now,' Patrick said.

Patrick's explanation provided a sliver of context but I still found it so hard to understand why he had done it. I realise that we are very different, and I have no interest in hunting and guns, and he'd explained to me that there's a fair amount of bravado surrounding men and weapons. Maybe Patrick had been shooting his mouth off to impress the undercover cop. I had no idea.

'One thing's for sure,' Amar said, 'whether it was from an informant or not, the police have invested a lot of money and resources in this operation, because they were looking for a big fish.'

It was clear that Patrick was no big fish but he'd been on a slippery slope. And when the opportunity presented itself, in the heat of the moment, he chose to break the law. No matter how you looked at it, he was no Andy Dufresne and this was no *Shawshank Redemption*.

Amar agreed to represent Patrick. On face value, he could see no way around the slingshot and firearm charges, and recommended entering a guilty plea. As for the other charges, relating to the crossbows, Amar believed Patrick had an excellent chance of acquittal. But that meant going to trial.

FIVE

In the movies, court cases are exciting. The lawyers look like Paul Newman or Matthew McConaughey, and, sure, they have their struggles with alcoholism and womanising, but their main problem seems to be living and breathing their cases. The courtroom comes alive with their impassioned outbursts and witty antics. In real life, being in court is right up there with watching paint dry.

On the first day of court proceedings Patrick's family all came along to show their support.

'You must be so proud . . . following in his father's footsteps,' one solicitor remarked to Patrick as he stood there surrounded by his extended family. We were in the corridor waiting for the courtroom to open and Patrick's father, a retired solicitor, had began to chat with some of his former colleagues. They thought that Patrick, in his fancy suit and tie and surrounded by his family, was there for his first big case. Neither Patrick nor his father corrected this mistake, but over the course of the day it became apparent that Patrick was in fact on the other side of the law and they quietly sauntered away.

I naively thought the matter would be resolved promptly. At worst, I thought, it might drag on for a couple of months but I'd hoped it would all be resolved in one day, as had happened with the bail hearing. If I had known that it was going to drag on for almost two years, I don't know if I would have had the strength to stay. But, like many difficult things in life, the magnitude of the mess unfolded bit by bit.

For months, our lives hung in limbo, travel plans were halted, money haemorrhaged from our account like blood from a gunshot wound, and the stress increased like a pressure cooker.

And all we could do was wait.

'What are you doing?' my sister-in-law Cathy asked as we waited in the courthouse corridor one day.

'Waiting for Godot,' I replied.

'Who?'

'Never mind.'

The pace of our lives was never more reminiscent of an absurdist play than during the long days in court. But instead of wandering around a barren landscape, or being buried up to our necks in sand, we waited. Shuffling from room to room, watching people in funny wigs use big words, periodically throwing buckets of money out the window, questioning our existence and trying to invent ways to amuse ourselves.

One day, we waited in the corridor with Patrick's best mate, Simon. It had been two months since the initial arrest and the strain was taking its toll. My face was ravaged from all the worry and dark circles had become permanent fixtures under my eyes. Simon, who is from a good middle-class family, was shocked to see so many colourful and obviously underprivileged people in one place.

'Look on the bright side, Mel,' he said. 'You've got a full set of teeth. You own a pair of shoes! They might not be the latest Nike

Air Mags, but they're not bad.' And I laughed despite myself; we all did.

'Come on, guys, cheer up,' Simon said, during another long day in court. 'There're huge business opportunities staring you in the face.'

'Here?' Patrick asked.

'Shoe and suit hire, ten bucks a pop. Or, if you want to make serious money set up a dentist in one of those rooms. That's the third person I've seen today with no teeth!'

Simon's comments amplified the tragedy of the courthouse. It didn't feel like a place of justice. It felt like a home for the destitute. A circuitous route for those trapped in a cycle of crime and poverty. Or was it poverty and crime? Some of those faces will be etched in my mind forever. Toddlers running down the courthouse corridor, trying to get even a smidgen of attention from their drug-addicted parents. A battered and bruised woman trying to find the courage to testify in court, afraid that her mere presence would cost her life.

Of all the tragic things we witnessed at the courthouse the most heartbreaking was a boy who only looked fourteen, though he must have been older, appearing at court wearing only a pair of old shorts and a singlet. His court-appointed lawyer requested that the magistrate wait until his mother presented before hearing the matter. The magistrate obliged, and we all waited and waited until well after lunch but his mother never showed.

And it wasn't just the days in court that wore us down; it was the ongoing dealings with the police. The first time Patrick reported for bail, he was told to come back because the systems were down. Under normal circumstances, he probably wouldn't have thought anything of it, only the junkie he'd been locked up with had advised him to be wary of the police: 'Watch out for the cops, mate. They make shit up, like saying the printer's broken, or the system's down, so you don't make bail.'

As a result of his arrest, all of Patrick's registered firearms were confiscated, except for one that was stored at a friend's farm near Tamworth. In order to retrieve the gun, the detectives came to see Patrick at our home in Blaxland, in the Blue Mountains. They served the documents and then, for no reason we could fathom, stood on our balcony for roughly twenty minutes and then sat outside in their car for close to an hour.

'Why are they still here?' Nick kept asking. And then later, 'Have you done the right paperwork, Dad? Are you sure, because they're still out there.'

Patrick had broken the law and we both knew there had to be consequences but, as far as I could see, he was reporting for bail, they'd served the documents and they had no reason to be out the front of our house.

In April 2011, three months after the arrest, things reached breaking point. Patrick applied for a bail variation in order for us to take the eight-night holiday in Coffs Harbour we had already booked and paid for. A procedure that, incidentally, cost more than the holiday itself, but we figured it was money well spent. We needed a break. The bail variation was granted, and Patrick was instructed to report to Coffs Harbour police station instead of Penrith.

It rained for most of the time we were away, so we didn't get to go to the beach. Patrick was preoccupied and unhappy. At the end of the first week, I found him digging through our recently dried laundry.

'What are you doing?'

'Nothing.'

I wasn't buying it. 'What's wrong? You've been moping around like it's the end of the world.'

'I've got three "Failed to reports",' he said.

This was serious. It meant that he could be taken into custody on remand, awaiting his trial.

'What? Aren't you meant to go to the police station?'

'I did, I have and they said they don't know anything about it. They told me to piss off.'

'Did you ask to speak to the . . . the person in charge?'

'Yeah. He told me to eff off.'

'No way.'

'I asked them to give me a receipt to say I was there, which they did, but it's not a bail receipt, and now it's been through the wash and you can't even read it.'

The stress of the situation was making us miserable. It was Easter Sunday. We still had another night left but we decided to head home early via Coffs Harbour police station. A phone call to Penrith station confirmed Patrick's 'Failed to report' status so, in desperation, all four of us went inside.

'And what can we do for this lovely family?' the officer on duty asked, offering Nick and Lexie Easter eggs. We explained the bail-variation situation and he promptly sorted it out.

In the months following Patrick's arrest, I could see that he was not himself. He was withdrawn, anxious and uncommunicative. I knew he was burdened by the financial and emotional consequences of his actions. Whenever I woke in the middle of the night, I would find him hunched over his computer, buried in spreadsheets. I told myself that it was his way of coping, of trying to maintain some semblance of control, when everything else in our lives wavered in uncertainty.

I felt the burden too. The legal costs were snowballing. Patrick was barely speaking to me. Though most of the time the kids seemed happy and well adjusted, their behavior was deteriorating; Nick was very anxious about Patrick's bail requirements and often worried about money. And Lexie was even more fiery than usual.

At times I felt worried, and even resentful, about the way our life had become unhinged, but mostly I felt an enormous amount of pressure to stay in control. 'Just a little longer,' I kept telling myself. And in the rare moments when I felt a phantom pain of sadness or anger, I pushed it further and further down inside of me.

Until one cold July afternoon when I received a call on my mobile phone. I was in Nick's room, putting his clothes away.

'Mrs Jacob, it's Naomi . . . Patrick's psychologist.'

'Oh, yes, hi,' I said, holding the phone to my ear as I tried to make some space in Nick's unruly drawers. 'He's not here at the moment. Did he miss an appointment?'

'No,' and she paused for an extended period of time. 'It's not usual protocol for a psychologist to break client confidentiality, unless there are concerns about self-harm.'

'Self-harm?'

'I don't want to alarm you,' she said but it was a little late for that. 'This is hard for you, I understand, but I need to disclose to you that Patrick made a noose and tied it to a secure anchor point . . . with the intention of . . . taking his life.'

It felt like I had been winded. I was beside myself with worry for the kids but mostly I was angry with myself. My maternal grandfather and my uncle had committed suicide. I should have known. How could I not have seen the signs? Patrick had been so withdrawn. So lifeless. He didn't talk to me. He didn't touch me. I couldn't remember the last time he reached across in bed at night to rest the palm of his hand on my lower back like he normally did.

I slid down to the floor, cradling Nick's clothes, and I cried. But almost as quickly as I started crying, I stopped. I couldn't fall apart now. I had to be stoic. I had to be strong. I had to put on a brave face.

It felt like an entire year passed as I waited for Patrick to arrive home that afternoon. When he did, we talked, really talked, for the first time in months. Tearfully, he confessed to me that he had been thinking that if he removed himself from the situation, everything would be resolved. He also figured that his life insurance—a staggering seven-figure sum I had had no idea about—would be more than enough to provide for the family in his absence. I was distraught.

Patrick assured me that the psychologist had spent hours explaining the flaws in his thinking. Suicide would create a multitude of problems, almost guaranteeing that each of our children would spend their adulthood on a therapist's couch, trying to deal with the irrevocable loss. Paddy promised that he no longer felt that way and that if any feelings like that returned, he would reach out for help. His assurances made me feel a little better but I still felt the crushing responsibility of having to hold the family together.

Weeks turned into months until, finally, it was November 2011 and time for the committal hearing we had been anticipating for so long. The hearing was tedious, because of the wordy and technical arguments. Essentially, the case rested on whether a crossbow is considered a crossbow if unassembled, and whether or not the metallic items were considered to be crossbows.

Patrick had managed to track down the director of the independent film the metallic items were used for. The director admitted that they were made for the film but was not willing to become involved in the case, for fear of being prosecuted. Amar and Susan were confident this didn't matter. The law was clear about unassembled crossbows, and the metallic items didn't technically fit the definition of a crossbow because the bow was not fitted transversely to the stock.

Our legal team was right. The magistrate dismissed the charges of ongoing sales of prohibited weapons, and the charges relating to the possession and sale of the crossbows. Of course, there was still the sentencing for the charges relating to the slingshot and the firearm, but they did not carry the weight of the charge relating to the sale of prohibited weapons.

Finally, there was light at the end of the tunnel. I could almost taste our unshackled future. We could make plans, travel. And I could finally sink my teeth into writing the novel that had been put on hold so many times.

And then, like some cruel joke, we received the news that the Director of Public Prosecutions had lodged an appeal and Patrick would have to stand trial in the District Court.

SIX

'It's Pommery,' Amar said to Susan, with a dark look. Panic flickered across her face.

'What's wrong?' I asked, standing up from my seat in the central corridor of the courthouse.

Susan immediately regained her composure, assuring us that when it came to drawing a judge, we could have done a lot worse. But when the proceedings in the District Court began, it was obvious why Amar and Susan were so alarmed.

As Pommery is a judge, I will make my description as delicate as possible. To say that his demeanour was cantankerous or surly does not paint the picture vividly enough. He looked like a man who had discovered his wife cheating, crashed his car, and arrived at work to sit on his haemorrhoids all day.

That day was a formality and the first of many more. It wasn't until September 2012, six months later and twenty months after the initial arrest, that the trial was held. And when that day finally came, it was clear that things were not going well.

We gathered in one of the small meeting rooms to regroup. Dealing with a lawyer is not dissimilar to seeing a doctor. There's a fair amount of prestige associated with their profession and they have spent years studying their respective fields. You go to see a doctor or a lawyer because you need their expertise. But it's more than that—it's a relationship. Similar to a doctor's bedside manner, a lawyer's disposition can impact on the nature of this relationship. In meetings at their respective office and chambers, Amar and Susan had assured both of us that they were more than happy to answer questions, but sometimes their tone and body language suggested otherwise. At times, they seemed so inert and uninterested that I wanted to reach across the desk and check for a pulse. But what really irked me were the eye rolls, the long sighs, the alternating abrupt and condescending tones that seemed so endemic to the profession. I began to suspect that undergraduates were required to complete a hubris module on how to appropriately belittle clients.

In the meeting room, Susan spoke in long, Latin-infused sentences and I didn't have the faintest idea what she was talking about. 'Would you mind rephrasing that?' I asked in one of our meetings, craning my neck up to look at her. Amar looked at me with all the disdain he could muster, and Susan just looked disappointed. I had studied Latin at school, but the finer points of the state's prohibited weapons schedule was not covered in the life and times of Caecilius. And, given that I had not studied law and was not a lawyer, I wouldn't have thought it would come as a great surprise. How much did they know about seventeenth-century Restoration comedy? Once again, I felt small and stupid.

Susan rephrased her wordy Latin speech into terms we could understand, explaining that although the atmosphere in the courtroom may have seemed hostile, it wasn't necessarily indicative of the judgement. She was still confident that Patrick would not be found guilty in regard to the metallic items, given they did not meet the definition of a crossbow because the bow was not fitted transversely to the stock. And that as one of the crossbows remained unassembled, he could not be not be found guilty because the weapons schedule stated that crossbows needed to be assembled.

But we were all blindsided. In a verdict that floored our legal team, Patrick was found guilty of all the charges.

'It's not over,' Susan said, as we gathered once again in the central corridor. She explained that the sentence wouldn't be decided until the end of January 2013. Three months away. 'There are still the character references and the sentencing report from parole.'

So we set to work, requesting as many character references as we could from friends and colleagues, and charities Patrick had been involved with. It's a humbling thing having to ask for a character reference for court. Not only does it need to outline the person's positive characteristics, it needs to demonstrate an understanding of the charges and the accused's attitude towards them.

Months passed slowly as we waited to find out what the punishment would be. Would he be fined, required to serve community service, or be on home detention? Or would our worst fears be realised and Patrick be sent to prison?

At the end of December Patrick and I waited in the foyer of the local community corrections office. I was wearing a black woollen suit and black high heels, like a mourning widow. It was a sweltering summer day and the office air conditioning had not been switched on. Beads of sweat gathered on my forehead and ran down the inside of my camisole. The wool felt thick and scratchy, but I had worn the suit because I wanted to make a good impression.

Finally, the door next to the reception counter opened, and a man wearing a singlet, no shoes, and a bold tattoo stating 'FUCK THE POLICE' emerged. I had spent hours applying concealer to the dark shadows under my eyes and straightening my wavy hair, and was wearing what felt like a hairshirt, and here was this man. It was all I could do not to follow him to the street and offer him my scarf. But seeing that man, part of me relaxed. I mean, if that's who we were up against, we had to be in with a good chance. Right?

'Patrick was the first person to wear a suit to this office and you are the second,' said Karlene by way of introduction. She seemed nervous, and covered her mouth with her left palm when she spoke.

She led Patrick and me to another office off the hall that adjoined the waiting room.

'I'm sure Patrick has told you about his meetings,' Karlene said after she sat down, and I looked at Patrick, who was seated in the office chair next to me. 'We are required to write a presentencing report that the judge will read and take into consideration before handing down a sentence.' I nodded, noticing the poster on the wall near Karlene's head. It depicted a small cartoon sheep climbing a hill a distance away from the crowd of other sheep. 'Don't follow the crowd,' cautioned the bold letters. Patrick put his hand on mine, reassuringly.

'Talking to a spouse, when that's possible,' Karlene said, and then emitted a laugh so brief and so out of place it resembled a sound effect, 'can create a fuller picture and assist us in writing the report.' When she finished speaking, she moved her hand from her mouth to the desk. Karlene's mannerisms were making me even more nervous than I already was.

'Do you understand the nature of his charges?' she asked, once again moving her hand to her mouth, and I proceeded to explain the charges as I had done so many times before.

'You'd be surprised how many partners don't know the full story,' she said when I'd finished.

Karlene asked Patrick to leave the room for the next part of the interview. 'The following questions are the types of questions we ask anyone in this situation,' she said.

'Okay.'

'Now, Melissa,' she began, 'has Patrick ever abused you in a physical, emotional or sexual way?'

'No,' I replied, thinking of him sitting out in the waiting room.

'Have you ever known him to use violence to respond to a situation?'

'No, never,' I said.

'Did he threaten or intimidate you in relation to today's interview or the responses you might give?'

'No,' I said, unnerved by the questions. I knew Karlene was just doing her job, and it was a positive thing that victims of domestic violence could get support from the department, but it felt surreal suddenly to be asked those questions about Patrick. For all his faults, domestic violence was not one of them. In fact, it frustrated me no end that he wasn't more assertive or confrontational. 'Tell them, say something,' I would tell him, frustrated at his passivity in many situations.

'Does he have any addictions?' she asked hopefully. 'Alcohol, marijuana, gambling?'

'No.'

'Shame,' Karlene said, shaking her head from side to side. And I recall thinking what a crazy, upside-down system it had to be for an addiction to be considered an advantage. 'Sometimes problems with addiction can lead to more lenient or flexible sentences.' Karlene scribbled some notes and flicked through the stapled booklet she had been writing in. 'Would Patrick be prepared to do community service?'

'Absolutely. And if for some unlikely reason he didn't, I would drag him down there and make him spike that rubbish.'

'We need more spouses like you.'

I smiled, relaxing into the interview.

'In my line of work, it's rare to meet someone as polite and punctual as Patrick. And he's taken every piece of my advice on board. He's so concerned about how his actions will impact you and the children.'

'He's prepared to do anything to stay out of prison,' I said.

At that Karlene put her pen down, dropped the hand that had been covering the large gap between her two front teeth and said, 'He's not going to prison, I'd bet money on it.'

SEVEN

For two years we had pivoted around the sentencing like horses tethered in a pen. The pace had been fast and slow, rough and rigorous. I had spent so much time thinking about the judgement that when 28 January 2013 finally arrived and we fronted up to the courthouse, everything seemed dull and anticlimactic. It was the same security checkpoint, the same grey–blue carpet with frayed rows that reminded me of ploughed fields. The same welfare ladies. The same lawyers.

In the weeks leading up to the sentencing, friends and family had told me how absurd it was that I was even entertaining the notion of Patrick going to prison. 'It's not like he murdered anyone. He's not a child molester,' people said. For two years I'd heard almost nothing else. Everyone seems to rank crimes beginning with the worst: murder, paedophilia, rape, down to what, depending on their own life experience, they considered to be trifling. At first, I didn't give a lot of credence to these opinions because, at the end of the day, their advice was free and was obviously coloured by their friendship with us. And Patrick might not have been charged with murder, but it's not like he had been jaywalking either. He had already pleaded guilty to several charges. But what if all these people were right? Even Karlene from community corrections was willing to bet money that he wouldn't be going to prison.

And that's without accounting for the stack of glowing character references and an excellent presentencing report. But my hopes were mainly riding on the fact that we had engaged the services of a Senior Counsel (or SC), having borrowed money from Patrick's brother James, in addition to the thousands and thousands of dollars we had already paid for legal advice. It was our expectation that the complexity of his argument and his presence would hold some weight in the sentencing. In the weeks leading up to it, I had foolish fantasies of this faceless SC. I imagined him citing such obscure laws and delivering speeches so rich in rhetoric that the case would be dismissed.

One look was all it took for these dreams to shatter at my feet. I stepped into that same courthouse meeting room to see Charles, the SC, ferreting through the detritus of his briefcase before pulling out some dog-eared paperwork. Susan made the requisite introductions, and he mumbled an indecipherable greeting before saying to no one in particular, 'Now, this Mr Brown, is this the one you think is the strongest?'

'Ms Brown,' I corrected. 'She's a friend of ours, a lawyer.'

'Right, yes, I see,' he said, rubbing his bald head and then proceeding to do the most thunderous throat clearing as we all waited awkwardly for him to finish.

Eventually, Charles continued, 'And Ms Ogle?'

'Dr *Graham* Ogle,' I corrected.

'So it is, so it is.'

Charles shuffled a bundle of papers before dropping them on the floor and it was amusing to see both Amar and Susan, both outranked by Charles, rush to pick them up. Susan eventually stood allowing Amar to collect the papers, while Charles attempted to untangle the mangy wig he had produced from his briefcase.

I looked down at the same old school desk and noticed the addition of a stream flowing out of the end of the penis drawing and onto a cowering stick figure. I wondered what had compelled someone to draw it. If the artist also felt that the king's ransom he had borrowed to pay for an SC could have been put to better use, such as kindling for a fire. If it hadn't been the last-ditch attempt at Patrick's freedom I might have found it all vaguely amusing, but it was beginning to feel like we were being tied to the tracks with the deafening sound of an oncoming train drawing near.

At ten o'clock we were in the courtroom. Patrick sat in the dock, and I sat a short distance away from him, in the front row of the gallery, between my mum and my close friend Frieda.

'All rise,' the court official said and we stood for the entrance of Judge Pommery. Some procedural matters were heard and then Charles began. His manner in the meeting room was a teaser for his performance in the court. He stumbled and stammered, and it felt like a combination of a drunken uncle's wedding speech and dreadful stand-up comedy. And, despite the fact that Ms Brown's reference had been lost and found several times in the meeting room, it was again misplaced in the court.

Just when I thought it couldn't get any worse, I heard, 'I call Melissa Jacob, the wife of the offender, your Honour.' There was a significant delay between me hearing the words and registering their meaning. The possibility of me being a witness had only ever been mentioned in passing, and I was furious and insulted at not being included in the decision to call me as the first witness. I should have worn the navy dress, I thought as I made my way to the front, as though our future hinged on my wardrobe choice.

Everything looked different from the elevated position in the witness box. Everything and everyone was in plain sight, even the gallery where I'd sat so many times, feeling far away and invisible.

Charles asked me a series of questions about the charges, my education and my employment. I spoke slowly and deliberately, worried that I might say the wrong thing, or do what I always did and go off on unrelated tangents.

Answering the questions wasn't difficult. The answers came quickly and intuitively. What was difficult was looking out at all our friends and family who had filled up every row of the gallery, and seeing all our worry, pain and fear reflected in their faces. For the first time, I could see how much Patrick's actions had bled into the lives of so many other people.

Charles's questions continued, eventually gaining flow and momentum. 'And is this your opinion, ma'am, that if you thought he was likely to commit any further offences, you would not have chosen to stay and support him?'

'I would not,' I said, feeling like I was drawing a line in the sand in front of every significant person in our life. I looked at Patrick, worried that my words would wound him, but he already looked so crushed that I felt nothing I said could have made him feel worse than he already did.

'His actions have caused you, have they not, significant pain, and financial and career setbacks?'

'Yes, they have.' I'd declined job opportunities, and even though the legal expenses had not cost us our house, there had certainly been many sacrifices. Financial and otherwise.

When Charles finished, the prosecution's barrister, a thin, wiry man, began the cross-examination, focusing on my employment and education. I explained that I had studied theatre and literature and then worked as a schoolteacher, resigning from full-time work when our children were young. I'd supported Patrick over the years as he built up his business, and the plan had always been that when our kids began school and preschool respectively, it would be my turn to pursue my career as a writer.

'But it's a choice that you've made not to return to full-time teaching while she's not yet started full-time schooling, is that right?' the prosecution asked, referring to my staying home with Lexie.

'It's a decision that Patrick and I both made with having our children, yes.'

'But that's the only thing that's stopping you from returning to full-time teaching, it's a decision that you made while your children are young?'

'Yes,' I said, feeling exposed and inadequate.

After I was dismissed from the witness box, I felt hot and nauseated and could not concentrate on the proceedings until I heard Judge Pommery say, 'I will formally stand the matter over to Friday, for sentence. A full-time custodial penalty is inevitable. I don't see any reason his bail is to continue. I revoke his bail.' Two corrective services guards who had been standing in the courtroom moved towards Patrick and, without thinking, I stepped out of the gallery and opened the gate that divided the public and the dock.

'Step back,' the guard said. And then, like a magic show, Patrick vanished.

'Where did he go?' I asked Amar, who had appeared at my side.

'The stairs are concealed behind the railing.'

'What happened? He said, "Revoke bail".'

'Because he's been taken into custody.'

I stared at him blankly, still not comprehending.

'He's going to prison.'

'For how long?'

'We're not sure, the sentence will be handed down on Friday.'

I have no memory of what happened next, as though I had blacked out and everything had been erased. My mother told me that I staggered out of the courtroom, pulling at my clothes and howling. Then I remember sitting next to Amar as he explained the appeal process to me.

It was two days before I heard from Patrick. A welfare officer had called and explained that he was in the holding cells at Surry Hills. Her voice was warm and empathetic. I'd called the inmate information line and all they could tell me was that he was in custody. I'd had no way of contacting him or knowing where he was, or if he was okay.

'Hey,' he said.

'Hey, are you okay?'

'Yes, I'm . . . good. Don't you worry about me. How are you, how are the kids?' he asked.

I had no idea what to say; every part of me ached with loss. 'The kids are good.'

'Can you put them on?'

I put the phone on speaker and called the kids over.

'Dad,' Lexie said.

'Now, I don't want you to worry about me, okay? I'm fine.'

'I'm not worried. Grandma gave me three dollars. I bought sherbet,' she said.

'Are there bars, Dad . . . in your room?' Nick asked.

'No, mate, it's clear perspex. You know, like a fish tank,' Patrick said.

'People can see in?'

'Yeah.'

'Have you got a bed?'

'Sure have.'

'A toilet?'

'Yep, it's just like ours but it's metal and doesn't have a lid.'

'Can everyone see you go to the toilet?' Nick asked.

'Yeah, but it's just other blokes, mate,' Patrick said in a light-hearted tone.

'Have you got a TV?' Nick asked.

'Yes, it's on all day and night,' Patrick said trying to sound deliberately upbeat.

'Why does he get to watch TV during the week?' Nick asked me.

'I want to watch TV,' Lexie added.

I heard the welfare officer telling him to wrap it up.

'I have to go now. I love you all so much.'

When the dial tone sounded, Nick began to cry. I let him nestle into my side, and when he stopped crying, he said, 'If he has to stay in jail, who's . . . who's going to buy my birthday present?' I couldn't remember Patrick ever buying the kids' birthday presents but I just assured Nick that I would take care of it.

I didn't sleep Thursday night, and when I finally got up and went outside to feed the chickens and the rabbit I stumbled on a dead rat. I had never seen a dead rat before and it threw me, both because it was the day of Patrick's sentencing and because it was the sort of thing that he normally would have taken care of. I rang Karl and he came over and sorted it out.

Later, in court, I stood among an even bigger crowd of family and friends than the last time I was there. So many, in fact, that they spilled out into the corridor. We stood as Judge Pommery entered, and Patrick appeared in the courtroom via the concealed staircase. In the instant that it took for him to turn to the front before he sat down, I glimpsed a dark brown stain at the back of his pants where he had obviously soiled his clothes. I felt like I was going to vomit.

'The offender comes before me for sentence,' Pommery began and it was as though everything were moving in slow motion. I remember my mother's grip tightening on my hand as I heard Pommery outline the nature of the offences, and the evidence that had been presented, some of which was presented in the form of character references and the psychologist's report.

And I told myself that there was still time and that, as Karlene had told me, the judge had several options at his disposal, such as home detention or community service. Pommery made a point of highlighting Patrick's 'otherwise good character' and his contribution to society, and then the focus shifted to me. 'He has now placed a considerable financial burden upon his wife to return to work, to enable mortgage payments to be met while he is custody. Fortunately, she is highly educated and will have reasonable prospects of obtaining employment, unlike the wives and partners of many who come before these courts. The hardships to be occasioned to her and the children does not amount to truly exceptional hardship.'

I could not believe it. I had grown up in a street where people sat in the gutter drinking and made fires in drums. I was the first one in my family to go to university, and now it felt like all my hard work was being used against me. It felt like my life had fallen off its axis, and was spinning wildly, violently, out of control.

'Mr Jacob, would you please stand,' said Judge Pommery, and Patrick stood, with only his back visible. He was clearly shaking. 'You are convicted. For the offence of not keeping a firearm safely, I sentence you to a fixed-term sentence of imprisonment for six months . . .'

Six months. I can do six months, I told myself. But Pommery hadn't finished.

'For the offence of possessing an unregistered firearm . . . concurrent terms of imprisonment for eighteen months . . .' Was it six months or eighteen months? My fists were clenched, my breathing was laboured and adrenalin pulsed through me.

'For the offence of possessing a prohibited weapon—namely, a slingshot—I sentence you to a non-parole period of twelve months . . .' I let out a small cry and leaned on my mother for support as Pommery continued undeterred.

Patrick turned around to face the large crowd of people who had come to support him. Tearfully, purposefully, he looked at every one of them. Some of his sisters had made signs with encouraging messages and they held them high.

He looked into my eyes and mouthed, 'I'm sorry.' One of the two corrective services officers took his arm and turned him, puppet-like, so that he faced front for the final part of the sentence.

'A total term of four years and six months. Commencing on 29 January 2013 and expiring on 28 July 2017. You are eligible for release to supervised parole on 28 July 2015.'

The thousands of times that I had played this scenario over in my mind, I had never imagined an ending so swift and so final. I had wanted to hold him, would have given anything for extra moments to say goodbye, to say something, anything . . . but he was gone.

PART II

EIGHT

'You have to tell them,' Mum said, breaking the silence that had followed us from the courthouse.

'I know.' The kids were due home any minute and I'd been going over and over what to say, trying to find the words to make it more palatable, less painful. The responsibility weighed me down like a ship's anchor. I felt that if I wasn't honest or tender enough, and if they didn't feel free to express whatever it was they were feeling, that this moment could fracture the rest of their lives.

'What do you remember about when your dad died?' I asked Mum, who was wiping down the island bench. She'd always been so open and honest with me, craving, I suppose, the intimacy she was denied because her parents died when she was a child.

'I knew something had happened because of all the whispering . . . a lot of people came to the house. And I remember the priest sitting us down to talk to us kids but I don't remember the funeral . . . I don't think we went to the funeral . . . and no one told me what happened.'

I'd known since I was young that when she was only six years old, Mum had lost her mother to cancer. And as the two-year anniversary of her mother's death approached, her father also died. So it came as a surprise one afternoon, when I discovered Mum sobbing into the lilac flowers on her bedspread. 'What's the matter?' I asked.

'My father . . . died,' she said, her voice hoarse with fresh grief. I sat on the bed next to her, confused. Her father had died long before I was born. Why, so many years later, was she so distraught? Eventually, Mum explained she had only just learned her father had committed suicide. He had gone to the common behind the town they lived in, and shot himself in the head. It might have been a generational thing, or perhaps due to the stigma of suicide, that the adults thought the kindest thing to do was to protect the children from the cruellest of truths.

But it didn't seem kind, as I watched her try to regain her footing as though the carpet had been pulled out from under her. The secret altered everything she thought she knew about her past and her father and, ultimately, herself.

Certainly, our situation was different, but it was serious. And I knew that, as difficult and as painful as it would be, I had to tell them the truth.

'Mum,' Lexie called from the front door, 'can I have a biscuit?' And when both kids appeared in the doorway that led to the kitchen, Nick looked up at me hopefully and I shook my head.

'How long?' he asked, climbing onto the barstool.

'Well,' I began, self-consciously, 'the judge said that because what Dad did was very serious . . . he has to go to prison . . . for two and a half years.' I expected Nick to cry but he didn't. He didn't say or do anything. He just looked defeated. And I felt a love for him so primal and so deep, I understood how mothers find the strength to lift cars.

I got two iceblocks out of the freezer, cut the corner off Lexie's and passed the scissors to Nick. Still neither of them said anything.

I wondered if, like me, they felt numb, or if they felt like it wasn't real and were expecting Patrick to walk in any moment, peel off his shirt, and say, 'Who's coming in the pool?'

I wondered if they would be haunted by distilled memories. Would they remember my black suit, the coffee percolating on the stove or the heat of the afternoon, the way I recalled each time I bit into a Granny Smith apple my mother telling me that she was not taking my father back. I had been eighteen at the time, and after years of him leaving and coming back she decided she'd had enough.

'Dad made a mistake,' I said, 'but it's nothing we should feel ashamed about . . . it's going to be hard, at first . . . but we will get through this.' Still neither of them said anything. I didn't know if it had even registered. If they had even heard me.

'Where's Grandma?' Lexie asked, panicked.

'Outside, getting the washing off the line,' I said, much to Lexie's relief. 'This is a big thing, a hard thing,' I continued, 'and I want you to know that it's okay for you to do or say anything.'

'Can I yell?' Lexie asked.

'As loud as you like.' And they both yelled at the top of their voices.

'Can I scream?' I nodded and they screamed.

'Can I hit Nick?' Lexie asked, delighted by the sudden behaviour amnesty.

'Do you think it's going to make you feel better?'

'Yes!'

'I don't think it'll make Nick feel better.' The conversation wasn't really panning out the way I'd imagined. I'd envisaged tears and tantrums, and holding them in my arms.

'Do we have to wait two and a half years to see him?' Nick asked, as the coffee hissed on the stove.

'No.' It had never occurred to me to explain that we could visit Patrick. It made sense that Nick wouldn't have understood this; he had no point of reference point from books or films or TV shows.

'Can we go now?' he asked.

'Another day. We have to make a booking.'

'Some people never see their dads,' Lexie said. 'Like Grace from preschool. Her dad lives in a kingdom far, far away.'

'He lives in the United Kingdom, in England,' I said.

'What's a moron?' Lexie asked.

'Another word for an idiot.'

'Grace said her mum calls her dad a moron. Sometimes she shouts into the phone like this: "You bloody moron!"'

'Dad's not a moron,' Nick said.

'No, he's not,' I agreed, although at that juncture, it was debatable.

Nick smiled in the wry, shy way he does. 'Can I make that pterodactyl noise?'

'Do you think it'll help?' I asked.

'Nah, I just like doing it.'

'Well, I'd prefer you didn't. It hurts my ears.'

'So we can't really do anything, can we?' Lexie observed. And then, as though I'd been talking about the most trivial thing in the world, she said, '*Now* can I have a biscuit?'

The phone didn't stop ringing. So many people stopped by to offer their support, or to drop off meals and flowers. And I hadn't expected that at all. Patrick hadn't fallen ill or been hit by a car, and I felt uncomfortable and undeserving about the enormous outpouring of generosity. 'He's gone to prison,' I said to my friend Bec, after the fifth lasagne had been dropped off at the house, 'for breaking the law. It's not like he has cancer.'

'Don't be stupid,' she said, 'they're your friends, they want to help. When people ask you what you need, tell them.'

At first when everything was so raw and so new, I didn't know what I needed. But Mum knew. She fielded all the calls, and took the kids to the park, bathed them and cooked dinner, as I stumbled through the day in a somnambulant daze. And on that first night, as tired as I was, I couldn't sleep. The court images played on a loop in my mind. Patrick's anguished face, his sister collapsing, the gavel hitting the desk, and him disappearing.

Sometime around five on Saturday morning I finally drifted off to sleep, and when I woke several hours later, I saw filtered light shimmering through the window, and, for that brief moment, I felt fine. Until I remembered what had happened and the pain returned, as salient and barbed as a needle.

I could hear the kids on the front lawn with Mum. I didn't feel like joining them; I wanted to stay in bed, where I could still smell Paddy. I held the green T-shirt he slept in and breathed in his scent. It was a mixture of sweat, and citrus from the deodorant he wore. I didn't know when would be the next time I would see him or even talk to him. I called the inmate information line religiously for any updates.

'You're just going to have to wait until he calls you,' the operator said, with an indifference I found cutting.

Late on Sunday afternoon, it was time for Mum to return to her home in the Hunter Valley. I felt panicked about her leaving. She was the only one aside from Patrick and me who the kids felt completely comfortable with. She'd already been at our place for a week and she'd given us all that she could. She worked full time, and she'd just bought a house and hadn't even moved in. 'You can do this,' she said as we said our goodbyes at her car. 'I know you can. You're a strong person.' I didn't feel strong. I felt fragile like blown glass.

Later on Sunday afternoon, Lexie began to cry. Finally, I thought, it's hit home. She understands. I imagined her erupting in grief.

'You okay?'

'Yeah, I'm just really sad,' she said, wrapping her arms around me.

'I'm sad about Dad too.'

She looked at me, puzzled. 'I'm sad about Grandma. Why does she have to go?'

Monday was tediously slow and fast at the same time. When I thought about Patrick, and wondered how I could survive without him for two and a half years, time seemed to pass at an excruciatingly sluggish pace. *I can do this. I can do this,* I told myself, repeating what Mum had said, but I didn't believe it for a second.

Only two days had passed since the sentencing. Two and a half years seemed like forever. And yet, dropping the kids to school, tidying the house, signing the power of attorney forms with Amar, buying groceries and walking to the bus stop to collect the kids, moved more swiftly than almost anything else I'd ever experienced.

When the school bus arrived, Nick was the first to step off, throwing his bag onto the ground with such force it slid along the gravel and into a nearby tree.

'You okay?' I asked, wishing I could see what was inside him, that I could read his thoughts like a diary.

'No,' he said and started walking home.

'Anything you want to talk about?' I asked, when we sat down to afternoon tea.

'Why don't you ask Lexie? She likes to talk . . . to people on the bus . . . about Dad!'

'Is that true?' I asked her gently.

'You said it was nothing to be ashamed of!' she screamed at me and ran out to the backyard. I was glad Lexie didn't feel shame but I was concerned her openness might invite teasing.

For some reason I couldn't figure out, the answering machine had stopped working, so I answered each and every call in the hope that it was Patrick. That afternoon the phone rang, and I steeled myself for another draining conversation about what had happened and how we were coping, but then a recorded message with an American accent played: 'You are about to receive a phone call from an inmate at MRRC Correctional Centre. If you do not wish to receive this phone call, please hang up now. Go ahead, please.'

'Paddy!'

'Beauty.' It had been a lifetime since he had called me that. Years before, when we first started dating and I would fall asleep on the long drives home from his place to mine, he began—somewhat ironically, I think—to call me Sleeping Beauty.

'Are you okay?' I asked.

'Yeah, I'm fine. It's so good to hear your voice.'

'And yours . . . are you sure you're okay?'

'Yes, yes. Can I speak to the kids?'

I called the kids, put the phone on speaker, and had a jumbled and overlapping conversation. We spoke for roughly five minutes before a series of beeps sounded. None of us knew then that this was a warning that the call was about to be terminated. It was the strangest thing, hearing the dial tone and not being able to call him back. In our pre-prison life, we had called each other countless times during the day, and often if I was in the middle of something I would call him back, but I couldn't do that anymore.

'You didn't do anything wrong by telling people on the bus,' I said to Lexie, as she helped chop vegetables for dinner. In many ways, she was the polar opposite of Nick. While he internalised and fretted over things, she was so expressive, she seemed transparent.

'So why can't we tell people?'

'We can tell *some* people but . . . but at this stage we're only telling our close friends and family.'

She chopped the zucchini with determined force. 'Can I tell Alice?' This was Lexie's best friend.

'You can, but she already knows, her mum wanted to explain it to her.'

'I wanted to tell her!' she said indignantly. 'Who else can I tell?'

'It's complicated, Lex. You've only just started at the school. It's going to take some time until you know who your close friends are.'

When I called the kids for dinner, Nick said, 'Mum, you set four places . . .'

None of us said anything. We didn't need to. We felt Patrick's absence so keenly; it felt as though a chasm had opened up around us. I'd always enjoyed dinners with the kids. There was a lot of laughter, and our stories flowed easily. Sometimes we had to stop the stories until more food was consumed. Our first dinner at home as a threesome was stilted and awkward.

I bathed the kids, we read books and prayed, and I tucked them into bed. And I went to the kitchen, to start washing up.

'Can you come up with us?' Lexie yelled.

Our house wasn't big, but it was long and the bedrooms were at the far end. 'Stop yelling!' I yelled back.

Soon afterwards, Nick materialised. 'Can you stay up with us? Lexie's scared.' But I could tell from his tone that it wasn't just Lexie who was scared.

The kids went to bed easily but were used to having one of us at that end of the house. So, I got into bed and picked up Robyn Davidson's *Tracks*, the book I'd started a month before. In the weeks leading up to the sentencing I had been so tired I'd only managed to read a couple of chapters, sometimes reading the same page over and over before falling asleep.

Reading it that night, I was riveted. As much as I loved my children and wanted to help them navigate this difficult time, another part of me longed to get as far away from the situation as I possibly could. I wished that, like Davidson, or other women I'd read about, I could embark on a solo journey across the Australian desert, or ascend a rocky mountain crop or meander along cobbled European streets. I wanted a journey of solitude and escape, one that could be plotted out on a map. Sure it would have its challenges, but they would be a welcome distraction from my messy inner life. Maybe I'd have an enlightening encounter with an enigmatic shaman. And there would be a recurring motif, like repeatedly spying an eagle or a striking red cardinal.

I just wished I could do pretty much anything other than what I was being called to do. I felt hemmed in. Trapped. Patrick was locked in the big house and I was stuck in a small one.

NINE

Maximum security. Maximum security. Maximum security.

Patrick was in the Metropolitan Remand and Reception Centre (MRRC), one of three prisons located in the Silverwater Correctional Complex, twenty-one kilometres from the centre of Sydney. MRRC is the maximum-security section of the complex, housing 900 inmates, most of whom are on remand (waiting to be sentenced), recently incarcerated or in transit between prisons. I read the description over and over again, trying to imagine Paddy in a maximum-security prison. Every possible scenario that sprang to mind was like oil and water.

For our first visit to MRRC, Patrick's brother James drove Rosemary, my mother-in-law, and me in my old beat-up Honda SUV. Patrick had been insistent that we not drive there in James's new car, and that I not wear fancy clothes, or make-up or jewellery. As I sat in the back seat, I kept thinking that I should have been feeling stunned or upset, but I still felt nothing. Even as James drove down Holker Street and coiled razor wire came into view, I was numb.

'We're here to see Patrick Jacob,' I said to the receptionist.

'MIN number?' she asked. Each inmate is given a master index number for identification.

'520764,' I read from my hand.

'ID?' she asked. There were signs everywhere warning visitors to remove jewellery and place personal items in the lockers provided. In our eagerness to comply, James, Rosemary and I had completely forgotten about identification and had to return to the lockers to retrieve it.

Next came the fingerprints. Then the biometric retina scans, which involved standing on a line and staring at a red dot in a machine similar to the one that was used at the optometrist. Rosemary, who'd recently had retinal surgery, was unable to provide a successful reading. At first, the staff insisted that she couldn't enter, but after numerous unsuccessful attempts, they gave her an exemption.

'Locker,' said the guard when we moved to the next security checkpoint, at the far end of the room. James and I stared at each other blankly. We had already been to the lockers numerous times. The guard eventually pointed at the twenty-dollar note in James's hand.

'The receptionist said we can take twenty dollars in. Is that correct?' I asked.

'Coins!' he barked and, like wide-eyed tourists, we returned to the lockers again.

After two more retina scans, a walk through a rectangular 3D metal detector, and having a hand-held wand waved over us, we exited the main building and walked across a small courtyard to another building. It opened into a long corridor filled with vending machines. I spent the full twenty dollars on things I knew Patrick liked.

At the end of the corridor, past all the vending machines, was another reception desk. The officer verified our details and we stood waiting, peering across through glass doors into the visitation room. From a door adjacent to the desk, I saw Paddy emerge in a skin-tight white visitation suit.

'Go!' an officer said. We just kept standing there. 'Go!' he repeated. James and I looked at each other, wondering if he was talking to us. The guard pointed to the double door.

When James pushed open the doors and we stepped in, all eyes turned to us. I felt a strange mix of repulsion and fascination. The visitation room was starkly lit, with neon lights. The inmates wore white jumpsuits fastened at the back, with 'VISITS' printed in large bold black letters on their backs. Some of the men looked like caricatures from prison movies, the most freakish collection of people I'd seen outside a Diane Arbus book. Some were monstrous, dwarfing the people sitting around them. There were shaved heads, rat's tails, tattooed and scarred faces. Others weren't especially large or scary, or otherwise unusual. They just looked like men you'd see anywhere.

All of the tables inside and outside, bar one at the very back of the room, directly in front of a guard, were taken. It felt like a decade passed as we made our way across to the back of the room. The table was small and circular and bolted to the floor, along with all the stools that surrounded it. We sat and waited.

I wonder what he did, I recall wondering about the inmate sitting at the table closest to ours. He had jagged scars down one side of his face, a short mohawk strip (which I later found out was called a brohawk), and tattoos creeping up from the neckline of his suit. I deliberately averted my gaze to the floor, worried that my curiosity might upset someone, the same way it sometimes did on streets and supermarkets on the outside.

'Black,' the guard said, standing next to Patrick at the table. We all looked up at him blankly; the remaining stool was white. An impromptu game of musical stools followed, and it was only when we were all standing that we realised one of the five stools was black, and was intended for Patrick—the black sheep of the family, as it were.

'Behave yourself,' the guard said, before moving to stand against the wall directly behind us.

I gave Patrick a peck on the cheek. 'You look . . .' I started and changed tack. He looked terrible. He had sunken, bloodshot eyes and an unruly mess of facial hair. 'What are you wearing?' I was referring to his skin-tight onesie, which looked remarkably like an ice-skating costume.

'I know. Lucky we don't want to have any more kids.' I was relieved to hear that he still had a sense of humour. 'CO's idea of a joke.'

'CO?'

'Correctional officer. They give out the wrong-sized suits and shoes, just to mess with you,' Patrick said, and then he talked and talked and talked. I recalled how during a playwriting course I'd taken, the teacher had said, 'In real life, people don't talk in monologues.' I'd disagreed because my paternal grandmother spoke in monologues that chronicled her entire TV-centred week, moving swiftly from one topic to another, without any variation in tone or pace.

Now Paddy was so desperate to talk to someone he could trust that the words poured out of him in a deluge. I found it hard to concentrate. I kept thinking that coming face to face with my husband in his white jumpsuit at a prison visitation should have been devastating. It should have made the situation agonisingly real. But it didn't. I didn't cry. I didn't speak mournfully about the kids. I didn't do anything, except observe numbly, because it still seemed like some kind of elaborate practical joke.

James and Rosemary listened intently, and they also had pertinent and comforting things to say. James talked about the business, and Rosemary spoke about the prison chaplain and about faith. I was stumped, though. I was so shocked, my mind had gone blank. And the more I tried to think of a question, the more one eluded me. About two thirds of the way through the hour-long visit, I finally thought of a question: 'Have you been keeping a low profile?'

'That's what everyone tells you to do,' Patrick said. '"Keep your head down, stay out of people's way." What they don't realise is that if you do that, people are suspicious. They want to know what you're in for and if you're rich, though that's a relative term in here.' A brief laugh escaped his lips. 'I was reading your letter, Mum—you were quick off the mark, thank you—and my cellie—cellmate—came in and snatched the letter out of my hand, and said, "Who do you know with a laser printer? You must be rich!" So you need a—'

'Backstory,' I interjected.

'Yeah, a backstory. So, when I was in Surry Hills and everyone was asking me questions about my business and my family, I gave them one.'

'What did you say?' I asked.

'It doesn't matter—'

'Tell me.'

'Just that . . . I lost everything and that my wife left me—'

'Your wife left you? That's what came straight off the top of your subconscious?'

'It was spur of the moment. I had to give them a reason for losing the business.'

'Is the business in trouble?' his mother asked, and Paddy and James laughed.

I slid the vending-machine purchases across the table towards Paddy. He picked up the mango yoghurt and, in the absence of a spoon, peeled back the lid and squeezed the contents into his mouth. A dollop of yoghurt fell onto his crotch and he wiped it away, resulting in an even bigger stain.

As I looked up, I caught the eye of the inmate at the table next to us. 'What did he do?' I whispered to Paddy, after the man had turned away.

'Brako? Trust me, you don't want to know.'

I sneaked another look. As I thought about him, for the very first time I started to feel something. Like an emotional thawing had begun. I'm ashamed to say that what I felt as I sat in the prison visitation room was not love or compassion, or even fear: it was the teeniest bit of smugness.

I wasn't required to wear a white suit or sit on the black stool, and when the visit ended I would be able to leave. And it made me feel different, elevated somehow, and that made me feel ashamed. And then I noticed all the other women in the room. Most of them looked really glamorous, with heavy make-up and tight, flattering clothes. I had on old baggy jeans, a plain T-shirt, and my unwashed hair was pulled back into a ponytail.

'You know what we need to do?' Paddy said, changing the subject.

'What?' I asked.

'We need a code to communicate on the phone.'

'About what?'

'Like, if you wanted to tell me something about the business or the kids, or if there's a problem in here.'

'Why can't I just tell you?' My brain is not wired for remembering numbers and codes. At various times, Patrick had tried to teach me Morse code and the NATO phonetic alphabet but I couldn't remember them. I could recall a celebrity's teeth whitening tip but not the internationally recognised sign for distress.

'What about numbers?' Patrick said. 'Like, number one's a person, and a colour represents an emotion. Like Nick—first born— and if you want to tell me he's okay, then you say, "One—yellow".'

'Here's an idea—why don't I just say, "Nick is okay"?' I couldn't remember numbers. I remembered stories.

'It sounds like you're drug dealers,' James said.

'What about if you want to tell me you got home okay, say something like "The chicken is in the coop."'

'Now you definitely sound like drug dealers,' James laughed.

'How would you know?' I asked him.

'The movies,' James answered.

'But, in all seriousness, if I need to tell you that something's wrong, I'll say something about our dog,' Paddy said.

'We don't have a dog!'

'Exactly.'

'Time's up,' said a turbaned CO and I looked up at the clock. It was 12.47. I worked out, without the aid of a calculator, that there were thirteen minutes of the visit remaining. And it had started late. The CO looked down at Patrick's yellow-stained crotch and shook his head.

'Gotta go,' Patrick said.

'You've hardly eaten anything!'

'I'm not going to eat junk anymore,' Paddy said, rising to his feet. He hugged me and said, 'Don't you worry, I'm going to make this count.'

We exited the visitation room and started to walk down the corridor.

'Been, been,' a heavily accented voice at the reception counter said. I wasn't sure what he was trying to tell me until he pointed to the rubbish bin. I held up all the unopened packets. The CO nodded and I dropped them into the rubbish bin.

TEN

MRRC Silverwater
5 February 2013

Beauty,

I'm in MRRC, Silverwater prison. No pen and paper till now. I'll explain things in sequence.

Taken into custody at the courthouse, guards took me downstairs to DOC reception, ordered to strip, squat and cough. Guard gave me a hard time for not squatting. Tried to explain inflexibility is genetic; most of my family can't squat or touch toes. He thought it was a wind-up.

Holding cells in Penrith and Surry Hills (as I was to later to find out) like Hunger Games in hygiene survival. Faeces and blood on every surface. No soap, small square toilet paper that doesn't absorb anything. Stood all day so clothes wouldn't get contaminated.

At 2.30 guards collect us to go in truck (milk run). Don't know why it's called that. Maybe because it's white. Learned from other inmates that it never takes direct route. Have to drop off and pick up from holding cells, courthouses, police stations and prisons all over the place. Difficult to put on seat belt with handcuffs but need to as metal bench seat v. slippery. Seats on either side of truck with men facing each other. Room for ten blokes. Given water bottle for journey.

Relieved, at first, truck is clean, but that's short lived. When moving, man gets cigarettes out of his butt (jail purse), v. impressive feat with handcuffs on. Chain-smoked all of them despite brown marks on cigs and hands (and he called me a dirty C!)

So much swearing (mainly F and C) even more than Army, more than Simon—which is saying something!!!

Inmates discuss charges/sentences. Didn't think you were meant to ask other people. Ray Stevens (truck driver) got six years for manslaughter for killing someone on the M4. Told me it's the second time he has killed someone in a road accident. Think I must be looking at 6–12 months at most.

Taken to Silverwater. Put in holding cell (3×6m) with 6 others. Handcuffs removed. Asked what I am in for? Said prefer not to say, everyone convinced I am undercover cop. Want to know why I have poxy haircut and no tats? Told them undercover cop that arrested me had a tattoo on his arm. All said bullsh*t!

After two hours, left Silverwater, in back of truck again. No one tells us where we're headed and guards ignore all questions and cop a lot of verbal abuse. Can hardly breathe—all men smoke courtesy of jail purse.

Placed in holding cell in Surry Hills (1×3m) with 8 others. Standing room only.

Bloke from Silverwater tells others that I am a dog (cop). Another bloke chimes in and says he recognises me from St George police station. Never even been to St George! Then demands to know where I live? Wants to know why my legs are so white when it was over 40 degrees in Western Sydney last week? Then a miracle happened: young bloke (junkie) I was in lockup with when arrested (2 years ago) materialises. Vouches for my story and it's obvious to everyone I wasn't making it up. Glad he didn't get off the gear (yet) like he said he would. Think he saved my life.

9pm moved to a cell with another inmate. Can't sleep. Cells are underground. Know it's morning by the sound of other men and lights are brightened, and see appalling state of cells. Stench of urine and faeces unbearable. Excrement, graffiti circa March 2010. No soap, no toilet paper and even the bubbler and light switch are covered in human waste. Can't believe this is Australia. Buzzed the guards for cleaning products. Said they would bring them down ASAP. They never came.

Inmates said we are only allowed to be detained in holding cells for 72 hours but so overcrowded. They said I should think myself lucky as men who can't speak English or mentally ill are taken out in milk run and brought back to Surry Hills.

On third day see welfare officer. V nice. Welfare and guards like different species. She tells me to keep being respectful to officers and I will be heard. Bollocks!

TV suspended from ceiling behind perspex so words are incomprehensible and muffled. Can't hear volume, don't know if on or off. Seems like Kerri-Anne Kennerley is on repeat. Is this prison or hell?

Friday morning taken to Penrith for sentencing. Cannot write about this yet. Still too raw. Thought I had prepared for the worst—not prepared for four and a half years.

Taken to MRRC at Silverwater. So shocked and stressed about sentence when welfare officer asked if I was withdrawing from drug use I was confused and obviously gave wrong answer, and they put me in Spinners (Mental Health unit like One Flew over the Cuckoo's Nest*) in padded cell. Men scratching skin off from ice or* *catatonic or delusional. Seeing wild dogs, imaginary friends etc. One inmate asked to buy medication from another. His response: I'd better not. Remember what happened the last time I didn't take my medication? I put that other bloke in hospital. Insisted he take prescribed medication.*

Healthcare professional is amazed by the speed of my detox. Explain that I wasn't on drugs and never have been. Out of Spinners and into Gen Pop. On first day men were sitting watching TV while I was standing.

Me: Do you think I'll get in trouble if I move a chair from the other room?

Inmate: Mate, you're in maximum bloody security, how much more trouble can you get in?

Moved chair but only stayed short time as brawl broke out about Home and Away *vs.* Neighbours *or similar (inmates get addicted to storylines).*

Know I'm not good with words but even if I was, don't know if they would be enough to describe how sorry I am for what I did. I have no excuse for the decision I made and I'm wrestling with that every day.

I don't know much but I know I want to spend the rest of my life making it up to you.

I can't change what has happened but I can promise you this: I am going to make the time in here count. I'm going to become a better person. I am going to get fit and read books and make a difference, not just in my life but also in the lives of others.

You are my great love. My sleeping beauty.

Love,

Paddy

ELEVEN

'But why?'

'Lexie . . .'

'They're only drawings—kids drawings!' Lexie said, for what seemed like the millionth time. In the first week, her grief, although only in its rudimentary stages, had been channelled into enough drawings and craft for her to show her first exhibition: *My Dad: A retrospective.*

'It's the rule—'

'But why?' I'd found with my children, and with Lexie in particular, the more evasive I was, the more they craved an answer. From the time they were very young, we'd tried to give them the age-appropriate truth.

'Well, you know the card you made for Dad the day he got sent to prison? An officer at the court told me it wasn't allowed because people can hide drugs under the glue and sticky tape.'

'We don't have any drugs!' Lexie said, as we made our way from the car park to MRRC reception.

'Not all drugs are illegal. When you have a headache or a cold, I give you legal drugs like Panadol or Nurofen . . . and I take medicine, a legal drug, that releases certain chemicals in my brain to make me happier,' I explained, a good octave lower than Lexie had been speaking.

'Why are those dogs here?' Nick asked.

'They're so cute! Can we pat them?' Lexie asked, finally moving on from craft.

'They're sniffer dogs,' I said, 'trained to sniff out drugs.'

'Are the brain drugs in your bag?' Nick asked, panicked.

'No. And it's medicine, it's not illegal.'

'That dog's sniffing the other dog's bum,' Lexie observed. 'Do you think there's drugs in there?' she asked and then laughed like it was the funniest thing she'd ever heard.

'No, I think that's just what dogs do.'

'It would be a good place to hide them,' Nick suggested blithely. It was their first visit to a prison and already they were thinking like criminals.

Children aren't required to have retina scans and I'd already been officially processed so we moved swiftly through the first two checkpoints.

'It's the glass elevator from *Charlie and the Chocolate Factory*!' Lexie said, as I emerged from the 3D scanner.

'Sometimes it breaks through the roof!' the officer said and I mouthed, 'Thank you.' I appreciated his effort to make the experience fun. Well, as fun as a prison security search can be.

'It *is* like *Charlie and the Chocolate Factory*,' Nick said, as we entered the corridor with the vending machines.

'You can choose *one* of anything you like,' I said.

'I'll have one cat,' Lexie said, jumping up and down. She'd been at us to buy her a cat.

'From the *vending machine*,' I told her and she frowned. 'You've already got a rabbit that you don't pay any attention to.' They both chose Crunchies and we made our way to the visitation room.

The kids were overjoyed to see Patrick. But after the initial embrace and then being required to sit on their own stools, they struggled.

'But why can't we sit on your lap?' Lexie moaned, after the fifth time she'd migrated to, and been removed from, her father's lap.

'I don't know. I think it's because of drugs,' Patrick said.

'Everything's about stupid drugs!' Lexie said, again at high volume. Patrick looked at me quizzically.

'Sometimes people hide drugs on their children,' I said.

Lexie rolled her eyes. 'They're parents, as if they would do that to their kids.'

Her innocence melted my heart. At her age, I was well aware that people in our neighbourhood did far worse things to their kids.

'Don't stare,' I whispered to Nick. I'd already noticed the man whose entire face was covered in tattoos. And I admit I also felt compelled to look, but I'd managed to do it with some level of discretion. Nick was unashamedly, open-mouthedly gawking at him.

'Stare at who?' Lexie asked, and turned to look at the tattooed face, like it was some sort of exhibit at a museum.

Paddy distracted Lexie and Nick by doing 'Round and round the garden,' on their hands and telling them jokes. He loved playing with the kids more than he did sitting down and talking with adults. At barbecues, you'd be more likely to find him running around with the children than standing with the men. He was a softie when I met him, but becoming a parent had softened him even more.

The last part of the visit proceeded smoothly, thanks to Cadbury's chocolate. Nick and Lexie ate their chocolate bars with such satisfaction and delight they could have been anywhere in the world except for a maximum-security prison visitation room. I wished I could be placated so easily.

At the end of the visit, the kids seemed different somehow. Older. Wiser. Although they couldn't articulate it themselves, I think seeing Paddy had cemented the awful truth. From the very beginning, we had told them simple kidspeak versions of what was happening, but that was far removed from what they had seen around them.

'You feeling okay after seeing Dad?' I asked Lexie, tucking her into bed that night.

'Actually, it gave me an idea,' she said, enthusiasm prompting her to sit up.

'Really, what is it?' I asked.

'We should break him out,' she said excitedly.

I laughed. 'Lex, I know you want him out, but if he got caught, he'd have to stay in for longer and we'd get in trouble as well.' Her face fell. 'Think of it like when you get in trouble and you have to sit on the step. What happens if you do the wrong thing on the step?'

'Consequences,' she said, exasperated. 'I was looking forward to it.'

I smoothed the sheets around her. 'Oh, Lex, I love your crazy little mind. Out of interest, how were you planning on doing it?'

'Well, you know how we saw that play in that old jail?'

'Old Dubbo Gaol.'

'Yeah, well, that girl escaped by tying the sheets together and climbing over the wall.'

'Do you remember what happened when she got caught again?' Lexie shook her head. 'She was put into solitary confinement, which means being locked up by yourself.' Lexie sighed and started looking through her book. Now that she knew the prison break wasn't an option, nothing about her body language suggested that she was the slightest bit perturbed by the visit or the conversation.

I had started clearing a path on her craft-strewn floor, ready to leave, when she asked, 'Do you think the guards will whip Dad?' in a tone that suggested she'd given it some thought.

'What makes you ask that?' I said, trying to conceal my alarm.

'Because in the play at the old jail, the guards said they whip the prisoners *and* put them in solitaire confindment.'

'They were acting out a play about a jail a long time ago. Guards aren't allowed to hurt prisoners anymore.'

'But how would anyone know if the guards hurt them when everyone is behind those high walls? How can anyone see?' She had a point.

'They have cameras,' I said.

'Okay,' she said, and resumed reading her book.

Later, when I was in bed, I worried about Lexie and Nick and Patrick. The images of the inmates played over in my mind: menacing tattoos, shaved heads, broken noses, missing teeth. And the energy of the visiting room was palpably negative and aggressive.

I wondered how I could help the kids: one minute they seemed fine and the next they were asking about government brutality. I was wrestling with both my own grief and the heavier weight of theirs.

I was exhausted, but with my mind so full and anxious, I couldn't sleep. As I lay there, thinking about the faces of the other inmates, another scenario popped into my mind. Once, years back, when Paddy and I were on the train from the city, a passenger stopped abruptly in front of us and started punching a small Asian man seated next to him.

Paddy stood up. 'Mate, what do you think you're doing?' he asked, trying to reason with the man. At which point, the accoster punched Paddy hard in the nose.

'Mate, if you do that one more time . . .' Paddy said, again trying to appeal to the man's good nature, receiving another hard blow, this time to the chin.

Paddy made no attempt to retaliate, or even shield his body by turning to the side or blocking the incoming advances with his hands. He simply stood, open-armed and optimistic, convinced, despite all evidence to the contrary, that common sense would prevail.

'Mister, you're skating on very thin ice,' Paddy warned again. No longer were they mates; the other man was now 'Mister' and Paddy received another punch, in the stomach.

The empty threat scenario played out several more times, until some male commuters intervened, restraining the attacker and calling for security.

Other men, I know, wouldn't have thought twice about retaliating—about kicking his arse, teaching him a lesson. But Paddy just didn't seem to have it in him to hit someone. I'd fallen head over heels in love with his gentleness. It had served him well in the regular world but I couldn't begin to imagine how he would survive in prison.

TWELVE

'So, the P & L . . .' Patrick's brother James said, sitting across from me at his favourite cafe.

'The P & L?'

'Patrick must've talked about the P & L.'

'Don't think so,' I said, thinking James was referring to a product code.

Paddy and James were entrepreneurs. I mean it in the nicest possible way when I say they both functioned as though they had giant calculators wedged in their cerebral cortexes. Not only could they do complicated calculations about cubic metres and fluctuating currencies in their heads, they had the ability to remember them.

'But you know what it is, right?' James looked over at me hopefully. 'It's the cornerstone . . . the foundation of any business.'

I racked my brain trying to think of business terms starting with P. P . . . pie chart, paradigm, power nap. These were the only P words that sprung to mind. But the L?

Normally, James functioned at a very high speed and was big on multi-tasking. He ate standing up, and returned phone calls in the car using his hands-free device. I knew he was making a concerted effort to be patient with me. 'Profit and loss ring any bells?'

'Yes, profit and loss!' I repeated emphatically. 'And the profit needs to be greater than the loss,' I said, thinking James would be impressed, but he just looked at me with a genuinely pained expression.

It was a Friday, two whole weeks since Paddy had been sentenced. During that time, James had been to our warehouse every day, working, keeping our business afloat. He had his own business and four children, but without hesitation had stepped into the gap. He coordinated staffing, managed the online accounts, and he'd organised for other family members to man the phones and wrap parcels for shipping. Patrick's family, my family, insisted that I needed to focus on the kids.

As we sat having our business discussion (though a discussion suggests an equal contribution), James dominated the conversation and I was ever so grateful. I didn't know the first thing about BAS or BOL or FOBs, or any of the other acronyms he mentioned.

'No problem,' he said after I'd thanked him again. 'Do you mind?' he asked as he started picking at my lunch. He'd only ordered a coffee.

'Can I order you something?' I asked but James insisted he didn't want anything. He assured me that he would keep the business going and gave me a list of things I needed to do when I felt I was ready.

'It's a good thing,' he said, still nibbling on my lunch, 'that he's not, you know, an orthopaedic surgeon or an employee, and that he has a business you can do.'

But I couldn't help feeling that if Paddy had been an orthopaedic surgeon, or the manager of a supermarket, or anything other than an archery-equipment importer, we wouldn't be in this mess. I appreciated James's belief in me. I was sure that, in theory, anyone could run a business. But he may as well have been talking about highly specialised surgical procedures for all the sense his business jargon made to me.

'Is there anything I can do for you?' I asked him. 'You're spending so much time at the warehouse.'

'Yep, next time order the avocado stack. I don't like that chicken thing,' he said.

As James finished my lunch, I recalled the time a woman in the mothers' group I'd joined after Nick was born asked me to be her business partner. This proposal had followed a doleful chat about the difficulties of finding childcare. As I'd pushed my pram up to the cafe for our first business meeting at Neutral Bay, my mind was ablaze with thoughts of business trips, long liquid lunches and a platinum credit card.

'So, what's the business?' I asked her.

'I'd like a business where I don't have to do anything, I just go in and pick up the cash,' she said with complete sincerity. I'd laughed because, coincidentally, that was the only kind of business I've ever really wanted to have too. Although, in an ideal world I'd prefer the cash to be dropped off to me. I suggested we waste no time copyrighting the idea before anyone else got wind of it.

Over the years, I'd had loads of business ideas: making piñatas; a mobile gelato van. But I could recognise, as James began fielding calls from his own customers and employees and I looked at my very long to-do list, that my business ideas comprised only overnight success, windfalls of cash, and very little in the way of actual work. Unfortunately, Paddy's business, as did all viable businesses, involved an enormous amount of work.

'You can do this! You can do this!' I repeated James's words aloud as I sat in front of my computer, trying to psych myself into action. My main stumbling block, as far as I could tell, was that I didn't see myself as a business person. Secondly, the business sold archery and camping equipment, and not clothes or books or make-up (the sorts of things I was interested in). However, I'd read in a magazine that it could be beneficial not to be in love with the product, so that you are able to focus on the business system.

I closed my eyes and imagined myself as the subject of a magazine article about female entrepreneurs. The focus would be on my inspiration for the multi-million-dollar business I had grown from a start-up and how I juggled its demands with those of my family. It would also be a great opportunity for me to talk about female role models—Arianna Huffington, Oprah Winfrey, Anita Roddick. The accompanying photos would be shot on the sprawling green lawn of our estate. Me and the kids in luminous white designer clothes.

That image was fresh in my mind as I opened my eyes to complete the first item on my agenda—paying bills. Patrick had always done the banking. And, to my shame, I'd never actually paid a bill before. But how hard could it be? I navigated the bank website, found the personal banking section, and attempted to log on using the folder that Paddy had left me, containing various passwords for all our different accounts. I entered the number and the password. Easy. But the log-in was unsuccessful. I tried again and again until the account was blocked.

I called the bank, to be told that Patrick was the only authorised person on the account.

'You'll have to get him to call us,' the customer service operator said.

'He can't. He's away. I have power of attorney.'

'Well, just pop into a branch.'

When I looked in the folder again, I realised that I had used the correct username and password, but for a different bank. Paddy had given me lessons, and got me to watch YouTube tutorials to assist me with most aspects of the business. However, all my lessons had had a very 'in the unlikely event of' feel about them, and I had applied the same level of attention as I usually do to the inflight safety procedures.

'I did some drawings—for Dad,' Lexie told me when I went to pick her up from preschool. Or, at least, that's what I guess she must have said. I wasn't listening. I was skimming the information sheet on the noticeboard in the foyer, worried that I had missed, or was about to miss, an important event.

'They're very good, very colourful,' another mother said, as if making a point about my apparent lack of interest in my daughter's creativity. 'I'm sure he'll love them.'

'He can't have them,' Lexie said, matter-of-factly, 'because people hide drugs behind the glue and sticky tape.' If I had danced naked around the preschool playground, I don't think I could have elicited a greater look of surprise from this woman. Her eyebrows couldn't have lifted any higher nor her eyes stretched any wider.

'It's not that I want you to lie,' I said to Lexie, en route to Nick's school, 'it's just that it's hard for other people to understand.'

'But I didn't tell her!' It amazed me that Lexie could be so articulate and so insightful but when it came to context and inference she was so aggravatingly literal.

'She could tell.'

'How?'

'Never mind. Remember, we're just telling people who are our close friends and family.' I remembered reading in a parenting book or on a website that it's good to give children a visual example of the point you're making. So I said to Lexie, 'People we spend time with *inside* our house.'

And that was exactly how, less than an hour later, Lexie came to tell a virtual stranger that her father, my husband, was in prison.

We were in the living room, having finished a tour of the house to our prospective new cleaner. She looked to be in her mid sixties, and was lean, most likely from all the cleaning. 'It's not a big house. I could fly through here in two hours,' she said.

We'd had a cleaner before, and though she had been excellent, I'd never felt entirely comfortable about the situation. She had been a single mother with three autistic children. She had seemed happy to have the work and did an excellent job, but I couldn't cope with the guilt. Not only was her regular life more difficult than mine, but her time away from her special-needs children was spent cleaning my toilet. And so I had started doing the cleaning before she came, which defeated the purpose of having a cleaner in the first place. When she was offered a part-time job at her children's school, I was ever so relieved.

'What sort of work do you do?' our new cleaner asked, handing me a quote.

'We . . .'—the pronoun slipped out automatically—'have an importing business.'

'And does your husband work from home as well?' It was an innocent enough question; she was making conversation and I could have simply said no. But she was the first person outside our immediate circle of family and friends I'd spoken to about Patrick and it caught me completely off guard.

'*My* husband?' I asked, sounding like I was either an idiot, or in the process of concocting a very bad lie. 'Well, he's, he's . . .'

'In jail,' Lexie said, without hesitation. The word ricocheted around the room, cartoon style, landing at our feet with a thud. I expected that the cleaner would excuse herself or find that her schedule was suddenly full.

She, like most other people I'd told, visibly recoiled. I felt foolish and exposed, and wished the floor would swallow me up. When other devastating things happen, like death or illness, it is, of course, difficult to find the right thing to say, but at least there's some known vocabulary we can call on. Some phrases, albeit clichéd, that express concern or sympathy. And if we can't find any words to express our feelings, there are cards to express it for us. I've yet to see a card that articulates the combination of horror, shame, fear and loss you feel when someone you love is sent to jail.

Of all the things the cleaner could have said or done, she opened her arms and she hugged me. This complete stranger hugged me. I was so moved by her kindness. And when she did finally speak, she said, 'Love, if there's one thing I've learned, it's that things are never as they seem, for any of us. Your life can be going along one way and, bam, everything changes.' By this time, Lexie had left the room. 'Happened to me,' she continued. 'Married almost twenty-two years when I found out my husband was having an affair. Life's got a way of teaching you what you need to learn.'

That night in bed, I tried to explain to Lexie that we didn't know the cleaner well enough yet to tell her about Dad.

'But she was *inside* the house.'

'I know she was *inside*, but, she's not our friend, is she? Not yet.'

'Don't you like her?'

'Yes, I like her, she seems very nice, but we've only just met her. It takes time for a friendship to develop.'

When it was Lexie's turn to pray, she said: 'Dear God, thank you for Mum and Dad and Nick. Please change Mum's heart, so I can have a cat. And can I please have some close friends, so I can tell them Dad is in jail? Amen.' Soon afterwards, Lexie fell asleep, and then Nick's breathing slowed and deepened, and he was off too. I loved it when they were finally asleep and everything was quiet.

The trouble was, they were in my bed. The sleeping patterns Paddy and I had diligently worked on had all, within a matter of weeks, completely fallen apart.

The following weekend, Patrick's mate Simon joined us for the visit to MRRC. It was the first time we were able to secure a table in the paved courtyard outside. Paddy hugged the kids so enthusiastically and so tenderly, it looked like he would never let go.

As I watched them, I became aware of my body solidifying, like water to ice, as I processed the shock of the surroundings. 'You sure you're okay?' I said to Paddy, as Simon talked to the kids.

'Yeah, I'm fine. The food's the worst. Brown slop, looks the same every day, it's just called different names. What I wouldn't give for some of your soup.' In fact, Paddy hated soup. He would eat it and then want to know what else we were having.

Then he played with the kids while I chatted to Simon. As Paddy threw back his head at one point, I watched him catch a glimpse of the sky. It was remarkable to see. He did a double take and then craned his head back up to look. He held his gaze for such a long time that the kids also looked up. And then Simon and I joined them.

'What are you looking at?' Lexie asked.

'The sky,' Paddy said.

'Is there a plane?' Nick asked.

'No, just the sky.'

We all stood there, transfixed by the sheer wonder of it. It was breathtaking; cornflower blue, with long, wispy white strokes of cursive letters. A love letter penned in the sky.

And the funny thing was, I wasn't in prison and had every opportunity, day or night, to look up at the sky and I couldn't remember the last time I had. As the visit drew to a close, Paddy said his goodbyes and said to me, 'It's funny what you miss. I miss you guys, of course, but I miss nature. I miss trees.'

As I drove through the prison gates, I noticed the trees that flanked the entrance on Holker Street, outside the prison. Gorgeous eucalyptus trees, skinny silver-hued trunks, with branches stretching up to the sky like open arms, towering above everything else as if mocking the laws of engineering.

THIRTEEN

Steph was wearing the most incredible strappy stilettos, with alternating pieces of black and snakeskin leather. In the years I'd been seeing her, I'd only twice seen her in the same shoes. Sometimes, as I sat across from her, I wondered if she had a walk-in closet, à la Imelda Marcos, or if she used clear shoebox organisers.

'So?' Steph said, breaking the ice. 'The sentencing?' Her pen was poised but her tone was light, so I knew that she, like everyone else we knew, had not expected a custodial sentence.

I'd been looking forward to my appointment all week. It would be an opportunity to let off some steam, and try to make some sense of what had happened. And then, sitting on the blue coach across from her, I realised just how many times I had already told the story and how tired I was of telling it.

I recounted the whole courtroom/prison shebang. He was taken into custody on the Tuesday, and brought back for sentencing on the Friday, receiving combined sentences of four and a half years, two and a half non-parole.

'Four and a half years!' Steph said, aghast. Like everyone, she winced.

'Uh-huh. Everyone's been so supportive—the fridge is filled with lasagne. People have offered to babysit and work, and do whatever it is we need.'

'And what does that mean to you?' Steph asked, once she had collected herself. I cradled my peppermint tea that was still too hot to drink. Recounting wasn't difficult. The what. The when. The where. What brought me unstuck, what made me tongue-tied and monosyllabic, were the questions about how I felt.

'And what does that mean to you?' was Steph's personal favourite. And even though Steph had asked me this question countless times during our sessions, I always found it difficult.

What does it mean to me?

It means I can't call him.

It means I now have to run a business.

It means I am essentially a single mother.

I shifted in the chair. 'Can you repeat the question?'

'What does that mean to you?' she repeated, crossing her long legs and, perhaps because I still looked dazed and confused, she reframed it. 'How does it make you feel?'

I stared at one of the two drawings displayed on the wall behind her. During one of our previous sessions, she revealed that she had two sons and the eldest had done the drawings. I would have given anything to spend the remainder of the session talking about them instead.

'How are your sons? How old are they now?'

'They've been on your mind a lot, have they?'

'Constantly.' I was sprung.

It was difficult to articulate my feelings, because I didn't know what I felt. When friends or family asked me, I filled the conversational gaps with anecdotes about the kids or navigating the prison. I didn't want to talk about the depths of my inner life, because at any given moment I felt an entire spectrum of emotions or nothing at all. Inside felt murky, like the dirty water that follows a flood. I couldn't make out any shapes in it and I certainly couldn't see the bottom.

'Not good,' I said eventually. 'Pretty impressive description, huh?'

'It's not about being impressive, it's about being real,' Steph said gently.

I couldn't give her anything else. As quickly as the clamshell had opened, it had shut again. Looking back, I can see I was in survival mode and thought that if I let my guard down, if I got emotional, everything would crumble. If the egg cracked at the wrong time or in the wrong place, it would create a gooey, unusable mess. I had to be strong for the kids and reasoned that it was far better to be hard-boiled.

So I kept it light. I told Steph about Lexie's conversation at the preschool. Steph listened, engaged and interested. Pen poised. She laughed in all the right places.

My little deflectionary excursion had relaxed me somewhat but I should have known better; I knew that anecdotes never washed over her. She listened carefully, gleaning for clues to what I was revealing or what I was trying to cover up. She usually said something like, 'I noticed that you made a certain expression when you did this,' or 'I'd like to revisit something you said about that.'

That session was no different. 'And what does it mean to you—in other words, how did it make you feel when Lexie spoke about jail to the preschool mother?'

'I don't know . . . embarrassed, mortified. I can still see the look on the mother's face. She had no idea what to say . . . Makes for a good story, I s'pose.'

In a previous session, Steph had pointed out how I often tried to steer the conversation away from things I found confronting.

During each appointment, I became more aware that the seemingly personal or revealing things I said served as conversational red herrings. To keep people at a distance. I was like one of those deceptively shallow beaches. The kind that make people into quadriplegics.

'And what does it . . . how did it . . . make you feel that the woman was shocked?' Steph asked.

'I mainly felt for Lexie; I didn't want her to feel put down or ashamed, like I did.'

A long pause followed, and just when I really wanted to jump in with singing or yodelling or chanting, anything to break the silence, she spoke. '*Like you did.* What did you mean by that?'

I shrugged. 'I didn't mean anything by it.' Wincing at my own defensiveness.

It was always the same. This was the part I hated most. I started the hour desperately wanting her to like me, and then, when her line of questioning honed in on something specific, something I didn't want to face, I turned on her.

A hundred and seventy-five dollars for a cup of peppermint tea, and a bit of conversation. It's a bit rich, I thought. And I only get a bit back from Medicare. I might do better buying myself some fancy shoes and chatting to a friend.

'You know, when Patrick first called from Surry Hills, he told me he was watching TV, and the kids said, "Why does he get to watch TV during the week?"'

Steph laughed before gently bringing us back to her point. 'It's interesting that you said, "like I did". Past tense. Did you feel ashamed when you were a child?'

'No. Well, maybe sometimes . . . a bit.' My throat was dry and the pitch was noticeably higher. A trait I associated with lying.

'Like everyone, I s'pose.' The room suddenly felt small and hot. 'Can I have some water, please?'

'Of course.' Steph stood on her long, long, legs, and for a moment she almost lost her balance and reminded me of a newborn foal. The request for water bought me time and as I waited I stared at the paintings. They both featured abstract splodges of colour: one green and blue, and the other yellow and red.

'Do you think everyone feels ashamed as a child?' She was like a dog with a bone.

'I imagine there are times when all kids are embarrassed,' I said.

'But you didn't say embarrassed, you said "ashamed". Were you ashamed as a child?' Steph asked, holding my gaze.

'I had a good childhood. No beatings. No child services.'

'And yet, you used the word shame. Why do you think that is?'

It was agony. 'My mum and dad got married young because of me. Shortly afterwards, my dad got sick and they struggled.'

'Financially?' Steph asked.

'Yes.'

'And you felt ashamed?' She would not let this drop.

I hadn't thought about this often but I was surprised to find how many memories were there, just beneath the surface. The flip clock on the side table next to me displayed 11.27, and yet I felt like I had been in there for weeks. It occurred to me that if Einstein had seen a psychologist, he might have discovered relativity even earlier.

'We were in government housing . . . housing commission . . . until I was eleven and then my parents bought a house on the other side of town.' Steph wrote a couple of notes and motioned for me to continue. 'This meant I changed schools. Within the first week, or sometime early on, a girl in the year above asked me where I lived. I was really proud of our new house, and the fact that it had three bedrooms, so my sister and I now had our own rooms, so I told her. She started laughing, like hysterically, and then called over a bunch of other scary-looking girls with extremely short dresses and dark eyeliner. "She's a 'Wollom," the girl said to the others.'

'A what?' Steph asked.

'A Wollom, cause that's where all the losers and the druggos and povos lived . . . in Wollombi Road.'

I looked out the window. Since I had started seeing Steph again, her office had relocated to the front of the building, which afforded me the best vantage point of her Lexus 4WD, and led to further deliberation about just who was benefiting from our psychology sessions.

'And then what happened?' Steph asked.

'After that,' I continued, 'I noticed that some houses further along the road—not all of them, some people were very house proud, just poor—had windows boarded up and furniture strewn across the front yard. And at night, groups of people would sit in the gutter and drink, and others would pour petrol or lighter fluid along the road and chase the flames.' I'd never talked to anyone about this before, and as I did, I realised that I had carried the shame with me my entire life.

'Did the teasing continue?' Steph asked.

'All through high school.' In fact, it intensified. 'Back then, the reputation of the area had grown and it was commonly known as The Bronx. And in high school, things like where you live and the clothes you wear, and what your parents do for a living, are such a big deal.'

'What springs to mind as you think about this?' Steph asked.

'There was this one girl who lived in my neighbourhood. I think her parents might have had problems with drugs or something, because they used to lock her out of the house, which is what some of them did when they wanted to get high. At school, I did everything I could to hide the fact that I lived in my neighbour-hood. I left the address section blank or whited out my address on permission slips, and only after I knew someone really well did I invite them over. Anyway, this girl knew where I lived and she knew how terrified I was of people finding out. So she became very evangelistic about it.'

I sipped my tea again. 'She used to follow me to and from school. Getting to school wasn't a problem, because I could vary or stagger the time, but in the afternoons when the bell went and everyone was dismissed, she would run ahead and wait for me. And on the way home, she'd throw stones at my back and yell out, "You think you're so good, but I know where you live!"'

'So in your situation now, with Patrick, do you feel ashamed? Are you afraid that people will find out?'

A couple of people had already asked me that and I'd said I wasn't. 'I suppose I am,' I said to Steph. 'On the first day after he had . . . gone away, at school pick-up, it felt like all eyes on were on me.'

'Do you think they were?' Steph asked.

'I told myself they weren't but when I talked to a school mother at a friend's house, I was surprised to learn that she knew.

'"Fraud?" she'd asked me. And it was good to know that she didn't immediately jump to the conclusion Patrick is an axe murderer, but the fraud assumption didn't feel all that great either. After that, I felt paranoid. My mother always told me it doesn't matter what people say but . . .'

'Go on,' Steph said.

'A few years ago, I was back where I grew up in the Hunter Valley looking at buying an investment property. I asked the agent about one pictured in the window. "You wouldn't want to buy in that area, people over there have two heads!" he said, referring to the street I was raised in.'

Our sessions were fifty minutes and at the forty-minute mark Steph would gather the various threads of our conversation into a recap. The remaining time would be spent on strategies. This session's strategies were as follows: (1) Tell people on a need-to-know basis. Friends, schoolteachers and the kids' friends' parents all should know, so they can support Nick and Lexie. (2) Say yes. People want to help and it's okay to accept those offers.

FOURTEEN

MRRC Silverwater

8 February 2013

Beauty,

Every morning I wake up and there is a gap before I remember what happened and where I am. Most letters and postcards I have written in the past (not many, I know) have all started with 'having a great time'. Not this time. Surreal, like bad dream.

Learning jail craft. Like bush craft but with the resources in here. Hot water made by DIY foil prong and inserted into power point. Water passed to others through space under door in a plastic bag.

In a 2 out (2 person cell) now and my roommate's (cellie) name is Charger. Everyone started asking me if Charger had been to the toilet (actually, they said, 'Has he taken a sh*t?') Said I better things to do than document bowel movements but, truthfully, nothing better to do.

Inmate: Want to keep it all to yourself? (????)
Inmate: Why not let others have a taste? (????)
Found out all waiting for heroin (called H in here).

Drugs are everywhere. In yard yesterday, bored out of my mind. Seemed like another miracle when tennis ball came flying over fence. First thought: handball comp.

Inmate: Is that your ball?

Me: Is now.

Inmate: Don't touch it. Get your family to throw one over for you.

Me: (confused) My family can throw one over?

Inmate: Yeah, just make sure it is no more than 5 grams.

Me: Can you get different sizes?

Inmate: What the eff are you talking about? (Hear that on hourly basis.)

Found out they hide drugs in balls and then glue them back together. Use dead birds for same. Curious: do they look for dead birds or kill living ones? Either can't be easy. Understand why tennis balls so popular.

Came as a surprise that Charger can't read. Couldn't believe my luck when I found the Good Weekend *mag (horse on front) in communal area. Read your story over and over. Think I know off by heart now.*

Charger: (threw letter onto my bed) I've got something you can read.

Me: I'm good.

Charger: Read it. (Started reading silently.) Aloud.

Me: Don't like reading aloud. (Twigging, then reading) Dear Tony . . . Of all the effing eff ups this one has to take the effing cake.

Charger: Did she write effing?

Me: I'm just abbreviating. I don't swear.

Charger: What the eff (didn't abbreviate) do you mean you don't effing swear? Just effing read what's on the effing page!

Me: It's against my . . . principles . . . if you want to get someone else to read . . . (tells me to keep reading).

Letter says (girlfriend?) thinks he is an idiot because he's charged with home invasion and torture. Read ahead and spoiler alert: she is leaving him, seeing his mate and has plans to sell his bike on eBay. Try to convince Charger he doesn't need to hear it. He psychs himself up like an Olympic weightlifter and clenches fists. Break news that she has been seeing Helmet (Charger says he is a dead man). He goes psycho and punches wall and storms out.

Hope he knows the phrase 'Don't shoot the messenger'. After dinner (3pm in here) he comes back. Has calmed down and thanks me for reading. Says that relationship is going through a 'rocky patch'.

Only 3 phones in unit. (1 broken, so only 2). Five men dominate one and the rest of us (approx. 60) share other. Decided to be proactive. Collected names and made a roster. 60+ men over the moon. Then . . .

Inmate: Are you effing crazy? Why are you picking a fight with the bikies?

Me: I'm not picking a fight with anyone.

Inmate that looks like bikie approaches.

Bikie: We own the phones. Comprende? (Sounded clichéd, like a B-grade movie. Didn't argue, he was size of large fridge.)

Finally understand significance of shoes. Inmates allowed to wear shoes they are arrested/sentenced in (explains attire in court). So brand names (Nike, Adidas etc) is mark of cool. I only have basic prison issue. Can buy more expensive (still green issue but not cool apparently) with buy up but prefer to use money on phone calls.

Sorry I couldn't be there for Lexie's first day at sessional kindergarten. I have never missed any of her other firsts and to miss this is so, so hard. Please take lots of photos.

Miss seeing you, my sleeping beauty next to me. I look forward to hearing your voice when I call (not much now with no roster).

Love,

Paddy

FIFTEEN

'Is Dad a bad person?' Nick asked.

'No, he's not a bad person. Why do you ask that?'

'Because you said the people in there—' he responded, pointing to a correctional centre nestled in the industrial area of Emu Plains—'are bad.'

I had taken the back way to the larger supermarket in Penrith, which just happens to be the site of a women's prison.

'I'm sure I didn't say that. Maybe I said they *did* something bad.'

'No, you said they *are* bad,' Nick insisted, tapping on the car door.

'Yeah, you did,' Lexie said, weighing in even though she would have only been a toddler at the time.

I had a vague recollection of the conversation. Nick had asked why all the women tending cows in the front paddock of the centre were wearing green. Maybe I did say they were bad people. I couldn't remember. Maybe it was a way of keeping the topic at a safe distance, a neat and convenient way of simplifying it for the kids. Before Paddy's arrest, I'd never engaged with the plight of prisoners. If I read or saw something about appalling conditions, or the perils of privatisation, or sentencing inequity, it didn't stir a fire within, or even prompt another thought, other than to change the channel. If I'm really honest, I suppose I thought they should have considered that before they broke the law. But saying that prisoners were bad contradicted my beliefs about human nature: that all of us are a mix of good and bad.

'If they put all the bad people together, won't it just make them all really, really bad?' Lexie asked, wiping what was left of her iceblock on the fabric of the car seat.

'Don't wipe it on the seat,' I said, so she proceeded to wipe it on her clothes, and it amazed me that someone could be so astute and so disgusting. 'Not necessarily,' I continued, unsure how to proceed. She had a point. 'Most of the people in prison are just like us, but they broke the law.'

'What laws do you have to break to get into prison?' Nick asked, brow furrowed.

'All sorts of things. Stealing, fraud, which is tricking people with paperwork, or lying.'

'Can you go to prison for lying?' Nick asked, with a considerable amount of self-interest.

'Not just any lie, but if it's a crime, or helps someone get away with a crime, then, yes, you can.' Nick looked relieved. 'But people can also go there for being violent, or robbing banks, or killing people.'

'Is Dad in there with murderers?' Nick asked, alarmed.

I hadn't thought through that last statement. 'No, of course not. There are different sections for people who have done violent or dangerous things.' I knew this was a big, fat lie but I also knew that Nick would have an aneurysm if I told him the truth about MRRC.

'Are they separated by walls or bars?' he asked.

'I don't know, Nick, but the really dangerous or disruptive ones would have to be separated.'

'Like Rory,' Lexie said. 'He has to be separated in class. And when that doesn't work he has to sit outside, but we can still see him making faces in the window.'

'Slightly different situation, Lex, being separated in class and separated from society,' I said. 'Kids don't go to prison.'

'Yes, they do,' Nick said. 'In *The Simpsons*, they call it juvey.'

'Not when they're six years old. A lot of people who end up in prison haven't had the best start in life. Their parents might be abusive or on drugs, so they end up on the wrong path.'

Nick found this funny. '"Excuse me, sir, can you show me the path that leads to prison?" "Yes, you turn left and then right, and follow it all the way along."'

'I think Rory is on the path to prison.'

'Don't say that, Lex,' I said, glaring at her from the front seat.

A conversational hiatus followed but there was still the sound of Nick's incessant tapping. 'Prison is the worst punishment there is,' he announced, after careful thought.

'There are worse punishments. In some countries, people can be sentenced to death,' I told them, and then instantly regretted it. I knew my kids and knew they'd never been exposed to such a violent concept as capital punishment.

'In *Horrible Histories*'—an historical sketch show the kids loved and knew by heart—'they said that in Tudor times, if you steal more than eleven pence, they sentence you to death. In one episode a lady gets money stolen and a policeman says he'll chop the robber's head off.'

'Tudor England was a long time ago,' I said.

I found these conversations hard. I wanted to be open and honest with the kids, but since Patrick's incarceration, so many of our discussions opened a veritable Pandora's box of issues that even adults had a hard time wrapping their heads around. Sometimes I felt like I told them too much; other times, I worried I wasn't open enough. Most of all, I wanted them to understand that Patrick had made a mistake.

'Dad made a mistake and everyone makes mistakes. You make mistakes and I make mistakes,' I said, as we pulled into the shopping-centre car park. 'Remember when I got that speeding ticket?' I said to Nick. The kids hadn't been in the car at the time but they had relished the fact that I, the CEO of the Fun Police, had finally done something wrong. I'd hoped that by reminding them of my very expensive traffic offence, I could rekindle their enthusiasm for my mistake.

'What if you get another speeding ticket and you have to go to prison? Who will look after us?' Nick asked, worried, still tapping.

'You don't go to prison for getting a speeding ticket.'

'But who would look after us . . . if something happened?' Nick asked, suddenly burdened by the prospect of orphanhood.

'Most likely, Grandma Laney.'

'What if Grandma Laney dies? She is very old.'

I loved Nick with all my heart but sometimes he made Woody Allen look optimistic. 'She's not that old, she's not even sixty.'

'She does have a wrinkly neck and wrinkly hands,' said Lexie.

'If Grandma Laney dies, Aunty Fiona or Aunty Cathy, but it's not very common for both parents to die.'

'It is in Roald Dahl books,' Nick said, and his questions finally abated. He was satisfied, for the time being. He could be so gloomy. Not that I'm in any position to criticise; he gets it from me.

Two days later, his ominously silent room roused my suspicions. 'You in there, Nick?' I asked and the sound of rummaging immediately followed from his bed. His head extended up from beneath the quilt, like a meerkat. His eyes were red and puffy from crying. He'd tried, unsuccessfully, to hide a box of tissues and a mass of snotty ones under the quilt. I shuddered at the thought of this and reminded myself to pick my battles.

'You okay?'

'Something's in my eye,' he said, turning away from me. I knew he didn't have anything in his eye, except the things he was supposed to have, like corneas and pupils and other bits that were too scientific for me to know about.

'Want me to have a look?'

He shook his head, confirming there was nothing in his eye, given he has the lowest pain threshold of anyone I have ever met.

'Are you feeling sad about Dad?' Once again, he avoided my gaze. 'It's okay to be sad, you know. It's a very big thing, a very hard thing that you're dealing with. I'm sad sometimes, and angry and frustrated . . .'

'You are?'

'Absolutely. And that's okay, that's to be expected. I miss him. And even though I know in my head what's happened, sometimes I come home and I expect him to be here, or I'll go to call him and then I remember. Yesterday, when it was time to leave for school, I was waiting for Dad to say, in that really bad English accent, "You've got your bag, you've got your—"'

'"Lunchbox, you've got your jumper,"' Nick said, finishing the sentence for me, and laughter momentarily replaced our solemnity.

'What do you miss?' I asked, sitting on the bottom bunk next to him.

'I miss computer games and wrestling and . . .' His voice was suddenly tremulous.

'It's okay, it's okay,' I said, as he collapsed into me, sobbing.

'It' . . . s . . . all . . . my . . . fa . . . ult,' came out in bursts between the sobs.

'What's your fault?'

'D . . . ad go . . . ing to ja . . . il.'

'No, no, it's not your fault.'

Nick cried long and hard. So hard that he couldn't speak, he just gasped for breath. I held him and stroked his hair and his back, and told him that it was okay and he didn't have to say anything yet. Finally, when he stopped crying and had used up the remaining tissues, he told me that importing archery equipment had been his idea.

It took me a very long time to explain that his suggestion was perfectly viable and legal, and that importing archery equipment was how we made our living. I also went to great lengths to explain that just because someone gives you an idea doesn't mean you have to run with it. Like my mother always said to me when I was a kid, 'If such and such jumped off the Harbour Bridge, would you do it too?'

Eventually, Nick stopped crying. He was exhausted but lighter in heart, and he smiled his beautiful, crooked, wry little smile that never fails to melt me.

'Is there anything I can do? Anything at all?' I asked.

'Can we wrestle?'

SIXTEEN

It had been seventeen days since Patrick had gone. It was the third week and it had been the hardest by far. I knew, intellectually, that my husband was in prison and that he couldn't come home, and yet, every time I heard the front door open or a car pull into the drive, part of me hoped it was him. But he did not come home, and as each day passed, the painful and inevitable truth of what had happened began to sink in for all of us. The kids began to grieve. And grief changed them.

In grief, as in life, Lexie was bright and explosive—a short fuse. Nick was a slow-burning flame. Lexie's behaviour regressed to the bed-wetting and tantrum throwing that she had begun to grow out of. Nick's bouts of melancholy were deeper and darker than ever before.

Life was already frantic with school drop-offs, work, music lessons, play dates and weekend visits to Patrick, and now their new behaviours had to be factored in. I had to learn how to manage things on my own. Everything was so delicately balanced that I clung to our schedule like a raft on the deepest part of the ocean.

The alarm would wake me at six. I showered and dressed, and made the school lunches. I drove Nick to the bus stop and waited with him and then dropped Lexie at preschool or, at least, tried to drop her there as she clung to my leg like a barnacle: 'I'm begging you, don't leave. Please don't do this to me!' On the way to the warehouse, I would ring the preschool and they would assure me she was perfectly calm and happy. Meanwhile, my mother guilt was off the scale.

I usually worked at the warehouse until midday, headed home for lunch, and worked there until it was time to pick up the kids at four. But that day I left the warehouse early, because I had woken with pain in my ear and by midmorning it was so intense I couldn't concentrate on anything. I was certain I had an ear infection but couldn't get in to see the doctor until later that afternoon, so I went home for a Panadol and a lie-down. I would have been in bed for no more than ten minutes when the doorbell rang.

'Nicola,' I said. 'You shouldn't have!'

Our neighbour from a few doors down was holding a homemade cake and some flowers. A lovely gesture, considering we weren't really friends. We were acquaintances at best, linked only by a mutual friend and our shared street.

'It's awful, just so awful!' she exclaimed. 'People out there doing real crimes, and Patrick gets this. He's not a criminal.' But by very definition, he was. He had broken the law.

'When I heard, I said to Steve, "I'm going to pop round there and encourage her."'

'Thank you . . . but you shouldn't have, really,' I said, unsure what to say to this woman and perplexed as to how she even knew about what had happened. I kept standing at the door, expecting her to leave. As I turned to put the container on the buffet near the entrance, Nicola walked in, muttering something about a vase.

'And I thought my place was bad,' she joked, referring to the pieces of brightly coloured craft and glitter that looked like they had been thrown, confetti-style, across the back end of the house.

'I haven't had a chance—'

'It's just so awful, isn't it?' she continued.

'Not what we were hoping for, no.'

Nicola unwrapped the flowers, and grabbed a pair of scissors that were on the table with Lexie's craft things, cutting the stems. 'I mean, if the same thing happened to Steve, I just couldn't cope. Lying in bed at night, hoping he doesn't . . . *slip in the shower.*' Her last words were whispered, as though that somehow diminished the horror of talking about my husband getting raped. I shuddered to think what it would have been like if she'd popped around to discourage me. Perhaps Nicola could visit the sick and the elderly— cheer them up as well. I tried to tell her that I wasn't feeling well but she's not a listener. She didn't once pause to listen to my answers; a drunk student at schoolies had more boundaries than Nicola.

When she finally left, a good hour and half later, she promised she would come around again soon. I did my best to say that I was on a pretty tight schedule but she just bulldozed right over me.

The medical centre was packed. 'Can you read this?' Lexie whined, waving a children's book in front of me.

'I'm reading a magazine.'

'You're not reading, you're just looking at pictures of people without any clothes on.'

'They're bikinis,' I corrected her and Lexie rolled her eyes. It had been ages since I'd read anything, and looking at stars without make-up and at celebrity cellulite was proving to be very good for my self-esteem.

Nick amused himself with his tapping but Lexie persisted with her whining, so I eventually succumbed and read her the shortest book on offer from the slim pile in the waiting room. Soon afterwards, another little girl approached me with a book. My ears were throbbing, and I was exhausted from the morning and Nicola, and life in general. I didn't feel like reading a book to my own children, let alone someone else's.

'Maybe your mum can read you a book?' I suggested, looking over at the woman whose genetic traits declared that if she wasn't her mother, she was somehow related.

'She doesn't read me books.'

'I'm sure she's read you *a* book.'

The little girl just shook her head and looked up with hopeful eyes, her arm stretching the book out towards me. Reluctantly, I started to read the book and when punctuation allowed, glared at the mother. As we neared the end of the longest book in the history of children's books, my mobile rang and I asked Nick to answer it.

'You are about to receive a phone call from an inmate at MRRC Correctional Centre . . .' announced the recorded message. Nick had put the phone on speaker.

'Nick, give me the phone. Nick! Take it off speaker, take it off speaker,' I raised my voice as he held it away from me.

'. . . receive this phone call, please hang up now,' it continued, for the listening pleasure of the entire waiting room.

'Dad!' Nick said, as the never-read-a-book-to-her-child-mother glared at me as if to say, 'I might not read books but at least my husband isn't in prison!'

'Hey, buddy,' Patrick said.

'Mum said we can have frozen yoghurt!' Lexie shouted.

'Mum's got an ear infection,' said Nick.

'That's great. Can I talk to Mum? I need to talk to Mum.' There was urgency in his voice. I took the phone off speaker and walked towards the entrance.

'They're moving me—six hours away. I've been classified as C2 and they are moving me to minimum security. I told them I'd refuse. That we can't survive as a family—they said I've got no choice. And if I don't sign the paperwork for Mannus, they'll send me to some other place nine hours away.'

'When?'

'I don't know.' The beeps sounded and the call ended.

Six hours? Life was already busy enough. I didn't have time to drive six hours and back. Weekends were spent shopping and cooking and cleaning in preparation for the following week. And we all relied on the continuity of the weekend visits to try to maintain some semblance of a family relationship.

'Melissa Jacob,' the doctor called. I didn't respond; I was still floored by the news.

'Mum, that's you,' Nick said.

I went in to see the doctor, who said there was no sign of infection. The pain was being caused as a result of grinding my my teeth.

'Feel this,' she said, and I ran my hand over what felt like a metal rod in the back of my jaw near my ear. She gave me some medicine to relieve the pain and suggested I buy a mouthguard to relieve the pressure.

In the weeks that followed Nick morphed into a distant and angry child.

'How was your day?' I asked as he walked in the door one afternoon.

'Brilliant,' he said, clearly having got the hang of sarcasm. Then he kicked his shoes off, sending one of them flying into the bookcase which caused a row of books to cascade to the floor.

'Pick them up,' I said to Nick, who was already en route to his bedroom. 'Come back here.' He ignored me. I marched up to his room, and, as I opened his door, trod on a marooned piece of Lego. Nick just sat there, which infuriated me even more. 'Get up, get up!' I yelled like a madwoman, grabbing his wrist and trying to force him to his feet. He was skinny but he was strong.

'I wish you were in jail,' he said. And it wasn't just what he said that stung, it was the way he said it—cold and calculated.

I felt so wounded; I had to leave the room. I made a cup of tea and went out onto the deck, and when I had finally calmed down, I took some biscuits in to him.

'There's a name for what you're going through right now, it's called grieving.'

He looked up at me, forlorn.

'It's what happens when you lose something, and you feel a mixture of all different emotions, like anger and sadness and confusion. It feels like it will last forever, but it won't.'

'How long does it last?' he asked, he asked, lips quivering.

'There's no set time, it's different for everyone. I'm grieving too.' The numbness I'd been feeling had been replaced with a physical ache in my chest. I tried to block it out and not focus on it, and then when it momentarily subsided and I felt like I had turned a corner, it would resurface and crash-tackle me to the ground. My friend Jen, a psychologist, had told me that the term 'waves' has been used in a lot of literature associated with grief and loss, but that more recently the term 'chaos theory' has been being used to explain the more haphazard way we experience it.

Nick cried and I soothed him like I had when he was a toddler. 'You will get through this,' I said, and tried to convince myself that this experience would make him more resilient and empathetic. But, as his mother, I wanted to shield him from every kind of heartbreak and disappointment, big and small. 'Sometimes, it can be helpful to think of other people who are having a tough time,' I said.

'What's worse than prison?' he scoffed and I berated myself. It was a stupid thing to say—I wasn't consoled by other people's suffering either—but I'd already started down that track.

'It's got to be hard for Caleb, with his dad moving out.'

'He gets to see his dad every single weekend, not for just an hour!'

'I know. I'm sorry.' I didn't have a clue; I was still flailing about in my own grief. I rubbed his back in soothing circular motions.

I wiped his tears away and he blew his nose, and then, as though he had a say in the matter, he said, 'I would choose divorce over prison.'

I smiled. It was interesting that Nick had started thinking about divorce. After Patrick's arrest, I just kept thinking we need to get through the court case, and then it became we need to get through the sentencing. As though I was waiting to restart my life. And now it was still going on. Perhaps Nick was right and divorce was easier than being a prison wife. Recently, thoughts about divorce had started to creep in and I wondered how long I could sustain a relationship which felt like it had been suspended in time. But that wasn't something for Nick to worry about. He needed all the support he could get.

'Will asked if you want to be on his soccer team,' I said to change the subject.

'My cousin Will?'

'Do you know any other Wills?'

And he laughed and shook his head.

First thing Monday morning, Patrick called to say he would be leaving sometime during the day. I rang Visits and made a booking, rang the school bus driver, collected Nick from the bus and Lexie from preschool, and drove straight to Silverwater.

'I'm very sorry,' the woman at the reception counter said. 'His profile says "Transit".'

'He just called. We wanted to see him, say goodbye.'

'He's probably somewhere on the grounds but once they've been moved, there's nothing we can do.' She was very sympathetic but the situation was clearly out of her hands.

'I wish the sniffer dogs were here,' Lexie said on the way out.

'I wish we could see someone busted for drugs,' Nick added, followed by, 'Not all drugs are bad. You take drugs, don't you, Mum?' much to the interest of passers-by.

I ordered hot chocolates in a nearby coffee shop. When they arrived, they were too hot to hold in the paper cups. I warned the kids not to touch them, but while I was at the counter collecting serviettes Nick, for some inexplicable reason, mimed drinking his hot chocolate and told Lexie to drink hers. She blindly followed, burning her lips and spraying chocolate milk all over the chairs and the table, and their clothes and my handbag. The morning had been so fraught and filled with so much expectation, and I was completely out of patience. 'You knew it was hot! I told you it was hot! Don't you ever think?' I yelled.

He just sat there looking at me, as did the other patrons. Then as though he was the one parenting me, he said, 'Have you had your brain medicine today, Mum?'

PART II

PART III

'THREE THINGS CANNOT BE LONG HIDDEN.
THE SUN, THE MOON AND THE TRUTH.'

Buddha

SEVENTEEN

Mannus Correctional Centre
4 March 2013

Beauty,

On the outside I was just Mr Average. Average job, average house, average marks in school. In Mannus, I am Stephen Freaking Hawking.

I'm in the unit they call The Bronx (roughest) but small fry compared to MRRC. Mainly drug related—possession, sales, petty crime to buy drugs (called earning). Smugglers are called Border Security (like the reality show).

In a 2 out with a guy named Jamie. Friendly, Indigenous, unintentionally funny and added bonus—not a bikie (I checked).

Sad to hear Jamie's life on the outside worse than prison. No real parenting, schooling. Eleven?? siblings, most of them have been inside. He's disappointed he didn't get a longer sentence so he can be in prison for winter. Told me he's had thirteen 'brushes with the law'.

Me: Have you been arrested thirteen times?

Jamie: (laughing his head off) No, bras, I've been in prison thirteen times. Been arrested heaps of times.

Me: Heaps? Like how many? Fifteen, twenty?

Jamie: (laughing) No bras, hundreds, hundreds.

Me: What did you do?

Jamie: Stole bacon from the supermarket, a lot of bacon.

Me: Were you hungry?

Jamie: No, I'm saving for a car, bras.

Jamie can't read either and Nick and Lexie know more about the world than he does.

After noticing me sleeping sun-up to sundown.

Jamie: If you keep sleepin' this much, bras, then you are going to sleep through . . . (extra long pause) . . . for a long time in your sentence.

Me: Half of my sentence.

Jamie: How'd you work that out?

Me: Because of the hours (he looks confused) 6 to 6 is twelve hours, half of 24 . . . And there are 24 hours in a day . . .

Jamie: Did you count them?

Me: No, someone else did.

Jamie: (rocking head in awe) Wow, bras, you are the smartest person I have ever met!

On the other hand, he knows things I don't.

Jamie: (after inviting him to a BBQ at our place once we're out) Bras, you don't want to invite me over for some grub.

Me: Why not?

Jamie: You don't have any Koori friends, do ya?

Me: Actually, no, I don't.

Jamie: And you don't have any crim friends either, do ya?

Me: No.

Jamie: Get yaself comfortable, it's time for me to teach you something. You invite me for some tucker and I come over with a coupla mates. We have some grub, some drinks and it's late, you ask me to stay the night and I accept. The next day we eat and drink some more, and some more mates arrive to pick me up and they stay for some drinks, and then we stay the next night and the next, until finally you kick us out of the house, and we'll get a 40-gallon drum and have a corroboree out on the front lawn, burn all the grass. Your neighbours are gunna complain about the noise and the smoke, so you call police, and get this: they can't do a bloody thing because you invited us.

Me: So, how do I get in touch with you?

Jamie: Remember that small town I told you I'm from? Go to the police station and they'll know exactly where I am.

Questions he has asked me in total seriousness:

Is Back to the Future *a documentary?*

What's all the fuss about recycling, bras? When this planet fails we're going to live on Mars (said trip will be as long as drive to Queensland).

Meant to be rehabilitated but prison is like apprenticeship in crime. So far I have learned how to:

Find a drug supplier

Sell drugs

Set up a drug mule

Steal a car

Cheat on other women

Do an insurance job

Defraud the government

My job here at Mannus is mowing the lawns. Ironic, I know! Raking in the big bucks now—$25 per week.

Me: Mowing's not that hard; when I get out, I might buy a mower.

Inmate: No one buys lawn mowers; you just 'borrow' them.

Me: I don't think it's unusual to buy lawn mowers.

Inmate: You probably buy toilet paper and newspapers too, ya mug.

Had a few offers to do insurance jobs. Inmate (Shane Malarkey) heard me mouthing off about a business competitor.

Malarkey: It's what I was born do. Teach people lessons. Bit of kero, packet of matches and I'll burn it to the ground.

Me: No, no, I do not want you to do that. I'm not telling you to do that.

Malarkey: But you said you wished they weren't around.

Me: I was angry. I was just letting off some steam.

Malarkey: Let me know if you change your mind, it's what I do and if I get effing caught, only get six months.

It's calmer here than MRRC and so good to be able to see trees/ nature. Most inmates are low risk (charges wise) or are at the end of their sentence. Some Spinners here, though. Turbo (nickname) moves around the yard doing sound effects and mimes driving a car. Always talking about the latest and greatest car models. XV72??? which means nothing to me. Yesterday Turbo tried to talk to me in the yard. Gestured that I couldn't hear him. He stopped suddenly and wound down imaginary window (old style).

Me: You'll cause an accident stopping suddenly like that, Turbo. Thought you had a new car?

Turbo then presses a button, which doesn't look as effective (mime-wise). Everyone jokes that one day we're going to see him wrapped around a pole.

Breakfast is jail-issue rice bubbles, or rice loops or Weetbix. Satchel arrives with dinner. (Get tea and coffee. Give to other inmates as gift.)

Lunch served between 10 to 11am (best meal of the day, wraps or samosas).

Dinner at 3pm. (Miss dinner with you and the kids more than anything.)

Food looks and tastes the same for each meal. Big disappointment when recognisable. #1 worst meal Five beans (as sounds) #2 Cold onion and cabbage.

One apple a day, sometimes a pear. Don't allow other fruits, as inmates can make alcohol. Nothing fresh apart from apples/pears. May be in danger of scurvy.

Locked in every night at 5pm. You would love it in here (apart from the sexism, criminals and food, ha-ha). All the time in the world to read and write.

Miss reading to the kids. Remember I made videos of me reading stories to the kids. Saved on desktop under Bedtime stories.

I love you,

Paddy

P.S. Please send more pictures of the kids (only postcard size 6×4 allowed).

P.P.S. So sad, a guy named Roger (only normal guy (relatively speaking!!!) in Bronx) hasn't had a visitor the whole time. Can you ask if Fiona or Cathy can book in to see him?

P.P.P.S. Another inmate's daughter is v. sick (leaking bowel?). Can you call Graham to see if he can help?

EIGHTEEN

It was dark when I pulled into the Club Motel in Tumbarumba, a small town on the western slopes of the Snowy Mountains. Population 1500. According to the map, the trip was 513 kilometres—or five hours and four minutes by car. But the map didn't account for repeated toilet and/or vomiting stops, a dinner break, and other interruptions, like searching for the *SpongeBob* DVD that had vanished in the time it took me to drive from the outskirts of Sydney into the dry, barren landscape of south-west New South Wales.

'Blink and you'll miss it,' is how my father would have described Tumbarumba. It's one of those small, sleepy towns, with one main street that doglegs around a corner to where our motel was located. It was not dissimilar to the town I had grown up in, though much smaller. The kind where everyone knew each other, and good old-fashioned trust and goodwill still existed. When I made the motel booking the week before, I had explained that I wouldn't be arriving until dark. Bill, the salt-of-the-earth proprietor, said, 'I'll leave the lights on and the key in the door. Fix me up when you see me.'

Sure enough, the lights were on and the key was in the lock of Room 10. I unloaded the car, and then, one by one, carried the sleeping kids and all our things into the room. When I had unpacked everything, I collapsed into the single bed furthest from the window and thought about all the food preparation I had to do the following morning. Mannus, unlike MRRC, allowed visitors to bring food. There was a long list of food that wasn't allowed—mainly, biscuits, cakes and sugar. All food had to be chopped and stored in clear plastic containers, and metal cutlery was also prohibited. Paddy's family had made the trip the week before, and told me that most people carried things into the prison in a clear 20-litre storage tub.

As I lay there, a yellow-tinged light flooded the room, moment-arily silhouetting the children's faces. They looked so angelic when they were asleep and even more so bathed in the glow of headlights. I always felt that whatever had occurred during the day, I could forgive anything when I saw their sleeping faces. They looked like perfectly formed cherubs, I thought, and my worries about the visit simply melted away.

'They've got ice-cube trays. And orange juice,' Nick said, when he woke me early the next morning.

'And there's a basket of little soaps and shampoos. What does this say?' Lexie asked, plonking her collection on the bed in front of me.

'"Country Life Conditioner. For smooth, shiny hair".'

'And this one?'

'"Country Life Soap",' I said, yawning. 'You can have them.'

'Really?' she said, jumping up and down. 'But isn't that stealing?'

'No, they're complimentary. Free.' I sat up.

'This is the best motel ever!'

I wouldn't have described it that way. It was in excellent condition, and everything was clean and well presented, but mostly it was nondescript. Apart from some mock-colonial features and the exposed brick wall, it could have been any of thousands of motels anywhere in Australia. But the kids loved it. They jumped around all morning, singing the praises of the wall-mounted television, and the miniature cereal boxes. I certainly couldn't accuse them of being ungrateful.

In the car park directly outside the door, it didn't escape Bill's attention that I, like many other patrons, was loading a plastic tub into the car. I had spent the morning chopping fruit and salad, and packing everything except a partridge in a pear tree into the tub.

'Made it here all right, then?' Bill asked and I told him I had. 'Make sure you take jackets out there today. It's only ten k's outta town but it gets a breeze up, being a plain.' It was his way of saying he knew where we were headed and it was fine by him. I appreciated it.

Having been treated with such kindness and respect at the motel, it caught me completely by surprise when, ten minutes later, we stood in front of a curt, portly female corrections officer.

'Do you have any mobile phones, recording devices, alcohol, prohibited weapons, illegal drugs, prescription medication or paper money?' she asked, looking me up and down, and then settling on an expression suggesting she'd recently had colorectal surgery.

'No,' I said, trying to make my response as brief and as bland as possible.

'Do you have any confectionery, sugar, chilli, seafood, nuts, cakes, sweet biscuits, muffins, or any other homemade baked goods, or screw-top bottles of any kind?'

'No,' I replied. And with that, the CO lifted the lid of the tub and started removing items. I knew from Patrick's sisters that this was simply part of the visiting procedure and I was confident I hadn't packed anything that was restricted.

'Oh, fancy. Like the brand names, do we?' she said, in a way that can only be described as catty.

I was at a loss as to what I had done to antagonise this woman. I had checked the website, and called the prison several times about requirements, and, as far as I could tell, I was meeting them. I thought back over the things I'd been told and read: no open-toed shoes; no short or revealing clothing (not in the last fifteen years); my mobile phone was under the front seat of the car; prescription medication was at the motel. I couldn't think of anything . . .

'Do you think you'll have enough food?' she scoffed. 'Anyone'd think you're catering for all the blokes.'

I looked down at my feet to try to focus on something that wouldn't lead to my own prison sentence. She was right. But the visit was until three o'clock, which was six and a half hours! That is an enormous amount of time to amuse and feed four people, all of whom eat different things.

Paddy had also asked me to bring the local newspapers, and paper for him to write down answers to my questions about the business, and then there were the games for the kids. It'd been like Tetris trying to fit everything into the tub. Lexie and Nick carried their own jackets and colouring pencils.

'Can't take these in,' she said, holding up a clear packet of savoury crackers.

'I called during the week to ask about the food and they told me savoury biscuits are allowed.'

'No, they'll have to go in the locker,' she said. 'And you've got too many games. We've got things for kids in the visiting room,' she snapped, and from where I stood, I could see a colourful hand-painted mural advertising 'Kids' Corner'.

I packed the permitted items back in the tub, and moved over to the counter to complete the visitor's information sheet, which required me to list my address, driver's licence number and car registration, and the person responsible for supervising the children. 'Jacobs,' was called over the loudspeaker. As I was doing this, a woman carrying a single transparent plastic bag entered reception.

'Now, here's a woman who knows how to pack,' the CO said. And I placed my handbag, along with the board games and crackers, in the locker with as much contempt as I could rally.

There were no retina scans or security wands at Mannus, and at first we didn't realise that. We just stood in the doorway until a male CO said, 'You can go in.' So then we simply walked in and sat down at a table close to Kids' Corner. The aspect was beautiful. The back windows looked out onto a small park-like area of trees and picnic tables, and in the middle of the yard was a sprawling, leafy tree, like something straight out of the pages of a storybook.

'Daddy!' the kids chorused, running up to meet Paddy. It had been weeks since we'd seen him. It had taken eight days for him to arrive at Mannus via the milk run with all the drop-offs and pick-ups and he had spent nights at Bathurst and Junee Correctional Centres. On his first weekend there, the kids didn't want to miss a friend's birthday party.

'You look nice,' he said, kissing me on the cheek.

'Thanks. You too,' I lied. Patrick was wearing a forest-green tracksuit, the uniform of inmates incarcerated in New South Wales. It was elasticised and tapered at the ankle, the style favoured by retirees and dowdy mothers, and very unflattering. As I spoke, I became aware of my body becoming tense. I had made the booking, and driven all those miles and signed the visitor's sheet, but seeing him in his prison-issue clothes I experienced the shock of it all over again.

'How are you?' he asked.

'Yeah, good,' I said, but I wasn't—I was bewildered.

'Come and play,' Lexie moaned, pulling on Paddy's arm as he wolfed down a large bowl of muesli, fruit and yoghurt.

'Why don't you play with some of the toys?' I suggested, directing her and Nick to Kids' Corner. They returned approximately thirty seconds later. 'What's the matter?' I asked.

'Everything's broken,' Nick said.

Kids' Corner was Blanche Dubois. From a distance, under the coloured lights and paper lanterns, everything looked new and shiny and full of promise. Up close you could see everything for what it really was; old and tattered and broken. The chalkboard had no chalk. The DVD player and TV had no visible cords to be plugged in. Only three of the toys (appropriate for a toddler) were in reasonable condition. All the books had ripped covers and torn pages. Kneeling down with the kids, I noticed a painted wall mural of library books. The mural's artist had written on the spines: *The Bill*, *The Great Escape*, *Escape from Alcatraz*, *The Green Mile*, *Midnight Express* and other prison-related titles. At least someone had a sense of humour.

'Let's go outside,' I suggested. To the right was a paddock, and then a cluster of sheds, small brick buildings and demountables. And for miles and miles beyond that, there were grassy acres of farmland. I was soaking in the beauty of the view Patrick had described to me in his letters, when he walked up, held my hand and leaned into me. At once, the kids were at our side.

'Want to wrestle, Dad?' Nick asked.

'I want to spend time with Dad,' Lexie whined.

'I don't think the guards'd be cool with that, mate,' Patrick answered, to Nick's enormous disappointment.

'Why don't you have a go on the slippery dip?'

We took refuge on a bench under the sprawling tree and watched Nick and Lexie on the playground equipment. They slid down the slide and balanced on the climbing poles, all the while saying, 'Look, Dad, look at this', and 'Did you see that, Dad?'

'What sort of tree is this?' I asked Paddy, pointing up to the sinuous branches.

'Oak,' he said, producing a perfectly formed acorn from his pocket. It was beautiful.

'There's nothing to do,' complained Nick, jumping off the equipment.

'Isn't there?' Paddy asked, and walked over to stand at one end of a cement rectangle. Nick and Lexie followed. He held the acorn in his hand, and hurled it down the impromptu pitch in a concentrated underarm throw. 'Reckon you can beat that?'

'It's my turn, my turn,' each of them insisted. They both took turns throwing the acorn, marking the spot where it landed by scratching the cement with a small stone. Soon, another group of kids joined in. After they had finished a round, Lexie stood open-mouthed, hands on hips, listening to Nick talk to a boy of a similar age. Then she marched over to us.

'Nick told that boy—Cody—that Dad's in jail!' Lexie reported and we laughed.

'Lexie, we're in a jail. You're visiting your dad and the other boy's visiting his.'

'It's his stepdad,' she said, oblivious to our point.

I went back inside to use the bathroom near the entrance. On my way through the visitation room, I noticed many of the tables had fruit and salad on them. The inmates must have also, like Paddy, been craving fresh produce. As I neared the front of the room, I noticed that on two of the tables were savoury crackers, exactly the same brand as the ones I had packed. On the way back from the bathroom, I passed another table with crackers. I was outraged.

'She's messing with me,' I said as soon as I reached Paddy.

'Who?'

'The guard, the female guard. She made me put my crackers back in the locker but nearly everyone else has them. What are we going to do?' I asked.

'Do?' he asked, confused.

He clearly did not understand what had happened, so I repeated the story of the female CO flagrantly abusing her power. 'What'll we do?' He still looked confused. 'About the crackers?'

'There's a bloke in here who got eight months for shooting someone in the leg with a stolen rifle, and I got twelve months for having a slingshot. Life's not fair and this place is certainly not fair. Some of the COs insist some inmates do one and not another. It's how it is.'

We went back inside for lunch. I had brought one of the lasagnes I'd been given but Paddy only wanted the salad and fruit. He ate like he hadn't eaten for weeks. After lunch we played Uno and Pictionary and Go Fish, and then we ventured back out to the yard. We sat at one of the shaded tables. Bill had been right. It was a warm day, but with the wind and the shade it was cold.

'I'm bored,' Lexie declared, and so Paddy started a game of hide-and-seek. Some of the other kids from the yard joined in, including Cody and his little sister, Crystal, who was besotted with Nick.

'Crystal is so cute,' Nick said, hiding behind a tree trunk near me, in one of the few places to hide.

'She's really taken a fancy to you, hasn't she?'

'She calls me "Ick" because she can't say N, and she keeps finding acorns and giving them to me.' The kids were beautiful and well-mannered and even Lexie, who normally has no tolerance for smaller children, had a soft spot for Crystal.

When everyone tired of hide-and-seek, Patrick started another game that, quite simply, involved throwing a hat up into the tree and then trying to get it down. It was interesting to watch Nick completely immersed in such a game because he was playing with his dad. I couldn't imagine him being as entertained by something like that at home.

Patrick continued to play with the kids as every time he ventured back to me, the kids demanded his attention. So I spent most of the afternoon adrift, meditating on the perfectly proportioned oak tree. The boughs grew out symmetrically, not drooping or bulging the way some trees did. And I marvelled at the way the top branches reached up to the sky like curled fingers and the lower branches hung low, but were still high enough to walk underneath.

At 2.22pm a tall male CO walked around the yard and informed us that it was time to leave. 'There's forty minutes to go,' I said to Patrick, after the CO had walked away. I'd hoped that we would get time to talk or enjoy our time together. Paddy just shrugged. He seemed to have surrendered to these minor injustices. I was upset, because it had taken me five and a half hours to finally relax into the environment and now it was time to go.

'We've still got tomorrow,' he whispered to me. And then Patrick put his arms around me and the kids.

The following morning, as I pulled the plastic tub out of the car, I vowed that I would be warm and present. But once again, as I sat across the table from Patrick in his green tracksuit, I felt rigid with shock. Sunday's visit unfolded much the same as Saturday's. On arrival, it was difficult to tell whether the female CO had been sucking on a lemon or a lime, and after a few curt comments about my preferred grocery brands, she instructed me to put the croissants in the locker, allowing several other visitors to bring theirs in. As on the previous day, Nick and Lexie were excited, then difficult, and then bored.

'Come and watch the muster,' Paddy said to the kids when the ten o'clock siren sounded. He led us to the edge of the yard, explaining that this was what they did each day. The inmates who didn't have visitors were required to line up outside the kitchen every two hours for a roll call. I found it fascinating to watch all the men in green step forward when their names were called, like they were still in school.

Lexie didn't find the muster as interesting as the rest of us and began playing with some plastic she'd found on the grass before promptly putting it into her mouth.

'Spit it out, spit it out,' Paddy said, forcefully. Lexie spat the plastic out and began to cry. 'Don't touch any plastic you see in the yard. It's, it's . . .' Patrick said.

'You don't know where it's been,' I said softly to Lexie, who'd curled into my side.

'We know exactly where it's been, that's the problem,' Paddy said. 'Up some guy's butt,' he whispered.

'Dad, that's gross,' Nick said.

'Paddy!' I said.

'Which is why . . . I don't want you putting it in your mouth,' he explained calmly and reached down to pick her up.

Mid morning a number of other kids arrived. Nick and Lexie met and mingled with them, most of them named Crystal or Destiny, Heaven or JD.

'What's your name?' I asked one little girl dressed in a T-shirt that said, 'If you think I'm hot, you should see my mum!'

'Teneesha Heaven Haley Butler-Reid,' she said, chewing on her bubble gum.

'That's a very long name,' I said.

'Not as long as my step-brother's,' she said, adjusting her sparkled tights. 'He's got four first names and three last names!'

I was anxious about the kids playing with some of the kids at the prison. They were only children, but some of them seemed rough and streetwise and I worried about their influence on Nick and Lexie. We stood close to the play equipment to keep an eye on them. The kids all played well together though; throwing acorns or hats, and chasing each other around on the grass, eager to do something other than sit down at a table.

At lunchtime Cody and Crystal arrived. They played with Nick and Lexie while Patrick and I sat on a bench at the back of the yard. It occurred to me that I should be trying to start a conversation or say something uplifting to Patrick but my mind was empty. I didn't know what to say. We were in a beautiful park-like setting, but we were being watched. No matter how hard I tried, I could not move past that. The time passed quickly and at 2.31pm a male CO walked out to the yard. 'That's it folks.' This time I didn't say anything.

During the long drive home darkness settled in and the kids drifted off to sleep in the back of the car. Watching the white line in the middle of the road had a hypnotising effect on me and I grew tired. So much so, that I had to pull over and close my eyes. I woke roughly twenty minutes later, bought some coffee from a drive-through and continued the journey. It was on the last stretch of the trip that I thought about Paddy. Mannus, it seemed, was safe and calm, surrounded by beauty. But there was no doubt in my mind that the new location was harder for me. He and I weren't just emotionally distant, we were physically distant, and he was relying on me to go the distance. All 513 kilometres of it.

It was just after nine when I finally pulled into the driveway, turned off the ignition and carried Lexie inside. As I laid her down on her bed, she said sleepily, 'It's okay, Mum, I don't want a cat anymore—I want a baby sister.'

NINETEEN

'It's called displacement,' Steph said.

'Sorry?'

'The name for what's happening here.'

'What's happening?'

I'd just finished telling her about Nicola, my neighbour, who continued to descend on me every week to 'encourage me'. During one visit, she seemed to think it might lighten my spirits to hear how inmates on *World's Worst Prisons* could transform any household object into a weapon. And on another, she told me to embrace Patrick's absence; meanwhile, her husband was in Hong Kong for ten days, making it 'just impossible to deal with the kids'.

When I finally took a breath, Steph said, 'So, Nicola has been coming over several times a week?'

'Yes. And we're not even close. I mean, before this all happened, I barely even saw her. It's not like we caught up for long chats before Patrick went to prison, so I don't know what gives her the idea we should suddenly be living in each other's pockets.'

'Who is she doing it for?'

'For me. She usually drops off a meal or a gift . . . which is nice.'

'But there's more to it than that, because she could just drop them off. Are you wanting her to stay?'

'No! She is driving me crazy.' And I felt bad about focusing on my frustration with Nicola, considering that everyone else had been so kind and generous. People had sent cards and flowers; my friends Frieda and Pamela had made small portions of Nick and Lexie's favourite meals that could be frozen; Paddy's sister Clare had written me a very large cheque; Cathy and Fiona often babysat; and Patrick's father had caught the early morning train from the south coast to visit him. Most of his family had been writing letters to Paddy, and made a visiting roster so Paddy would see someone every week. And all I could think about was Nicola. Talk about glass half empty.

'So, who's she really doing it for?'

'Patrick?'

'Does she know him?'

'Not really.'

'Who benefits from the visits?'

I shrugged, astounded at just how dim I could be.

'She does it for herself. She does it because it makes her feel good. Sometimes, following a trauma, people—I call them "rescuers"—like to swoop in to help, but they're not always helping in the way that other people want or need.'

Steph stood precariously on her stilettos and made her way over to the small whiteboard. I always found it amusing that she used a whiteboard just for me, when it would have been far easier to use a notepad. She'd told me she felt it made more of an impact.

Steph began with one small circle in the centre of the board. And inside it, she wrote my name. Around the first circle, she drew another and another, until she had drawn approximately ten concentric circles. It looked like a target. She explained that each circle was representative of the different circles, or layers, of people in my life, stemming from my immediate family to the outer circles of acquaintances.

'Each circle is representative of the different levels of intimacy you share with the people in your life,' Steph said. 'In grief, as in life, it's best for people to respond in a way that is in keeping with the circle they are in. For instance, if you hear that a distant friend's partner died, you might send a card, but popping over to the house would not be appropriate. Of course, things can overlap and change, and sometimes people can have a strong connection with someone they barely know, but typically this is how it works.'

Steph walked back to her chair and sat down. 'Where does Nicola fit into your circle?' she asked.

I explained that I thought she belonged in the sixth or seventh layer. We knew each other by name and lived on the same street, but we hadn't shared life's challenges or bonded over broken hearts.

'So, Nicola is not responding in a way that corresponds with the way you see her in your circle.' I nodded.

The circle metaphor was a revelation to me. It crystallised not only where I saw the people in my life, from the inner sanctum to the furthest ring, but also how sometimes, in my eagerness to befriend others, I had misinterpreted my place in their circle, heading straight for the nucleus.

'The tricky thing,' Steph continued, 'is that people can see their own circle differently to the way others do, and vice versa. With that in mind, any thoughts on how you can change the situation with Nicola?'

My first thought was hiring an assassin. My second was moving house. 'I don't know,' I replied.

'There is a simple solution,' Steph said, holding my gaze in a way that unnerved me.

'Really?'

'You say no.'

I felt uneasy. The word 'no' has always terrified me. More than public speaking, or the dark, or snakes or spiders. I was afraid that by saying it, I might offend or disappoint someone and they then wouldn't like me. And, because I'm not naturally assertive, when I do say 'no' it comes out sounding sharp and caustic.

'I want to revisit something I mentioned earlier—displacement. We've *established* that Nicola has been getting on your nerves,' Steph said, firmly, as though another diatribe about Nicola would send her into spasm. 'And you're feeling frustrated and angry.'

'Yes.'

'In psychology, displacement is when someone replaces a person, or a goal, or a feeling, for someone or something else. For instance, and this is a very simple example, it is common for someone having issues at work to come home and take it out on their spouse.'

'Okay,' I said, not seeing the relevance.

'Now, I'm not suggesting that your feelings for Nicola are unwarranted. From what you've said, she doesn't seem to have much insight or empathy into who you are or what you're going through.' I nodded, and Steph quickly continued, presumably to stop me beginning another anecdote. 'But on a scale of one to ten, how angry are you with Nicola?'

'About a hundred thousand,' I said, trying to find a comfortable position on the couch.

Steph smiled. 'But, in this whole situation, who is it you are really angry with?'

'Nicola's parents.'

Steph managed a smile but I could see that, once again, she wanted me to dig deeper. And, once again, I was resisting.

'Is it Nicola who caused you to be a single parent? Is it Nicola who caused you to forfeit your own dreams of finishing your novel to run a business?' Steph lifted and smoothed the end of her skirt, and as she did, I saw a glimpse of her black slip. I bet all Steph's male clients are in love with her, I thought. I bet the man who was here before me is head over heels.

'When you think about the depth of anger you have felt for Nicola, is it possible that your feelings are disproportionate to what she has done?'

'No.' I'd studied English literature, and I could deconstruct texts and identify characters' flaws and motivations with my eyes closed. Well, maybe not with my eyes closed, as it would have to be an audiobook, but those things were glaringly obvious to me. But when it came to the deep waters of self-analysis, I hadn't a clue. I was flailing around like someone who'd never learned to swim.

'Who put you in this position?'

Nicola had been tactless and thoughtless but she hadn't dismembered any family members, or put me in this situation. My anger with her was misdirected, I could see that. But I was paying Steph so I was going to make her work for the big bucks.

'It can be easier for people to direct their anger and blame onto someone else, rather than face the truth of the situation. Who broke the law?' Steph prompted again.

I was silent and once again fascinated by the splodgy paintings.

'Who broke the law?' she repeated.

It felt as though every part of me were bending in resistance away from this question. Of course I knew the answer but despite all the bravado and the glib comments I didn't want to face it.

'Who put you in this situation?'

'Paddy,' I whispered.

'Who?'

'Patrick,' I repeated at greater volume.

After which, Steph didn't say anything at all. She just let me sit there, feeling the sharp edges of the truth. And I hated her for it. I knew that when Steph did speak again, she was probably going to ask me what it meant to me. And I didn't want to think about what it meant to me. I didn't want to think about anything.

So I told Steph how Lexie's teacher had called to say that my daughter had taken the Country Life shampoo and conditioner in for show-and-tell, and told the class she got them when she went to see her dad in jail. After that, I told Steph about the kids' disastrous session with a child psychologist. Lexie was so insulted by the woman's condescending manner that she refused to answer any questions, claiming, 'My mum said not to talk to strangers.'

'I can recommend someone else,' Steph offered.

'That'd be good.'

We remained in shallower waters for the rest of the session. At last I could stand up and paddle around.

'Are you doing anything for yourself?' Steph asked.

'Myself?'

'Yes. Things just for you.'

I ate. I took care of my personal hygiene. I had the occasional coffee or lunch out but it was always for a purpose: a business meeting, or a meeting with someone from the school to work out how best to support Nick and Lexie. Aside from that, my time was absorbed by the kids, work and visiting Patrick.

'I read.'

'For work or pleasure?'

'Both. It's pleasure but, yes, I s'pose they're linked, in a way.'

'Is there anything you would like to do?'

'A solo trip around the world . . . for a year.'

'Really?'

'Yeah, but I can't . . . because of the kids.'

'But there are things you can do. Within your situation, you still have choices. You can choose who to see, and what to think, and how to respond. In the small windows of time you have, you can choose to do things for yourself, like having a massage or a coffee, or seeing a movie.'

The thought of doing something for myself when I had such big responsibilities seemed selfish. Every time I thought of something I wanted to do, I felt guilty about the kids, as though I was their personal court jester.

Eventually, Steph said, 'I understand your concern for the kids, but you are doing everything you can to make them feel secure and loved. You've told them the truth and you're helping them to work through it, and you've told their teachers and their friends' parents, who can also support them. Doing something for yourself every now and then, or even on a regular basis, is not only good for you, it's good for them. You're frowning . . .'

'Sorry, it's what I do . . . apparently . . . when I'm thinking.' I sipped my water.

'Consider it this way—you're putting your oxygen mask on first. You can't give anything to them if you have nothing to give.'

At the end of the session I felt a tiny surge of hope. That I didn't have to wait another two years to start living again. I could start today. I saw that since Patrick's arrest, I had been a piece of driftwood being swept down the river, hitting and whirling around everything in my path. I knew that I needed to make my way over to the riverbank, hoist myself out and stand up.

Then I arrived home to relieve the babysitter, who had met the kids at the bus stop. 'Why didn't you meet us? Where have you been?' they cried. And my resolutions about journal writing, and fancy restaurants and quirky little bookshops quietly crumbled.

I chose instead to do what I'd done so well for so long—be a martyr.

TWENTY

'We've been through this,' I said wearily. 'I can't have another baby because Dad's in jail.'

All Lexie wanted for her birthday was a baby. Her preference was for a sister but she would be willing to settle, she said, for a boy.

'You do remember how babies are made?' I prompted. After endless questions and my vague, wishy-washy answers, I had finally relented and bought the book *Where Did I Come From?*

'You do the sex,' she enthused.

'Yes, so even if I wanted another baby'—and I needed a newborn baby like I needed a hole in the head)—'I couldn't make one on my own, could I?' In New South Wales inmates are not entitled to conjugal visits and, on top of that, Patrick had had a vasectomy.

Lexie paused, tilted her head to the side and rubbed her fingers along her chin, like a wizened old professor. It was so adorable, and so incongruous, on a five-year-old girl wearing rainbow leggings and a crowned-kitten T-shirt. 'Do you think Dad would mind if you made a baby without him?'

'I don't think he'd be all that thrilled, Lex.'

'Because I was thinking that you could just find another man, do the sex, and then, when you've got the baby, you can get rid of him. You don't have to be married, you know. Aunty Fiona isn't married and she had a baby.'

'I'm quite aware of how babies are made, Lex, but I have too much on my plate to have another baby.'

'What plate?'

'Never mind.'

I couldn't give Lexie what she wanted for her birthday but I could give her the next best thing—a visit with her dad. In the first year of Patrick's sentence, Lexie's birthday fell on Good Friday, and Mannus Correctional Centre advertised that it was open for visitors on public holidays. Lexie knew that she couldn't take her birthday presents into the prison to show Patrick, but a visit was all she wanted, apart from a baby or a cat.

All plans were in place. I secretly bought, assembled and hid Lexie's bike, made and froze the birthday cake, and booked a house in Tumbarumba for the long weekend visit. Then a week prior to the visit, when I called to make a booking for a friend, the receptionist informed me that the centre would not be open on Good Friday.

'The visiting hours on the website say you're open on public holidays,' I said.

'We haven't opened on public holidays for years,' she said.

I was disappointed, Lexie was disappointed, and I was determined that, whatever happened, I was not about to be manipulated into getting a cat or having a baby. So, having limited experience with the prison system and being a little slow on the uptake, I did something very, very foolish and asked to speak to the manager. I'd found this strategy to be very effective in the outside world. I'd introduce myself, tell a joke, explain the broken-hearted daughter/ birthday situation and appeal to the person's good nature.

I anticipated a friendly chat with the manager, during which time he would share a tale about his grandchildren, then he would apologise for the mix-up and organise complimentary Twix bars from the vending machine.

The first thing the acting manager of the centre did after I explained the situation to him was chuckle. 'We haven't opened on public holidays for *years*!' he guffawed. I made another appeal to his good nature, and explained that the visiting hours published on the website and on the sign outside the visits building advertise that they are open on public holidays.

At which point, he laughed even harder. 'I've got better things to do with my time than spend it with people like that,' he said.

'People like what?' I asked. I had expected that sort of attitude from people on the outside but he worked in the system. He had men in his care.

'The sort of people who end up in here.' He went on to explain that the centre would be open on Saturday and Sunday as per usual, and that a weekend was ample time to visit someone.

I was furious when I got off the phone, and even more furious that I couldn't ring Patrick to explain what had happened. I had to wait for him to call me. When he did finally call, I told him the story using all the colourful words I could think of, forgetting that inmates' phone calls are recorded.

At that stage, Patrick was eager for me to report the issue to the Corrective Services Ombudsman. The representative I spoke to on the phone verified that the visiting hours were published on the website—it was a clear breach. He suggested I email Corrective Services directly to ensure it would be open.

Several days later, I received an email from Corrective Services acknowledging that I had spoken to the acting manager regarding visiting hours and that it 'appears that I may have misunderstood the information'. Mannus was open on public holidays after all.

I was astounded. Appears that I may have misunderstood? It appeared that the acting manager was lying through his teeth, I thought to myself. The email went on to say that the centre would be reviewing its policy regarding public holiday visits.

After that, whenever I tried to talk to Patrick about it on the phone he shut the conversation down and started talking about our non-existent pet dog. This, I knew, was his way of telling me that something was wrong.

'You don't want to check inside?' I asked the guard at reception on Good Friday, steeling myself for a dressing-down. My twenty-kilo plastic tub was in front of him at the security checkpoint.

'Looks to be all in order,' he said, after giving Nick and Lexie the colouring books supplied by Shine, a charity that supports children with parents in custody.

We sat at a table near Kids' Corn, as Lexie called it. Paddy fussed over Lexie and explained that he couldn't give her a birthday present, but that he had used part of his buy up to purchase a basket of Easter eggs we could share on Sunday morning.

The kids went out to the play equipment and we stayed at the table. 'He threatened me,' Paddy said.

'Who?'

'The manager, the acting manager.'

'No way!'

'He called me up to his office . . . twice . . . and said, "If you don't get your wife to shut up, we'll tip you."'

'"Tip"?'

'Move me to another prison. I tried to allude to it on the phone
. . . about our dog, Rover.'

'Why'd you call him Rover?' I asked.

'Does it matter?' Patrick said, as he started on the second punnet
of strawberries.

'They are meant to be open. The inmates are entitled to see
their families on public holidays, that's what the ombudsman told
me,' I said, drawing in one of the colouring books.

'The acting manager doesn't think so. He said if anything else
happens, he will charge me with inciting.'

'Inciting? Inciting what? Inmates to see their families on
public holidays?'

'It doesn't matter. The COs do what they like.'

'They can't do that.'

'They can and they do.'

His voice sounded different. There was no passion, no fight. It
was a voice of defeat.

We walked out to the yard. It was autumn, and the leaves had
begun to change from green to earthy hues. Deep red, russet,
rust and orange-coloured leaves decorated the ground. Lexie ran
through the yard in her gumboots, crunching them underfoot.

'It's hard for you to understand,' Paddy said. 'It's not like out
there. One guy in here had a toothache and the COs said it was
too much paperwork to take him to the dentist. Wouldn't even
give him painkillers. So he asked a CO for an ombudsman's form
and they put him in the Breezeway.'

'What's the Breezeway?'

'Solitary.'

I couldn't believe that the COs could be so mean-spirited. Of
course, I didn't want to place Patrick in harm's way, but it sickened
me to know what he was dealing with.

We watched the kids run around on the grass. There were just a handful of visitors that day. Paddy said he'd only told one inmate, Jason Bird, about his meeting with the acting manager. Most inmates and their families probably didn't realise the centre was open for visits that day.

But some did. 'Thank you,' said one of Jason Bird's visitors as she walked past me in the yard. 'You're very brave. It's been a long time since we've had visits on public holidays.'

Paddy and I didn't talk much after that. I didn't know what to say. My usual numbness had been replaced by burning indignation. I looked at the oak tree. Trees had only ever been a blur in the background. Since my visit to MRRC I had become enamoured with them. I noticed how some were tall and spindly, others short and plump, and how leaves had such a vast spectrum of colours and shapes and textures. Sharp, spikey, waxy and shiny. The oak leaves were strikingly beautiful. And as I stood next to Paddy I marvelled at the way the visit, like life, could be filled with such pain and such beauty.

Lexie had always been drawn to nature and I joined her on the ground making garlands of leaves. Up close, they looked different. The green leaves were thick and strong, with large veins in the underside, and strands as fine as human hair growing out from the curved ends. The older ones that had already fallen to the ground were thinner, and felt like paper.

'These leaves are friendly,' Lexie said.

'What do you mean?'

'See,' she said, holding out an orange-tinged leaf, 'these are the arms and the legs and the head.' She was right; most leaves had four parts stretching out to the side and another on top.

'This one's saying hi,' Lexie said, laughing at the way one section curved out and up like a hand. The leaves were our precious little gifts. Soon, two other girls joined us and together we linked the leaves. When we finished we unravelled the chain to see how long it had become. I was amazed to see what we had created—a chain that stretched from one side of the yard to the other.

'Where are the eggs?' Lexie asked, running to Patrick on Sunday morning.

'Have you hidden them for a hunt?' Nick asked.

'I'm really sorry, guys, but they didn't arrive. Mum will get you something from the vending machine, okay?' he said, trying to mitigate their disappointment.

Patrick's Easter eggs arrived a week later, speckled white with age. Not only were they late, the use-by date indicated that they had expired. Around the same time as he got the eggs, I received a letter I'd sent to Paddy. 'Not at this address' was clearly marked on the front of the envelope. I rang Tumbarumba post office and they informed me that someone at the correctional centre would have done the redirection.

TWENTY-ONE

No. No. No.

No matter how many times I said it to myself, the word 'no' sounded harsh. As much as I found Nicola irritating, and as much as I dreaded her plunging into the centre of my circle, part of me still wanted her to like me. But I had no choice. I had to work and I needed to redefine the boundaries of our relationship.

From the moment I decided it was time for action, I didn't see her. Every time the doorbell rang my endorphins were pumping and I was ready to say the speech I had prepared. For two whole weeks she didn't show. And then early one morning she caught me bu surprise.

'Sorry I haven't been round, I've been *so* busy,' she said and I smiled sympathetically. 'Coffee?'

'Look, Nicola, I appreciate you coming over,' I began my hand firmly planted on the doorframe. '*But no*'—and, just as I feared, 'no' sounded abrasive—'I'm sorry, I can't.'

'Just a coffee,' she said. 'You've got to take a break.' Nicola's response was just the impetus I needed to keep my resolve. I had said no and still she persisted. I knew from countless other times that if I invited her in, it wouldn't be for a quick coffee, it would be a long visit. Then, when she left, I would be riled up and snowed under.

'No,' I repeated, emphatically, 'I can't take a break, I'm working.' Nicola didn't look disappointed; she looked furious and I was ever so tempted to invite her in just to please her. But I knew that later I would curse myself, because I would be behind with my work, eating into the time I had with Nick and Lexie. I didn't back down, and as I watched Nicola walk towards her car I didn't feel triumphant, I felt awful. It took me a few days to let go of those feelings.

As it turned out, saying no to Nicola proved to be an excellent training ground for another situation that required me to be assertive: Nick's first foray into the competitive world of children's sport.

As we drove to the field for his first soccer-training session, my mind was awash with fantasies. Nick scissor-kicking the ball into the net; his masterful footwork and fortress-like defence culminating in him being hoisted onto his teammates' shoulders.

'Do I have to go to training?' Nick said when the car stopped. 'I already know how to play.' It was the first inkling he might not have the heart of a champion.

Nick was one of three new players in a team who had played together for several years. As the weeks went by, I noticed that Nick, along with the other new players, always started on the bench, and their spells off the field were longer and more frequent than anybody else's. Nick didn't seem too bothered about this, although he did ask me about it a couple of times.

Saturdays mornings were also a minefield of awkward conversations. 'So, you're married to James's brother?' one of the other mums asked as we sipped our takeaway coffees.

'Yeah, but don't hold that against me.'

'Does your husband work Saturdays?' she asked and I knew she was just being friendly. She'd explained that her husband worked every second weekend, but still the conversation unnerved me. I didn't want to lie but I couldn't bear seeing another horrified expression.

'He's away,' I said.

'For long?' she asked.

'A while,' I responded and moved further along the field to watch the game.

Unlike most of the other boys who loved soccer, Nick's chief motivation was the promise of a slushie.

'What's deadwood?' Nick asked, as we stood in the line for the post-game slushie.

The question struck me as odd. Nick had built a lot of fires with Patrick. And we didn't pay a small fortune for him to attend the hippy school not to know about deadwood.

'You know,' I said and he looked confused. 'Why do you ask?'

'Something Trent said.' Then he shrugged. There were two coaches, Trent and Trevor.

'What did he say?'

'He was talking to Sebastian, and he said, "The team's good, there's only a bit of deadwood—Archie and Nick."'

'Really? He said that to his son?'

'Yeah, when he was putting the balls in the net.' I don't think he knew I was there. My first thought was to contact Shane Malarkey, the inmate who 'taught people lessons' by burning things to the ground. My second was to talk to the coaches. I chose the latter.

I'm only five foot three and it was intimidating looking up at Trent and Trevor. The men denied everything, insisting that it was all fun and fair and then the conversation was over. I couldn't help feeling it had been a complete waste of time. But when I arrived at the field for the next game, they had a list of players and a stop watch, and Nick was over the moon to start on the field for the very first time.

Nick's involvement in soccer turned out to be worthwhile for other reasons.

'Got a drummer in the family,' one of the fathers said during a match one morning.

'Sorry?'

'Look at him. There's a rhythm inside, trying to get out,' he said, and we watched as his fingertips fluttered up and down his torso.

'You think so?'

'I know so, used to play. You need to get that boy some sticks.'

For the first time I considered Nick's action. It was a response to something from within. Something that could be nurtured and channelled.

More poignantly, through soccer Nick met a boy whose suffering eclipsed his own. 'Mum, you know Ethan in my soccer team?' Nick said when we were driving into the city one afternoon.

'Yes, I know Ethan in your soccer team.'

'His dad committed suicide.'

'Oh, Nick, that's awful,' I said, looking back at him in the rear-view mirror. His tapping slowed as if keeping with the mood.

'How did he . . . do it?'

'I don't know, darling. How did you find out?' I asked.

'At Will's house. Someone said not to talk about our dads because it might make him feel sad.'

'That's very thoughtful,' I said.

'And I thought, *What about my dad?* but then I started thinking about Ethan. He'll never get to see his dad's face or hear his voice or play PlayStation . . . ever again.'

Tears welled in my eyes, both for Ethan who had lost his father, and because Nick had grown so much that he could empathise with someone else's suffering in a way I hadn't been able to even as a grieving adult. Kids see the world in a way that is so clean and uncomplicated, and it filled me with awe, and with heartbreak, to bear witness to Nick's discovery that our lives are nothing like that.

'Suicide's worse than prison,' Nick stated, in the way he might repeat a fact from *The Guinness Book of Records*.

'You're right,' I said. 'Suicide's forever . . . and it is very sad for Ethan . . . for everyone in his family . . . but it's still okay for you to be sad,' I said making eye contact with him again. 'I'm proud of you . . . that you can step outside your own pain and see what someone else is going through.' I looked at him again, in the rear-view mirror. He'd resumed a morely lively rhythm.

'But divorce is still better than prison,' he said.

TWENTY-TWO

After settling on martyrdom, it came as a surprise both to myself and to James that I finally agreed to join the extended Jacob clan on a holiday to Bali. Initially, I balked at the cost. We had decided to go ahead with the appeal, and an overseas holiday was an unwarranted expense. But a number of things happened that convinced me to to reconsider.

'Your eyes are yellow,' Lexie said as she lay next to me in bed one night.

'No, they're not.'

'They are. They're really yellow, like your teeth!'

'Thanks, Lex. Anything else you'd like to mention?' I asked. It was a rhetorical question.

'Well, you are getting a bit wobbly,' she said, and I cursed myself for not living in a period when children were seen and not heard. Lexie was right about my weight, and our conversation was the catalyst for a visit to the doctor, who told me that I needed to find some strategies to relax. 'Go on a holiday,' he suggested.

'Don't worry about the cost,' James said when we met at his favourite cafe.

'I don't want you to pay for it,' I said.

'Neither do I, so I've talked to Fiona and she's going to rent out your house. It'll almost cover it,' James said, picking a large slice of avocado from the salmon and avocado stack I'd ordered.

'Why don't I order you something?' I suggested.

'Nah, I'm not hungry,' he insisted. 'So you'll come?'

'I don't know, I feel guilty,' I protested. I wasn't comfortable with the idea of frolicking on a tropical beach while Patrick languished away in prison.

'Mel, I've got one piece of advice,' he said—which was unusual, because James normally had a lot of advice. 'Order the lobster.'

'What?'

'Order the lobster,' he repeated.

'I don't really like lobster,' I said.

James looked at me in the exasperated way I sometimes looked at my children. 'It's an expression,' he said, 'my expression. You can't just put your life on hold until Patrick gets out. You've spent thousands and thousands of dollars on legal fees. Live a little, enjoy yourself. If you're going to go under, it won't be because of an eighty-dollar lobster. So Mel, order the lobster!'

While James's argument was certainly persuasive, bumping into a friend I hadn't seen for some time was the deciding factor.

'How are the kids? How's Patrick?' she asked, and when I told her what had happened, she winced and let out a small moan. And it was at that precise moment I realised I wanted to go to Bali. I wanted to go somewhere where I could disappear. Somewhere I wouldn't constantly be asked about my husband.

I'd never been to Indonesia before, so it came as something of a surprise that the very first question I was asked when we exited the gates at Denpasar airport was: 'Miss, Miss, where your husband?'

Family is the heart of Balinese culture and they find it incomprehensible that people would choose to holiday without their whole family. So every single day, everywhere I went, to the market, to a restaurant, to the beach, I was asked the same question: 'Where your husband?'

On the second day on Seminyak beach, I accepted an offer of a massage from an elderly but remarkably acrobatic woman named Made. I explained that my neck and shoulders blades were sore, and she welcomed me onto the large woven mat she had set up under the shade of a palm tree.

Made began by pushing the upper part of my back, then she poured oil down my spine and rubbed it in with strong circular motions.

'You hit car?' she asked, banging her hand and fist together.

'Sore neck and shoulder,' I repeated, slowly.

Made continued to knead the oil into my back and, after a short while, said, 'No, you have sore heart. Very sore heart,' placing her hand on her chest. Then she proceeded to give me the most robust massage I'd ever had. And as her bare hands touched my skin, I realised it had been months since anyone else had.

Made's oiled hands moved up and down my back, focusing on the problem areas with the full force of her weight. After months of pain, I finally felt some relief.

I left the beach feeling rejuvenated and then, as night fell, I had the most acute spasm of neck and back pain. I spent the night whacked out on painkillers, and in the morning, when Made finally arrived at the beach, I explained that the pain was infinitely worse than it had been before the massage.

I expected Made to give me an age-old remedy but she just sat there, cross-legged, eating a banana. 'Is pain. First worse, then better, yes?' which was not what I wanted to hear. I don't like pain,

I do everything I can to avoid pain, and I was on holidays. I wanted to relax, and run along the beach with the carefree abandon of someone in a tampon commercial.

The pain increased. My temples pounded and my neck felt as though someone were hammering nails into the base of my skull. At one point it was so intense, I began to cry. I didn't know it then, but it was part one of what I now refer to as the 'Trilogy of Crying.'

Part one was merely the introduction, characterised by stifled sobs. The pain continued for roughly three days until, on the fourth, some of the pain I had been carrying around for months finally began to ease. And when it did, I pulled myself together and began to enjoy some world-famous Balinese hospitality.

The kids and I had pedicures, and a spa that involves tiny fish eating the dead skin off the bottom of your feet, devoured platters of seafood and fruit, fed monkeys and rode on elephants, learned to surf, and offered ourselves up wholeheartedly to the buffet—I ate the lobster!

As our time in Bali came to a close, I could see that the small amount of comfort I received from being a martyr did not come close to the pleasures the world had to offer.

'Where your husband?' the woman at the airport check-in asked and I explained that he would not be joining us.

'So, one adult, two children and one coming?' she asked. And I turned to see if there were any other children that she may have mistaken for mine.

'Sorry?'

She smiled. 'The baby . . . inside,' she said, pointing her floral-patterned nail at my abdomen. I shook my head—that was my Bali belly.

Our holiday to Bali was something of a turning point in our lives. Although I couldn't see it at the time, it brought me closer to acceptance. But its real significance was that it was the first overseas trip for the kids. Memories were made that did not include Patrick. This was highlighted on our first visit to Mannus afterwards.

'So, you learned to surf?' Paddy asked the kids enthusiastically. 'What was it like?'

'Yeah, good,' Nick replied flatly. 'Where's Cody and Crystal?' he asked, looking straight past Patrick and around the room to try to see the kids they had grown so fond of.

'I don't think they're coming this weekend.'

'Oh,' Nick said, disappointed.

'And you rode on an elephant,' Paddy said to Lexie. She nodded but did not elaborate. He tried so hard to engage and connect with the kids, but their responses were short and laboured, the way they are when they walk in the door after a long day at school.

It dawned on me that for many children telling is closely associated with showing or doing. *I made this. I drew this.* At that time, Lexie was really interested in growing seedlings and sewing but, for obvious reasons, wasn't allowed to bring her samples to a visit. Added to that, a lot of what children share with you is spontaneous. Little gems that occur to them when you're doing something mundane, and when they feel secure and relaxed, which is a very difficult atmosphere to create in a prison visitation room.

Sometimes the conversations flowed and funny little observations popped out. During one visit we were sitting at the table near Kids' Corn and Lexie was busy drawing pictures of corn, as she liked to do, when Nick asked, 'Dad, how come all the people in jail have big muscles, like Simon?'

'Not everyone,' Paddy said, pointing to a scrawny old inmate.

'Most of them.' And we looked around at all the buffed and toned physiques in green tracksuits. 'How do they get like that?' Nick asked.

'The gym,' Patrick said, eating a slice of the pizza he'd requested for lunch.

'There's a gym here?' Nick asked, surprised, and Paddy nodded.

'You should go . . . so you get muscles like that,' he offered helpfully.

These conversations were rare. Mostly, it was like pulling teeth: forced and painful.

The starkness of the visitation room did nothing to promote our connection as a family. I'd like to think our home is comfortable: we have couches and scatter cushions and throw rugs, and a deck with outdoor sofas. We have 1000-thread-count cotton sheets and lambs' wool rugs. By contrast, the visitation room is austere. The chairs and tables are moulded plastic, the floors are cold and bare and the fluorescent lights are bright.

Attempts to make the visits more entertaining or comfortable were not allowed. Balls were considered dangerous because of the possibility of injury or because drugs could be concealed inside them. Picnic rugs and tablecloths were not allowed because, as one guard explained to me, couples had been caught fondling underneath them.

I understand that for security reasons a prison visitation room has no couch to curl up on or music to listen to or movies to veg out in front of. And I'm not trying to suggest there should be, I'm merely explaining that it was difficult for the kids, especially Nick, to connect with Paddy in such an environment. Lexie was usually happy to draw, make up stories and play with leaves, but without wrestling, balls to throw, and computer games, Nick was lost.

Paddy tried so hard to engage them, but after our trip to Bali, the reality of driving six hours to sit across from their father and twiddle their thumbs in a prison visitation room began to sink in. On that first weekend back it rained, and the usual reprieve of running around on the grass, or throwing acorns or hats, didn't come. And there's only so many times you can play Uno before you lose the will to live.

'Can we go now?' Nick groaned after lunch, tapping furiously on the table.

'Stop it,' I snapped at him. He was upset because I was trying to take away the only fun thing he had left.

'Yeah, I'm bored,' Lexie added. Patrick looked wounded.

We were all tired. Even though we hadn't been doing anything, we weren't able to relax in such an artificial environment, knowing we were being watched. In our regular life, part of our weekend was spent napping or reading, or cooking or listening to music. Visits didn't allow for this.

'It's fine. They look tired. We'll see each other tomorrow,' Paddy said.

As I carried the heavy plastic tub from the visitation room to the car park, I could see that we had begun to move in different orbits.

TWENTY-THREE

Mannus Correctional Centre
17 June 2013

Beauty,

I'm moving up in the world. Out of the Bronx pod and into Manhattan (white collar—lawyers, actuaries, accountants. Range Rovers, pastel golf pants! All university educated. V. intimidating. But like James said, 'How smart can they be? They're in prison!' Goes for me too, I know.

Whitey's always correcting my slang. Horrified I was teaching English in the Bronx. Reckon I need to do an ESL course and pay compo to my former students.

Not mowing lawns anymore. Got promotion to admin job in the main office. Grateful to be working for CO named Mr Metcalfe. Have so much respect for him. Not a pushover or naive about people (keeps his distance) but treats everyone with humanity and respect rarely witnessed even on the outside. Sometimes his kindness drowned out by pettiness of other COs.

Understand that it's prison, procedures to follow etc. Popovic is heavy handed. In routine search of room, threw things for pleasure.

Even family photos etc. Edwards is also mean spirited. Paid for two pairs of winter pants with special buy up and only one arrived. Reported it to Edwards on duty.

Edwards: (leaning in close) Can you hear that? It's the sound of the world's smallest violin.

Same response to my mouldy/out of date buy up food.

V. hard to work out mentality of most in here (not all). Some great people, Andrew, Tom, Glen, Steve, but for the rest I've never seen such selfishness. Gave tea and coffee away until inmates started standing over me for it and demanding other things from my satchel. Had to refuse and then throw out because it was getting to be a huge problem. When I was still in the Bronx I made a going away meal for an inmate who was getting out. All of the guys ate it while I was at a visit. On the outside, generosity was always repaid with generosity. Not in here.

Getting v. cold here now. Frost on ground outside. Winter will be freezing. Thanks for sending money. Bought 2 quilts and more clothes. Issue blankets are thin and no heating yet. Another inmate asked to borrow my spare quilt. He took oath on dead mother and he promised to give back when I want/need. Has no family to send money and I really feel for him.

Mainly work with Zhao Lin—actuary done for insider trading. Owns a string of houses in North Shore. We're both rolling in it now—$46 a week in our office jobs. Need it. Phone calls to your mobile are $2.20 a pop. Buy up food costs way more than supermarket. Someone is making money from us being in here.

Full scales of economy in here.

Inmate: You're on the phone a lot. Reckon you must have some dough. Got a cracker deal; I've got a mate who works at the wharves in Sydney. This could be huge. Been racking my brain and can't think of anyone who can come up with that sort of money. All I need is eighty and in two days I can turn it into 160.

Me: I don't have eighty thousand dollars.

Inmate: No, mate, eighty dollars.

On the other hand, there's Tom. English, Eastern suburbs, ex-cocaine dealer. Real high-flyer, yachts, house on the beach, Pablo Escobar-style parties.

Tom: When I get out of here I'm going on the straight and narrow.

Me: Good for you.

Tom: I'm prepared to do anything, start at the bottom. All I need is $200k a year.

Me: Tom, no one's going to give you a starting salary like that. You don't have any qualifications, any education, apart from teaching those disabled kids to kayak that weekend and you couldn't even hack that.

Tom: How can anyone live on less than that? I made 4 million last year.

A lot of the blokes in here give me a hard time for being naive. Can hardly blame me when I have my mum as a mum. Mum visited on Saturday. At lunch Mum pulled out a small foil packet with white powder in plastic wrap. Looked like large packet of cocaine.

Me: Mum, what is that?

Mum: It's salt, for my lunch.

Me: You can't bring that in here.

Mum: Bit of salt isn't going to hurt anybody.

I just shook my head.

Fiona and Brigette came on Sunday. Olivia was very cute.

Olivia: Where are the bars?

Me: We don't have bars in this prison.

Olivia: (sad) I wanted to see you behind bars. What's that (isolation cubicle with glass divider)?

Me: That's for the men who've been naughty.

Olivia: Can we go in there then?

Nothing like getting to know your sisters over five-hour face-to-face visits!

Glad kids had a great time at the lantern walk at school. Did the candles stay lit this time?

I love you.

Paddy

P.S. Zhao Lin teaching me how to cook. Made five-spice chicken. I'll make it for you when I get out. His wife is heavily pregnant with second child. Do you think you could drive her down? Zhao's due for work release. Was wondering if you might be able to help him write cover letter for job applications? So many inmates are daunted about getting work when they get out.

P.P.S. Can you please get an update on progress of appeal?

TWENTY-FOUR

Days crept into weeks, and then months, until it was the final week of June. Five months since Patrick had gone away, and a week away from my fortieth birthday and our fifteenth wedding anniversary. There was something about these milestones that brought the derailment of my life into a glaring new aperture of disappointment.

Every trip I made to Tumbarumba was draining. Physically, financially, emotionally. None more so than the trip before my birthday. I had left it to the last minute to book accommodation and could not get a room anywhere. I decided I wasn't going to let this stop me and got a crazy idea that camping would be a blast. The kids were ecstatic.

I borrowed a tent from my nephew Dylan, and we arrived at the lake near Tumbarumba around eight o'clock at night. Using the car headlights, I chose a flattish spot and unpacked the tent. I'd grown up camping and had helped my parents to put up our tent, but it was only when I was down on my haunches on the cold, damp ground that I realised it had been a good twenty years since I'd erected a tent. And the tent of my youth had been old-style, with straight vertical poles, not the curved-dome variety I'd been given.

'Mum, we believe in you. You can do it!' Nick and Lexie shouted in encouragement. It was nice to hear the words that I so often said to them echoed back to me. I had no mobile or internet access, and not a clue about what I was doing. But I kept at it. I joined the connector poles, threaded them through the loops on the top two diagonals so that it was dome-shaped. The kids shouted and waved the torch up and down from the warmth of the car.

Despite their unwavering faith in me, I could not do it. I tried so many different ways but did not realise that the small pins needed to be inserted back up into the poles, not into the ground, as I had done. So, the tent, while dome-shaped, would not stay up. The kids were still desperate to camp and with no other place to go, I laid out some ground sheets, then, using McDonald's straws I tied a tarp from the car's roof racks to the wire fence next to us. We hopped into sleeping bags underneath a layer of quilts.

I looked up at the blue plastic tarp.

This was my life. This was what it had come to. A paddock and a tarp.

'Look at the stars,' Lexie said.

I couldn't see any stars. All I could see was an ugly blue tarp. I turned my face towards Lexie, but she was facing away from me; all I could see was her penguin beanie.

'They're so sparkly,' Lexie said, enchanted, as I noticed she wasn't looking up, she was looking out. It was a clarion moment. If I wanted to see the beauty, I had to move. I had to change my perspective. And I did. I lifted up onto my elbows, so I could see the black sky and the incandescent stars. It was idyllic. It was magic.

And then.

Mooooo. Mooooo. Mooooo.

'We're going to get trampled,' Nick said, panicked.

'Are they going to stomp on us?' asked Lexie.

'No. You're forgetting that I grew up in the country,' I said. 'Trust me, the cows are miles away. The sound carries.' My explanation satisfied them. And I told them a bedtime story as they drifted off to sleep, and soon afterwards so did I.

'Buuulll!' I woke up to Lexie shouting.

'Muuum, there's a bull!' yelled Nick.

'It's not a bull, it's a cow,' I said nonchalantly, rising to my feet, seeing my hot breath in the cool air.

'Then what are they?' Nick said, pointing at the large testicles at the back end of the bull.

'Right,' I acknowledged. Not only were we looking at a very large bull, but during the night the paddock had filled with cows. The kids clambered into the car, while I untied the tarp and shoved the camping gear in the back. Then I edged out of the clearing as slowly as possible, careful not to hit any animals.

The COs on duty that morning were polite and the visit went smoothly. It was winter and the oak tree had shed its leaves. The once round-shaped tree bursting with leaves had been replaced with a curved and skeletal frame. Although it was cold we moved outside for privacy. Looking out from the yard to the grey, frost-filled morning, the tree looked haunted.

The ghostly appearance of the tree didn't deter Nick and Lexie. While Paddy and I were engaged in conversation they climbed up into it. Soon afterwards a CO advised them to get down. We played Mr Squiggle and some board games and as soon as Paddy finished his lunch, we left. The kids were bored and I was tired.

It had warmed up that afternoon so I laid out a blanket next to a willow tree in the grounds near the caravan park.

'Those kids were at the jail today!' Nick and Lexie shouted, having no interest in resting when there were other kids to play with.

The kids all played under the large willow trees, whose leaves hung down low, like straggly beards. I rested on the blanket and closed my eyes, listening to the kids talking, marvelling at the way they could befriend each other so quickly. They moved further along the tree line and when I could no longer hear them I went for a walk, finding the group outside a cabin near the amenities block.

'Mum, it's the lady from the jail,' a chubby boy about Lexie's age called to his mother. She looked to be in her mid to late twenties, sitting on the balcony of a cabin smoking a cigarette. Even in her puffy winter clothes she had the kind of looks that turn heads on the street,

'I'm Mel, Nick and Lexie's mum,' I said.

'Trish. Crystal, Bailey and Jayden's mum. If no one knew where we were today, they do now,' she said and we laughed.

'Far to travel?' I asked, unsure about the etiquette for prison-spouse chitchat.

'Four hours. Near Wollongong. You?'

'Bit over five. Blue Mountains. The things we do,' I said, with thoughts of the wilderness and the cows at the forefront of my mind.

'Fancy a drink?' Trish asked, and the truth was, I was dying for one. But while Trish seemed nice, there was a part of me that wondered if I could trust her.

'Why not?' I finally said, and she went inside, returning quickly with two glasses and a red Chateaux le Cask.

'To the things we do,' Trish said and we clinked glasses.

'Visiting your husband?' she asked and I nodded.

'Yours?'

'Fiancé. We're getting married as soon as he gets out . . .' Trish said, taking a long drag of her cigarette. 'Never thought I'd end up with someone in the big house.'

'Me neither,' I added.

'I met Sione after he'd been charged. Driving an unregistered vehicle. Didn't think he'd go in but it was too late, I'd already fallen for him.' I was tempted to judge Trish. On a certain level, I could empathise with her. We both had children to look after, both had partners inside, but, as I sat talking with her, I found myself wondering if I would have stuck with Patrick if he had been sent to prison after we'd just met. I didn't think so. I suppose it's hard to say if you're not in the situation. I didn't judge Trish and I'm glad because she went on to tell me her story.

Trish had met Sione, a Samoan construction worker, after escaping the clutches of domestic abuse. Her relationship with Sione was the only non-violent one she'd ever had. He had a regular job, treated her kids like his own and even supported her financially.

Trish took another long drag on her cigarette and I recalled how I had smoked at university. I had been cast as a smoker in a play and I'd coughed and spluttered through my first cigarette, so I'd smoked a couple of packets for practice. I liked the rush it gave me and the sense of control. I craved her cigarette, wanting to suck that nicotine deep into my lungs.

'You know what's weird,' she continued, 'my family loved Michael, my ex, bloody idiot, and they can't stand Si because he's in prison. A record only tells part of someone's story, it's not the whole story.' I was touched that Trish had shared her life with me. And it made me think about my life. I was so afraid of people finding out about Paddy's sentence, and yet, as I sat there listening to Trish, it struck me that knowing her story was what was drawing me in to her. Drawing me close.

Trish's words stirred something deep within me. What if being sent to prison is just a mistake, no worse than any other? What if it's just a flaw, a blemish, like anyone else's? I shared some of my story with Trish and we finished our drinks.

My phone beeped indicating that I had a voicemail. It was the motel letting me know that, due to a cancellation, they now had a room. I was desperate to get there and have a long, hot shower, but Nick and Lexie still wanted to play with the other kids.

'We'll see them tomorrow,' I said, accompanying them back to the car, 'when they see their dad.'

'He's not their real dad,' Lexie corrected, 'he's their mum's boyfriend.'

'I know,' I said, 'but she said he's like a father to them.'

'Where's their real dad?' Nick asked.

'You mean their biological father? The one who made them?' I qualified, folding the blanket.

'Yeah.'

'Because anyone can make a baby, but being a father is a whole other thing,' I said, opening the car door.

'So where is he?' Nick asked again.

'I don't know.'

'Happy birthday,' Patrick said, sliding a handmade card across the table at the beginning of the Sunday visit. 'You might not want it though . . . when you see the back.' The front was a beautiful, detailed Aboriginal artwork; and the back featured a drawing of a penis, similar to the one on the courthouse desk.

'I only put it down for a minute,' Paddy said. 'When I showed the CO, he said, "Charming." I didn't know what he meant until I sat down.'

'It's . . . original,' I said.

'And I got you this,' he said, producing the most exquisite origami vase and flowers. The vase was made from pink and white paper, the flowers were multi-coloured, and if you looked closely, camouflaged on the yellow flower was a small golden butterfly. It even had tiny black paper antennas.

'This must have taken ages. How did you—?'

'Jason Bird made it and I'm not going to tell you how much it cost me, in trade,' he smiled, proud of his industriousness.

'The guy who murdered the policeman? He made that?'

'You said Dad wasn't with any murderers!' Nick said, suddenly interested in the conversation.

'It was a very long time ago,' Paddy explained. 'I know him, and there were mitigating circumstances.'

'What are miti—, whatever you call it?'

'It means it's complicated. He wouldn't be in here if they thought he was still dangerous,' I reassured him.

'Is he here?' Nick asked, looking around.

Patrick nodded.

'Where?'

'Don't all look over at once,' Patrick said, and then whispered that Jason Bird was the tall, extremely muscly man sitting across from us, near the back window.

We all looked over at once.

From where we sat, I could see that Jason had greying hair, the beginnings of a bald patch and thick jail-issue glasses.

'I'm going outside,' Nick announced, and walked to the other side of the room past Jason Bird's table and straight back over to us. 'He doesn't look like a murderer, he just looks like a normal person,' he said and then ran outside to play.

All the kids usually played together but the yard dynamics had changed when a new inmate—some hotshot lawyer—arrived at Mannus. At visits his family dressed and acted as though they had just stepped out of a sailing boat or a Ralph Lauren photo shoot. The boys wore chinos and polo shirts and jackets with the collars turned up.

Both Nick and Lexie, despite being corrected several hundred times, still called the COs police, as did many of the other kids. On this day, Lexie made a comment to one of the Ralph Lauren boys, Tarquin or Hamilton or something. He rolled his eyes and said, 'They're called correctional officers. And besides,' he said to Lexie, 'we're not meant to talk to you!'

'Which one is he?' I asked Patrick, fuming. It was difficult to tell the men apart, they all had green tracksuits and bad haircuts. Patrick pointed out a slight man in his mid to late forties—the hotshot lawyer. He didn't look different from the other men. A tracksuit is a great leveller. But he and his family were right to keep their distance. His only error was misappropriating half a million dollars in clients' funds for his own purposes. He wasn't a real criminal low-life like the rest of the inmates and their families.

The car park was a testament to the diversity of the prison population. You had the Range Rovers and the Audis and the BMWs, and then there were the old, beat-up cars that would be lucky to pass a rego inspection. Inside the centre, it was the same. You would see visitors wearing the finest clothes and people who were obviously struggling. During one visit, I saw a family sit around with a single loaf of sliced white bread from the Tumbarumba bakery. At $3.50, it was the cheapest thing you could buy. And at the end of the visit they asked around for a lift into town so they could get the bus back to the city.

After lunch, Nick and Lexie were allowed to choose something from the small shop the COs operated. Interestingly, there had been a hefty price increase. Most of the items had gone up by fifty per cent.

'Pretty steep price hike,' I said to an enormous CO named Popovic. 'Any reason?'

'Inflation,' he said. I laughed aloud, thinking he was being ironic. He glared back, uncertain as to why I was laughing.

Usually, the kids chose a chocolate bar. Lexie bought and ate hers at lightning speed, and asked for another one. I said no, at which point she proceeded to take some change out of the plastic tub.

'You say something to her,' I told Paddy. I felt for him. The visitation rules precluded him from handling money or approaching the entrance, and it must have been emasculating. But he was still their father and I felt resentful that the responsibility of disciplining them always fell on my shoulders.

'No, Lexie,' Paddy said.

Lexie clenched her hands into fists and stamped her feet. 'I want another chocolate!'

'You can stamp all you like,' said Paddy, who has always been worlds more patient than I, 'but you're not getting another one.'

She increased her volume and repeated, 'I want another chocolate!'

Patrick looked her straight in the eyes. 'No!'

It was a battle of wills. And Lexie's is as unbending as iron. She put her hands on her hips and looked at Paddy as if to say, I raise you with this. 'You're not even my *real* dad,' she shouted. 'You're just the stupid man my mum married!'

Patrick blushed and laughed, and then tried to explain to the people around us that he was, in fact, her biological father. People offered sympathetic nods and words, and a CO who had walked over to the table said, 'Either way, I wish you luck, mate. You're gunna need it.'

At my mother's insistence, I had a low-key birthday party in my hometown in the Hunter Valley. I didn't want to have a party. The thought of it only highlighted the gap between the life I wanted and the life I had. The party was nice, though, and it was good to catch up with old friends and family I hadn't seen for a long time. Amy, my sister, had made a PowerPoint presentation with photos from my life. I knew it had taken her a lot of time and effort to put together, and it disappointed her when I asked her not to play it that night. Seeing the photos of myself growing from a child to an adult, and a parent, only emphasised the way my life had imploded. The photos in the presentation captured the very best parts of my life but my mind replayed the worst.

As part of my birthday present, my mum and sister organised for me to stay in a hotel at Bondi Beach while they babysat Nick and Lexie. I'd still been working as a freelance writer and I had some looming deadlines and research to complete. And I also hoped to use the time for personal writing.

I checked into what used to be a grand hotel but was in a state of disrepair, due to the fact that the building was being sold off as luxury apartments. The room looked out onto Bondi Beach. It was too cold to sit outside on the balcony, and the water that was normally blue and soothing raged before me, grey and unforgiving.

After unpacking, I went down to the main street to buy some supplies. The wind was icy and whipped my bare ankles as I walked back to my room. I poured myself a glass of wine and began to write in my journal. I wrote unconsciously, just letting all the words flow out onto the paper, regardless of order or purpose or punctuation. As the words flowed out, so did my tears. Part two of the Trilogy of Crying. And, unlike the words I allowed to pour out in scrawled and scribbled jumbles across the pages, I put up an emotional wall to try to stop the tears. I didn't want to be celebrating my birthday, and soon-to-be wedding anniversary, as a blubbering mess on a hotel floor.

I remembered the smell of Trish's cigarettes, and craved the taste and that exhilarating rush of sucking back smoke. I walked back out to the hall, past the peeling paint, caught the elevator down to street level and headed straight to the little tobacconist I had seen earlier.

'Do you have any clove cigarettes?' I asked.

It had been years since I'd bought cigarettes, and when the cashier reached underneath the counter and showed me a packet of Djarum Kreteks, I was shocked to see a horrifying picture of an emphysema-affected lung. 'Or these?' he said, holding up a different packet featuring an eyeball pulled back with a pin-like apparatus. Even more alarming was the price tag of seventeen dollars and twenty cents. I paid, and walked back to the hotel balcony to cough and splutter my way through one cigarette.

It had the desired effect, though: the cloves and nicotine coursed through my veins, giving me the rush I had been craving and making me feel that, even just for a moment, I was in control. I poured myself another glass of shiraz, and then another, until I had the warm, giddy feeling of the alcohol taking effect. Life felt better; easier, smoother. Drinking is what I should have been doing from the very beginning, I thought, and proceeded to get horribly, disgustingly drunk.

The following day, our fifteen-year wedding anniversary began with me on my knees, heaving into the toilet. My temples throbbed so hard I felt like they were going to burst, and my head ached as though it had been bludgeoned. I drank glass after glass of water, and threw up each one, until finally all I had left to retch was the acrid taste of my own bile. I spent the remainder of the day in bed, nursing my hangover and waiting for Paddy to call me. I was too sick to write or read, or barely even move, and all I could do was wait. I stayed in bed until 5.30pm, when the prison phones are switched off.

I could usually see the funny side of situations. It was like a game I played, to stop myself becoming too dark. I could see the irony when at a recent kids' birthday party, the girl's father whispered that he was an undercover cop; something, he said, he didn't tell most people, adding that I seemed like a good person. Shortly afterwards his wife asked if my husband and I would like to join them for dinner. I could see the absurdity in all the hours I'd spent on the phone with our service provider trying to explain that my husband was incarcerated. On one occasion, the Filipino customer service operator said, 'That's very nice, ma'am. Can you please ask him to get out of the car?' And I'd laughed so hard when a friend sent me a link to a *Sesame Street* Tool Kit that had a scene with a Muppet's parent in custody. Nick and Lexie and I giggled and sang along with the sad blue-haired little Muppet.

But I could not see the humour anymore. I wasn't asking for the world. I hadn't expected to be whisked up the Eiffel Tower or given a two-carat diamond, but I thought that after fifteen years of marriage, I could have done better than a card with a penis drawn on the back, and a vase of paper flowers made by a murderer.

I was drunk, hung over and alone. All I craved, all I wanted, was for someone to hold me.

TWENTY-FIVE

Mannus Correctional Centre
5 July 2013

Beauty,

Sorry I couldn't call for our anniversary. Jail in lock down for whole day. No phones. Asked Jamie or Uncle Dingo (other Aboriginal artist) if he can make you another card. Sorry. Worse than high school in here.

Promise to make it up to you. Whiteys were discussing engagement rings and said I am cheap bas%^$d for not buying you diamond. I didn't have much money then but we could afford to buy one now. Or maybe pearls. Know you love them. Or antique ring with those tiny pearls you love and rubies??? Would be nice to get you something good to have as heirloom for kids. I can't buy for you until I get out but you could pick something out now and buy.

Went to parenting course (unfortunately titled Hey Dad). Some good tips. Being consistent. Setting boundaries. Spending time each day. Statistic from course said something like fathers spend less than ten minutes a day with kids. It kills me that I am not with them now but at least I smashed that statistic before I went in. Still believe it's all about quantity time, not quality time.

Some interesting conversations about this with other dads.

Me: Want to come to the Hey Dad course?

Inmate: Nah, don't think there's any room for improvement.

Me: Good for you. How many kids you got?

Inmate: Three but haven't seen them for 18 months.

Other courses offered here but there is an internal war. Mannus is a working prison and there's a lot of resistance to educational programs. There is a charity called Kairos (prison ministry). Misread form and told other inmates we got to travel to Wagga so a lot of them signed up.

Inmate 1: When's the bus from Wagga arrive?

Me: I might have misread the form . . . the volunteers are from Wagga.

Inmate 1: You mean we have to stay here all day listening to bloody God botherers?

Inmate 2: Lucky for you, Jacobs, the cakes are good.

I love you so much and thank God every day for you.
Paddy

P.S. I know I wasn't v. consistent with the kids. Promise to work on it when I get back.

P.P.S. Can you ask the school if I can call the kids during the day? Phones aren't on when they leave for the bus in the morning and often miss them in the afternoon.

PART IV

'THE WORLD BREAKS EVERYONE, AND AFTERWARD,
SOME ARE STRONG AT THE BROKEN PLACES.'

Ernest Hemingway

TWENTY-SIX

I'd tried to enrol Nick in a music school, for private drum lessons. However, being mid-term, there weren't any vacancies. I put his name on waiting lists but all the schools said they'd be surprised if anything came up before the end of term.

'Have you tried Hands, Heart and Feet?' the school receptionist asked, whose kindness in caring for my children has never ceased to amaze me.

'No, but I've heard of them.'

'I'm not surprised—they're pretty special.'

I learned from the website that Hands, Heart and Feet is a Blue Mountains percussion group run by a husband and wife team—John and Emily. I called to see if I could book Nick into a drumming class. On the phone, Emily explained that the classes were drop-in only. Children were encouraged to attend the adult evening classes with their parents, absorbing the rhythm of the African style music.

I wasn't keen on African drumming, or any drumming, for that matter. I wanted to sit outside a classroom, and read a book or drink coffee. But Nick's tapping was sending Lexie and me to the brink of insanity, so we went.

The drumming class, like so many other things in life, was not at all what I'd expected. First of all, John and Emily were not African. They are a white Australian couple. When we arrived, Emily was sitting at a small desk on the stage. She was the antithesis of me—calm and glowing with health and vitality.

John was tall, silver-haired and dressed in garish patterned clothes. He was unstacking blue plastic moulded chairs and placing them in a circle. He'd already put out about twenty, which I thought was pretty ambitious, when he strode over to introduce himself.

'John,' he said warmly.

'I'm Nick.' He placed his Balinese drum at John's feet. 'I can't stop drumming. Mum said I'm driving her crazy.'

'Bet I can get you to stop and I'm already crazy,' John said, pulling a face and instantly endearing himself to Nick and Lexie.

People started pouring into the primary school hall, many of them also wearing brightly coloured clothing. We sat opposite the entrance, and it felt like being at the airport, watching people arrive and greet each other with such affection. When they hugged, they held onto each other close and tight, like they had really missed them. Like they would never let go. The cynical side of me wondered if there was a catch to all this congeniality. I wondered if, at the end of the class, someone might try to con me with some network marketing scheme.

When everyone had arrived, thirty-seven in all, John started drumming. He began with a dramatic flourish, which, I found out much later, is known as a call, then settled into a continuous and repetitive rhythm. The majority of people, presumably regulars, knew each other, had their own drums, and followed the beat effortlessly.

It wasn't effortless for me. It was frustrating. I could hear the rhythm and I knew what I had to do but I couldn't do it. It was as though my hands wouldn't cooperate. The more I tried, the more I thought about it, the more difficult it became.

'If you're not getting it, don't worry, your brain hasn't formed that neural pathway, but it will. Let go. If it's not getting in here,' John said, pointing to his temple, 'let it in here,' placing his hand on his heart.

The drummers in the circle played *djembes*, goblet-shaped drums covered with animal skin and bound together with an elaborate series of tied ropes. At the front of the room, a handful of people played large barrel-sized drums with sticks. As the *djembe* rhythm increased in difficulty, the standing drummers continued their pattern with the constancy of a heartbeat.

For those of us who were still struggling, John introduced a phrase: 'Two hundred pineapples, a rich red tomato, and an apple, and an apple—a really, really big one.' The word felt more familiar to me, like something I could cling onto. Then, John instructed all of us to get on our feet and together we stamped out the rhythm and the phrase. We moved as a group, swiftly changing from one direction to the next, like a school of fish. I felt silly and self-conscious until I saw Nick, a smile stretched from one side of his face to the other. He had found his tribe.

After the phrase was introduced, I finally managed to get the opening part of the rhythm. It had an up-and-down feel to it, like riding a horse. The rest was beyond me. But it didn't matter. The sheer difficulty of the drumming, combined with being in the circle, demanded that I be fully present. I had no time to brood about the past or worry about my future. My drumming ability aside, I had to admit that there was something special, otherworldly, about the way the empty school hall had been transformed into this pulsing hub of energy.

As John had predicted, about three-quarters of the way into the class, Nick stopped drumming. At seven-thirty, when the lesson ended with a team building 'Whoosh,' Nick leaped out of his chair, making a beeline for John's psychedelic pants.

'You like my pants?' John asked, amused by his unabashed admiration.

'Yes,' Nick blushed.

'I sewed them myself. These are my conservative ones,' he said, and we all chuckled. John thanked us for coming, before chatting with a long queue of others who were waiting to speak with him.

The *djembe* drummers restacked the plastic chairs, and the standing drummers moved their barrel-shaped drums onto the stage as a large influx of people filled the space for a dance class.

Nick, Lexie and I went to the drumming class for the next two weeks and, on the third, I arranged a babysitter to take them home so I could stay for the dance class.

Emily began the class with a rigorous physical warm-up, before slowing to stillness. The quietness enveloped me like a soft, warm blanket.

'Let go of anything that has been on your mind,' she said, gently. It was difficult to let go. Heaviness weighed me down. It was mostly that same nagging question of why? Why did Patrick break the law? Why did this happen?

'Worries or fears or events of the day. Let it all go,' Emily repeated.

It seemed like an impossible task. My worries were wrapped around me like tentacles.

'And connect with the reason you came to class,' Emily continued.

I had come to class because I liked dancing. I wasn't particularly good at it but I wanted, like Steph had suggested, to do something for myself. Something for the pure unadulterated fun of it.

'Now, bring that intention to be present in the class,' Emily soothed.

After the warm up, she instructed us to bring our awareness back to the room, as she began to teach the routines. Unlike other dance classes I had been to over the course of my life, this one was welcoming and fluid. Usually, the two front rows of a class are taken up by the most experienced dancers and they cling to their positions like tightly held pieces of real estate. Emily's class was different. After each sequence she instructed the dancers to move to a different position in the room, in order to experience a new perspective. She moved through the routines in a patient and nurturing way, showing us that the triumph was in trying. And that if we didn't have it yet, it didn't matter; it was only a matter of time. Everything about the class was like a spiritual lesson for me. Even though Emily explained the steps in small sequences, thinking about the routines didn't seem to help. It came from a deeper part of me: that part that feels. In those brief and uninhibited moments as I swayed and gyrated and shimmied, I felt alive and sensuous. Perhaps even a little bit sexy.

The class ended the way it had begun, in a large circular formation. 'We thank our bodies,' Emily said, demonstrating how to massage our own bodies. 'Even the parts we don't usually like. Especially the parts we don't like.' As I massaged my stomach and my buttocks and my thighs, it occurred to me that I have a relationship with my body outside of the physical relationship I shared with Patrick.

'We thank each other with our eyes,' Emily said. I joined the rest of the class, who were all looking, deeply and purposefully, across the circle into each other's eyes. 'And, finally, we send our thanks to Africa.' The circle dispersed.

'Nick's doing well,' John said, walking up to me.

'He loves it.'

'He's a natural.'

'I can't thank you enough. He's had a tough time . . . this year . . .'

'Everything okay?' John asked, looking at me with deep concern.

'His dad . . . my husband . . . well . . . he's in prison.' I have no idea what John was expecting me to say but it wasn't that. And of all the facial contortions I had experienced his was, by far, the most dramatic. He looked horrified, involuntarily jerking back as though he'd been burned. And for the briefest moment, I was worried that we might not be welcomed back to class.

And so in the Springwood school hall, part three of the Trilogy of Crying began. I felt so ashamed. All the sadness and tension and shame that had built up over the past few years was threatening to come pouring out. And in a public place. I turned to face the wall. I had to snap out of it. Pull myself together.

John moved in front to face me, placing his hands on my shoulders the way a father might. He bent down so that he was the same height as me and he hugged me.

'Sorry, sorry,' I kept saying. 'You don't have to . . . you're bending right down,' I managed to say, embarrassed.

'When you hug someone, it should always be heart on heart.'

At first, my body was hunched over, my hands balled up at my chest. John didn't attempt to move me or tell me what to do, he just held me. Slowly my hands unclenched and dropped to my side. My face pressed into his chest, relaxing into his embrace, and I bawled. It had been so long since anyone had held me. Really held me. Tears and snot came pouring out of me and onto John's shirt.

'Sorry, for crying . . . sorry about your shirt,' I said, when the sobbing had died down to a whimper.

'Crying is good for you, it's healing . . . it releases chemicals and toxins from the body. My wife cries every day,' he said, including Emily, who stood a short distance away, in our conversation. The love between them was obvious. The way they called each other 'my love', and gently brushed each other's arm when they were near.

'Sorry about your shirt,' I said again.

'That's the beauty of these crazy patterns, there's all sorts of things on here and you can't tell.'

I cried all the way home in the car, as I paid the babysitter and I was still crying when I clambered into bed without removing my make-up or cleaning my teeth. As I lay in bed, fighting so hard to hold back the tears, I could see the situation for what it really was. I felt like a character from a children's book that had attempted every route except the one she knew she had to take. I had tried to go around it, dig under it, jump and fly over it, and pretend it didn't exist. I'd tried to numb myself with food and cigarettes and alcohol. But I knew in my heart that there was no way to avoid my suffering: I had to go through it.

And so I surrendered to the pain I had been so dreadfully afraid of. As the Balinese masseuse had told me, 'First worse, then better.' I felt like my chest cavity had been wedged open, and the dull ache I had been feeling for so many months was replaced with a sharp, stabbing pain, as through I'd been cut.

I cried for Patrick being in prison and for what our relationship had become. I cried for all the things he was missing and for all the things I now had to do on my own. I cried because every night I went to bed alone and because each day was a long, hard slog with no break. And because I hadn't been able to reconcile the faith I once had, the faith that had brought Patrick and me together, with all the hurt and pain and anger. I cried because the pain wasn't just emotional or metaphorical, I was in actual physical pain. My eyes stung, my shoulders throbbed, my stomach was knot of tension. Every part of me felt wounded and broken because I had been holding on to everything so very, very tightly.

I continued to cry on and off for roughly two weeks. Sometime during part three of the Trilogy of Crying, I received a phone call.

'Is that Melissa?' asked a well-spoken man on the end of the line.

'Yes. Who is this?'

'It's Zhao . . . Patrick's friend . . . from Mannus. I'm out now.'

'Hi . . . congratulations,' I said, recalling he was the actuary charged with insider trading. And then immediately felt guilty. He was so much more than that. He was married with two children. He loved real coffee and couldn't stand the instant stuff he was forced to drink on the inside.

'How are you? How is Cynthia? How is the baby?'

Zhao told me that they were all well and he was taking time out to be with the new baby, something the demands of his previous job had not allowed. He asked me if, when he started looking for another position, I might help him with his cover letter. I'd never written a letter disclosing a prison sentence, a federal charge at that. I didn't know if I'd be of any help but agreed to take a look.

'Do you just keep asking why?' I said, after we'd exhausted all other topics. 'I just keep asking, over and over, "Why did this happen? Why did he do it?"'

Zhao paused, and then after a long exhalation said: 'It's good to analyse a situation, so that you understand it, but I'm Chinese, it's not part of my culture to ask why. Usually, you're not asking why, but why me? That doesn't help you move forward. In my culture, we say, "It just is."'

His words felt like the sun, enlightening but out of reach. However I knew that my questions weren't bringing me any peace. For a brief moment I entertained the possibility that there might not be an answer and something inside me shifted.

TWENTY-SEVEN

Mannus Correctional Centre
2 August 2013

Beauty,

Sorry to hear Theo escaped. Do you want to get Lexie another rabbit? I hope this doesn't upset her but I have a dog. One of the COs helped me apply and I now have a Jack Russell named Bella. If I'm allowed I could bring her home to the kids. She's v. well behaved. Came from elderly deceased owner in Snowy Mountains. Can't tell you how comforting it is to have her.

So weird, the inmates (especially the ones, charged with violent crimes (armed robbery and GBH against humans) are like different people around the dog). Give me a hard time and call me names (mainly a slack ba$%&d) for not letting her sleep in my bed (single) and not taking her to work (in office!) Tried to explain she has 164 inmates fighting over her and slipping her extra food. She has four walks a day minimum. Mannus is dog heaven.

V. cold. Asked inmate for quilt back and he refused. Others said if I want it back I will have to fight him for it. Can you send money for new quilt? ($60?)

Sometimes life brings you surprising teachers. Getting to know Jason Bird after asking him to make you the origami vase. His parole is coming up and he started coming to visit me for advice about the outside world. Ironically, he's the one teaching me. He's been in prison for sixteen years, since he was eighteen or nineteen. Never used a mobile phone or a DVD or the internet or an iPod. Hard to imagine what it will be like for him getting out, it's like he's been frozen in time.

Heard his story from other inmates. Apparently, Bird tried to sell drugs to some off-duty policemen who'd been at the pub for hours, drinking. They accepted, took him around a corner and then started attacking them. He retaliated first with fists and then with a knife he had on him, killing one and injuring another. Most in here idolize him because of what he did and everyone hates the police in here. V. interesting to see, as Bird won't tolerate others degrading policemen or praising his crime.

Inmate: Way to go, Bird. One down, about fifteen thousand to go (referring to policeman).

Bird: Don't let me hear you say that again. All I did was make a widow.

People listen to him. Looks like cross between Superman and The Incredible Hulk. He did a lot of years in A1 Class (Highest). Stabbed three times by other inmates and had to have surgery for one of them. He showed me the scars on his chest and stomach. Now is C2 like me.

Bird has a deep respect for the police. Told me that in his appeal one of the officers couldn't live with himself and testified that they didn't disclose to Bird they were policemen. If he didn't do that Bird would have got life, never to be released.

Said most people rejected him after what he did. The only person who was there for him was his father, who had abused him most of his childhood (dropped wardrobes on his head, woke him in the middle of the night and beat him for drinking remaining milk in fridge etc).

Me: What chance did you have if you had parents who did that?

Bird: I had every chance, there's no excuse for what I did. Everyone has choices. Everyone.

Refreshing to hear someone take full responsibility for what they have done. Most of the men seem to want to blame everyone else and I have been guilty of falling into that trap. Bird explained how every day he wrestles with the fact that he took someone's life, which unlike everything else is irreversible. He's incredibly self-aware. Speaks about himself in the third person and admits that his old self was going nowhere and deserved everything he got.

After I got arrested nearly everyone said to me, 'It's not like you murdered someone!' I see not only the way that others look at him but how hard it is to know you did something that is irreversible. So hard to not let it define you. Most people only see him as his crime. But in my conversations with him I can see that he is more than that. He's knows all about anatomy and fitness and he knows a lot about plants. Taught me how to propagate a fig tree and he can make anything with origami.

I used to think things were black and white. Right and wrong. Now I can see it's only shades of grey. Way more than fifty! There's context and motivation and fear that all come into play.

There's blokes in here that got such light sentences and there's others who got worse than me. From the outside it might look like black and white but it's anything but that. Andrews told me he requested a ruling from the tax office for some creative thing his accountant wanted to do. They approved it and then, despite the ruling, he, his accountant and a whole bunch of clients were all *prosecuted. Interestingly, they are all in here together. When the accountant arrived, several blokes offered to bash him for Andrews but he said, 'NO WAY!' Most men only speak one language in here—violence.*

Another inmate, Gaffey, was charged with manslaughter after a female driver fell asleep at the wheel. She drove onto the wrong side of the road, he swerved to avoid a collision, then she woke and corrected. It was her fault but he was charged because he was on the wrong side of the road. His whole life has been ripped apart. Lost his job, his wife left him so he can't see his kids. He's so depressed.

Most inmates don't believe my charges. Wouldn't matter except they think that I'm deliberately lying or am an informant. Hard to try and accept things when blokes telling me every day how I got ripped off.

Printed out my charges to shut people up.

Typical conversation.

Inmate: How long did you get?

Me: Two and half on the bottom (when eligible for parole). Four and a half, on top (full sentence).

Inmate: But there must have been a victim.

Me: No, no victims.

Inmate: Didn't you have a lawyer?

Me: Yeah, I did.

Inmate: Must have been an effing useless one.

Bird suggested he become my personal trainer. I agreed and then in the gym he started punching me in the stomach while I was doing chin ups (said is maxo style and how you become hard). Decided to have a break from the gym for a while.

Heard from one of the other inmates that Jamie (first cellie in Mannus) broke parole and was arrested again. Hard to believe someone would prefer prison to life on the outside. He said his three squares a day on the inside are better than what he ever had on the outside.

Surprised that there is so much humour in here. V. black and sarcastic. For example, after a visit yesterday, Summer (border security) played a practical joke.

Summer: (to the CO) After every visit you search me and you've found nothing but it's (drugs) still getting in here. Have you ever searched Jacobs?

Thanks to Summer, I got strip-searched. On that note—thinking of you!

I love you.

Paddy

TWENTY-EIGHT

'So, tell me about your father,' Steph said, crossing her legs and flicking out her ankle, causing the laces on one of her strappy shoes to flutter. I'd thought we'd talk about the dual disappointments of my birthday and wedding anniversary, but Steph wanted to get all Freudian.

'I think we've covered that,' I said, firmly.

Steph flicked back through the pages of her folder, skimming her notes and diagrams. 'Your father was nineteen when you were born. Divorced, remarried, has teenage sons?' She looked up for confirmation and I nodded. But Steph and I both knew that a person's life encompasses so much more than the scant details you would tick on a form. Marital status. Children. Occupation. These things are categories. They only scratch the surface of our deep, complicated lives.

'Are you like him?' Steph asked, pen poised, and I looked down at her shoes again. Does she only wear them once or is she fanatical about cleanliness? I wondered. None of my shoes looked like that.

'Not really. I get my dark features from him. My mum and sister both have blond hair, and blue eyes,' I said, noticing a new addition to her wall. The roughly drawn figures floated, weightless, mid-page, with wild curly hair, and smiles that extended beyond their angular faces.

'Tell me about him,' Steph prompted.

Why is she doing this? I thought. 'He's a dichotomy, I s'pose, like the rest of us.'

'Tell me about that,' she said.

'He's incredibly social, always telling jokes, a great storyteller. People have often told me how he's such a nice guy, but when it comes to me . . .' Steph jotted down notes in her folder and then paused, as if waiting for me to continue. I was waiting for her to speak. It was a conversational stand-off.

'Nineteen's young to become a parent,' Steph said. I'd won.

'Yes,' I agreed.

'Was it planned?' she asked, with her perfect posture, perfect everything.

'No. Mum was only seventeen.'

'And how did their lives change?'

It's difficult to think of your parents as people with lives and aspirations of their own. Being a parent myself had given me a speck of insight into how my children only saw me in my one supporting role—their mother. What was my mother like when she was seventeen? I didn't know.

'Apparently Mum was very good at school, in all the top classes. She had to drop out because of the pregnancy. I'm not sure about Dad,' I said. 'I know he was on his way to becoming a professional footballer and he was a state champion boxer. And suddenly he found himself with a wife and a baby and a job he hated. Then he got sick, I'm not sure what it was, but I know he almost died, had to have an ileostomy bag . . . that put an end to contact sport.'

'So his life got derailed as well,' Steph commented as I sipped my water. It was the first time I'd ever thought about my father's life in those terms.

The conversation moved on to depression and Steph mapped out a family history. My maternal grandfather and uncle had both committed suicide; clinical depression snaked through my mother's side of the family like a mineral vein. There was no denying that it was in my make-up. I'd always been a brooding pessimist.

'And your father, did he struggle with depression . . . after his illness perhaps?' Steph enquired.

'Come to think of it, he did,' I said, taking another sip of water as the memories seeped in.

'What comes to mind?' she asked eventually, holding my gaze for so long I had to look away.

'I remember him lying on the couch, next to the stereo. Mum was out, so the music was turned up loud. It was The Doors, he loved this song called 'Peace Frog', from *Morrison Hotel*,' I said, recalling it so specifically and vividly, it felt like it had happened yesterday. 'I must have been about fourteen. I came in and turned it down, oblivious to his existential crisis. I asked him something and he didn't respond, it didn't even register . . .' I started crying.

'Take your time,' Steph counselled.

'And then . . .' I said, still crying, 'he said to me, "I can't think of a single thing, worth living for . . ."'

Years before, a kid on my street had accidentally shot me in the face with an air rifle. I remember the sting of the pellet penetrating the skin. It was deep and sharp and foreign. My father's words felt like that. I could feel the hole where they'd gone in, but, unlike the pellet, it was difficult to tell where they had lodged and impossible to extract.

'And what does that mean to you?' Steph asked gently, passing me a tissue.

'In retrospect, I suppose I see it as selfish,' I said, continuing to cry.

'But that's an adult's perspective—possibly how someone may have described it to you—how did it make you feel back then, as a child?' Steph was firm, steeling herself for our usual mental tussle.

I cast my mind back to that time, to that place. The brown leather. The speed of the guitar. The pain in my father's eyes. And I remember I was determined to be better, smarter, so that I could give him at least one reason to live.

'I can see . . . now . . . that it was a call for help,' I said, dabbing at my eyes.

'That is still you as an adult. How did you feel as that little girl?' Steph asked, and I started to cry even more. After the past weeks, I was surprised I had so many tears left.

'Hurt . . .'

Steph looked at me, tenacious and tender, imploring me to go on.

'. . . like I wasn't enough . . .'

I looked over at the picture of the happy family, the irony not lost on me. And I said what had been buried deep down inside me for so long.

'Unloved.'

It was there, in Steph's office, I remembered that my father had tried to kill himself. 'My family had gone out to my uncle's farm, bushwalking. Dad didn't go on the walk, said he wanted to stay back at the house. The others cut the walk short for some reason . . . and they found him in the garage . . . He'd run a piece of hose from the exhaust into the window with the intention of . . . you know . . .'

Steph nodded.

'I wasn't there, I was at my part-time job at the video shop, but that didn't stop me thinking about it. Imagining what it must have been like for him in that car, what was going through his mind? The fumes. I was afraid that if he'd tried suicide once, then he'd do it again. I always felt this worry, this responsibility to look out for him.' I noticed the clock. We were only halfway through the session but it felt like I'd been in there for hours.

'For years, it haunted my dreams. I dreamed that I was the one who'd discovered him, and I was coughing and spluttering, trying to pull him out. I always woke exhausted from that dream. I tried so hard to lift and carry him and I couldn't do it. I couldn't save him. In my dreams, it was always smoke, not fumes and the room was filling with smoke . . . I couldn't see, I couldn't breathe. I had to get out.

'I'd wake from that dream and walk straight down the hall, to check he was still alive. He has this breathing pattern, where he does two or three regular breaths in a row and then there's a long pause until the next one. And I'd wait, frozen, till I heard the next breath.'

'What does the dream mean to you now?' Steph asked and I shrugged, focusing on the shiny tip of her shoe.

'I don't know.'

Steph smiled, even though the session was a long, hard slog. And, as the clock indicated, time was passing with a deathly slowness. I wondered if that's what it felt like for Paddy in prison.

For years I felt like I'd failed my father but now new light had been cast on our history.

'That he had to save himself, that we all do,' I finally answered. 'And he has. He's remarried and he's got two great boys. He's enjoying being a father the second time around—I'm happy for him.'

'Is he involved in Nick and Lexie's lives?' Steph asked.

'Yes, whenever I go back to the Hunter, the kids ask if they can go to Pop's lolly shop. He used to have a shop, now he just has a large collection in the cupboard.'

'When you met Patrick, did you consider him different to your father?'

'Yes.'

'Consciously or unconsciously?' Steph asked.

'Consciously,' I said, thinking about just how different they are. Chalk and cheese.

There was no doubt in my mind that Patrick loved me. We had bonded over the pain of our fathers' infidelities and Patrick had promised that he would never ever betray me.

The session had gone over time, so we ended there. Unlike my other sessions with Steph, this one didn't end with the feeling of neatly folded corners. Everything felt unresolved. Unfinished.

I wasn't until days later, after mulling things over, that I finally got some perspective. For the first time in my life, I felt enormous compassion for my father. We weren't so different, he and I. He had taught me to love stories and I will always be grateful for that. I could see now that my father's life hadn't turned out the way he'd planned either and it had broken him.

And, as it turned out, Patrick wasn't that different from my father. Deep down, in that messy, murky core, I was afraid Patrick would abandon me and he had. He hadn't neglected me or replaced me with another woman, but I could see now with crystal clarity that he had betrayed me. Not in the way I'd feared, but it was betrayal, nonetheless.

TWENTY-NINE

Mannus Correctional Centre
3 September 2013

Beauty,

Awkward weekend visit with Dave Pete and Geoff. Geoff only wanted to talk about World's Worst Prisons *TV show. Highlight for him was hearing about unsuspecting prisoners attacked in their sleep with DIY weapons. Comforting thought! Geoff failed to understand why he couldn't bring iPhone or iPod to visit (tried to explain to CO, Popovic, of all people, that he likes to listen to music).*

CO: Do you have anything to declare? Any prohibited weapons, sharp objects (whole spiel)?

Pete: Only my rapier wit.

Popovic didn't laugh.

COs wanted to know what time I was finishing my visit as some new inmates had to be processed and they needed me to do the paperwork and computer entry.

Pete: It's like the Shawshank Redemption.

Me: Funny you should say that because right now my boots are in the warden's office.

Pete: Why?

Me: Long story. But I'll have to remember to swap boots when I leave.

Bella the dog is causing problems for me. Tom is up for parole and all the inmates are hassling me to let her go with him.

Inmate: Don't be a slack bas%&$d, Jacobs, this is Bella's chance at freedom. Her opportunity to finally get out.

Me: She's on 47,000 acres. She chases cattle and sheep and she can roam . . .

Inmate: Why would you want someone to be in prison?

Me: Bella is a dog. She doesn't have her civil liberties taken away from her.

*Inmate: But this is her chance, her one chance, Jacobs, to get out, you selfish effing *rick.*

COs pride themselves on knowing what is going on but they don't have a clue. There's a Vietnamese inmate, Nguyen (border security), so tiny he looks like he's about 12 years old. COs are always worried about him because he's so freaking small. Some of the Asians do Chinese medicine on each other with small stones from paddock.

Nguyen was coming down with something and went crazy rubbing himself all over with a stone, and asked another inmate to do his back so his entire body was covered in bruises.

CO: Tran, Wang, you're coming with me.

Tran: Why?

CO: We know you've been laying into Nguyen. We've seen the bruises.

Tran: Sir, you've got the wrong idea, it's not what you think—it's Chinese medicine.

CO: *What sort of idiot do you think I am, Tran? There's no doubt in my mind he's been beaten and you've had it in for him since he got here.*

So Wang and Tran both got tipped because Nguyen had a cold.

Jason Bird was granted parole. Have so much admiration for his self-awareness. One of his parole conditions (20 years) was a ban on alcohol and he requested they make it a lifelong ban.

Me: *Really? For the rest of your life? I don't really drink but what if you want to have a Baileys and milk or something?*

Bird: *Baileys and milk? Who drinks Baileys and milk?*

Me: *I do.*

Bird: *Mate, I wouldn't go telling anyone that if I was you, especially round here. And if you'd seen me after I'd been drinking, you'd put in a request as well.*

Thanks for the photos, esp. of Lexie's drawings. That girl is a craft machine.

And I know I have already asked for so much but would mean the world to me if you could wait till I'm out to watch the rest of Breaking Bad. *It's not on in here.*

I love you.

Paddy

P.S. Can you please ring Amar and ask what is going on with the appeal? If their case loads were too big and they can't start on it yet, they should have told us.

P.P. S. Please record and engrave all our personal items with our details.

THIRTY

There's no doubt that day-to-day life without Patrick had a much heavier sense of drudgery. It was like ploughing a field (I imagined, having never actually ploughed a field). Up and down. Up and down. Doing the same thing over and over again. But the anxiety caused by the significant events left me longing for the predictable.

'I *don't want* to go to the Father's Day concert!' Lexie yelled, having worked herself into a frenzy. I'd explained, many times, that she didn't have to go to the concert. I offered to be a stand in for Patrick, or she could come to work with me or we could go out for ice-cream. But none of the scenarios appealed to Lexie. She was furious her dad wouldn't be there, and even more furious that, post concert, she couldn't give her handmade craft and chocolate crackles to him. Even Grace's dad, who lived in a kingdom far, far away, could receive his gift by mail.

After much angst we reached an agreement that Lexie would go to preschool for the morning, and I would pick her up at midday, before the concert started. But when I got there Lexie had spent the morning practising the songs and wrapping the chocolate crackles and didn't want to leave. I was delighted to see she'd had a change of heart, but I was neither dressed nor emotionally prepared for seeing the other parents.

'How's Patrick?' one of the other dads asked, and the question filled me with dread. I didn't want to lie but he was not in the inner layers of our circle. We only crossed paths at school functions and kids' parties, and our children weren't close friends.

'Good.'

'Still working from home?'

'Not at the moment.'

'Oh, don't tell me that. Can you ask him if we could have lunch, talk business?'

The afternoon was peppered with similarly elusive and nerve-racking conversations. Every time Lexie yelled 'Mum!' I experienced a mild panic that she was going to blurt out Paddy's whereabouts. But she didn't. She sang the songs and ate Patrick's chocolate crackles with a blustering enthusiasm.

Not only did Lexie enjoy the concert, she noticed the absence of several other fathers. Of course, there was Grace's father, but Isla's dad was sick, and several other fathers either had to work or were separated from their partners and were not able to make it.

Nick's birthday is in October and in a moment of weakness, I had agreed to a pool party/sleepover. All the preparations were in place. I'd bought the food, including ingredients for a Millennium Falcon birthday cake, and Nick's tight circle of friends and parents all knew about our situation, so there was none of the apprehension that normally accompanied social functions.

'You seem like you're doing okay?' I said, tucking him into bed on the eve of his birthday.

'Yeah, I feel happier.' Nick's outlook had improved exponentially. John had helped him channel the rhythms and the emotions that had been building inside of him into his drumming. He'd also given us some exercises to help him release his tension, like me holding a pillow while Nick punched it. Plus, I'd outsourced the wrestling to my nephew Sam, who babysat one night a week, and he had Nick begging for mercy.

'Are you still going to see Martin?' I asked Nick. He was the school literacy teacher and someone Nick felt very close to.

'Yeah, he's a good listener, tells jokes and he's gluten free,' he said, as though this last were a prerequisite for wise counsel.

'I'm glad you can talk to Martin, but is there a reason the need strikes every Monday morning, during orchestra?'

'Orchestra makes me feel sad.'

'Really?' I glowered at him.

'Mum, the violins sound like dying cats!'

'I don't want you taking advantage of Martin's good nature, seeing him just to get out of orchestra.' Nick smiled his beautiful crooked smile.

'You okay about Dad not coming to the party?' I asked, brushing the side of his face with my hand.

'Yeah,' he responded, his mood suddenly pensive. 'I wish he could come, but I'm okay.'

'You know you can tell me . . . if there's anything bothering you.'

He looked down at his feet and then tilted his head back up to look at my face. 'There is one thing,' he started, and stopped, clearly embarrassed. Even though he was only turning eight, I wondered if the question might be about a girl. I'd heard from Lexie that different girls had crushes on boys. And I wished Paddy were here to navigate us through the conversations.

'I'm worried . . .' he ventured and I held his hand in support, letting him know I loved him no matter what, 'that you'll wear your bikini to the party.'

'I don't wear a bikini!'

'You do sometimes.'

'Not when people are over,' I said, relieved. If that was his main worry, things were going brilliantly.

The pool party was a great success, thanks to my nephew Sam, who spent the best part of three hours wrestling eight year olds into the pool. At one point, when he was fending off ten other boys, it occurred to me that hiring out a teenage male could be the answer for many boys craving fatherly affection. Certainly the idea was fraught with insurance issues but his presence made for the easiest party I have ever hosted. The boys were completely enthralled with Sam, and come bedtime, they were so exhausted they slept like babies.

It was a long grind to Christmas, and as it drew near, both Nick and Lexie, who seemed to have adapted to our new situation, were distressed that Patrick wouldn't receive anything for Christmas.

'Don't worry about me,' Patrick said, wiping the tears from Nick's face, in the first part of what turned out to be a very interesting visit to Mannus. 'I don't need presents. Andrews in the kitchen is making us fish and chips.'

Nick looked unconvinced but his melancholy quickly vanished with the arrival of Cody and Crystal.

'Before you go,' Paddy said, 'Andrews' kids are coming today—'

'Yeah, I know. Please, thank you, no excluding. I got it,' Nick said, edging backwards towards the door.

'That's good manners,' Paddy said, holding Nick's arm, 'but they're coming for the first time and he asked me to have a word with you because he hasn't told them this is a prison.'

Normally it was difficult to tell what Nick was thinking, but on this occasion, as his eyes moved from the various signs to the CO who was walking brusquely through the room, not to mention all the green tracksuited men, I could tell verbatim.

'He told his kids he's been working overseas and the company makes him stay in a camp,' Paddy continued.

'That doesn't explain why everyone's wearing green . . .' Nick wasn't so much critical as confused.

'He told them it's an army camp,' Paddy explained.

'It's not even camo or khaki.' Nick knew about the difference because, prior to his incarceration, Patrick had been in the Army Reserves. 'He lied . . . to his kids?' he asked.

'Not real—. Well, yes,' Patrick said.

'Why?' Nick asked.

'I don't know . . . maybe he thought it would be easier that way.'

It hadn't occurred to Paddy and me not to tell the kids that he had gone to prison, but, thinking about the events of the past few years, I could see how much easier my life might have been if we had.

'We're not asking you to lie. Just don't say it's a prison,' Paddy said, as Nick circled the room with his eyes again.

'I won't say anything, it's definitely an "army camp",' he said, using his fingers to indicate inverted commas. Paddy and I laughed, not just at the absurdity of the situation but because it was the first time either of our children had managed to use that gesture appropriately. Our little boy was growing up.

During that visit, Lexie took a tumble from the play equipment and a large egg-like bump appeared on her forehead. We soothed her with words and cold water but she continued to cry hysterically. So I went to the office to ask for an icepack.

'We don't have any,' replied Popovic, unmoved.

'Look she's injured, as you can hear. I've tried everything and she needs an icepack,' I said, appealing to his blank expression. I didn't want to leave the centre, because visitation rules prevented same day re-entry.

'Are there icepacks anywhere else in the jail?' I asked. 'For when the inmates hurt themselves?'

'Yes,' he replied, unable to make the connection.

'Any chance you might be able to radio someone to bring one up?' I asked, as politely as I could manage, and he agreed.

Soon afterwards, a female CO arrived at the visitors centre, with an icepack and a chocolate bar for Lexie. She was lovely, and stayed with us until Lexie was back to her usual exuberant self.

Later in the afternoon I asked Popovic if I could fill our used water bottles and place them in the office freezer for Lexie on the trip home.

'Can't have people freezing clear liquid. Could be vodka,' he said. I didn't respond. There was no point arguing, clearly he'd been handpicked from the Mensa Society.

Throughout the course of the day, Nick provided us with updates on the army camp scenario. 'They still think it's a camp,' he said at lunch, and, 'They said their dad doesn't call much because he's in a remote area with high mountains, and no reception.' At the end of the day, after we'd said our goodbyes and wished each other a merry Christmas, Nick said, 'I didn't say anything . . . to the kids . . . they don't know it's a jail.' A contemplative beat followed. 'They must be stupid kids.'

The late December trip to Tumbarumba provided several other happy coincidences that helped in the lead up to Christmas. Lexie had been insistent we buy a Christmas present for Patrick when we walked past a small shop displaying an eclectic array of wares, including a circular rack of forest-green tracksuits. I couldn't for the life of me think why anyone in Australia would want to buy one. But then I recalled that my father had once owned such a tracksuit and had rather unwisely chosen to wear it to visit a mate in the local prison. A wardrobe choice that caused a great deal of confusion for the guards on duty that day.

Though Patrick was only allowed to receive new and sealed socks and underwear from family members, Lexie was delighted by the serendipity of it.

Further along the street, outside the main supermarket in town, we saw the female CO aka the croissant and cracker Nazi.

'Hello,' the CO said, as I began descending into panic.

'Hello,' I managed, before remembering that I was in a public place. And, as far as I was aware, she had no jurisdiction. I could fill my trolley with all the pastries and crackers my heart desired.

'Down this way for Christmas?' Her question seemed friendly enough but our previous interactions made me wary.

'We're going to Grandma's. She lives in Muswellbrook,' Lexie said.

'That sounds nice,' the CO replied and I wished that Lexie hadn't given anything away. 'What would you like for Christmas?' she asked Lexie, while Nick eyed the cans of drinks and lollies in the specials baskets outside the shop.

'I would like a cat but Mum said I have to be realistic, so I'd like my own actual cooking utensils,' Lexie said and I noticed a smile creep onto the CO's face. Lexie had a way of charming people with her candour, often receiving comments and, on some occasions, gifts.

'Would you like to be a chef when you grow up?' the CO asked, as Lexie began the chin-rubbing thing she now did habitually. And at that moment I felt confident that the CO would finally see our core family values: hard work and education.

'It's not definite,' Lexie said. 'It's a toss-up between a waitress on roller-skates and a cat.'

'A cat?' the CO said, laughing.

'Yeah, they just laze around most of the day.' Which struck me as ironic, because Lexie has never been interested in lazing around. She woke at the crack of dawn and went like an Energizer bunny all day until she collapsed into bed. And I had no idea where Lexie might have heard about waitresses on roller-skates.

'Sounds like you've got it all figured out,' said the CO, uncrossing her arms. 'I hope you get those actual cooking utensils.'

'You're making the right decision,' the CO said to me after Lexie had joined Nick to stare wistfully at the soft drink. 'Prisons are no fun at Christmas and no place for families. I hope you can still manage to have a nice time,' she said. And for the first time I saw her humanity. It can't be easy being a correctional officer. Even in a minimum-security facility like Mannus I had witnessed some inmates and their families being aggressive to the guards.

'Merry Christmas to you as well,' I said.

Nick and Lexie still loved Christmas. The food, the presents, the extra people, were a great distraction. I was the one who found it difficult. Christmas is a time when most people set aside their petty squabbles and travel from all over the countryside to spend time with people they love. I was stronger than I'd been at the start of the year but being in the company of people I rarely saw, even though they were people I liked very much, only amplified Patrick's absence.

THIRTY-ONE

Mannus Correctional Centre
27 December 2013

Beauty,

Glad you still had a good Christmas with your mum. Nick and Lex sounded upbeat. Thanks for organising the presents from me. Nick said he loved the blow-up boat and Lex the 'actual real life' cooking utensils and a fluffy toy with large eyes (cat?). As if she doesn't have enough!!!

Couldn't call again Christmas Day. 2+hours queue for phone and also called Mum. Guys who don't usually use the phone wanted to make calls.

Glad you visited the week before Christmas. Overbooked. They turned many people away. Lots of guys lost it (smashed things). Andrews in kitchen made an effort to make a Christmas special (fish and chips) and I made chocolate mousse for my unit with buy up money. We aren't allowed sugar but yoghurt and Nutella works well. Not as good as yours, though.

New inmate named Ravi. Singular talent for antagonising people. Started saying pro-Israeli things to the Lebanese. Went down like a hand grenade. Instant enemies.

Everyone has delusions about their own abilities but Ravi's are astronomical. There's a prison book club where inmates read and discuss books (you would love it!) Shantaram *and Steve Jobs biography are like rites of passage in here. Glen (v. smart) inmate librarian is happy to order books for people. Only lets me borrow one at a time and only thin books (max 250 pages). Said I'm too slow.*

For reasons obvious to no one except Ravi, he is convinced that he is cut from the same cloth as Steve Jobs.

Ravi: After finishing the book I can't help but think that Steve Jobs and I are exactly the same.

Me: Oh yeah, how so?

Ravi: We are both visionaries. Both of us think outside the box, believe in taking risks and LSD.

Me: Steve Jobs created the most successful business on the planet and you're . . . well . . . we're in prison.

Ravi: I see your point but, apart from that, we're identical.

Exactly the kind of insight you want in a CEO of a company. Inspired by Jobs, Ravi is starting his own social media company.

Ravi: It's going to be bigger than Facebook, bigger than Twitter.

Me: Oh yeah, how's that?

Ravi: It's like Facebook but you can do groups.

Me: You can do groups on Facebook.

Ravi: (disappointed) Really? Well, that's what's known in the business world as a setback. It's still going to be huge. Net worth prediction: twenty billion dollars.

Me: Good for you.

Ravi: I'll let you buy a share for two hundred and fifty thousand dollars.

Me: That's an outstanding return but I'm afraid I have to decline.

Ravi: Are you telling me you don't want to share in twenty billion dollars?

Me: I'm asking this purely for business purposes but don't you still owe hundreds of thousands of dollars to a Colombian drug cartel?

Ravi: A trifle, a . . .

Me: And do I recall you saying that, at a low point, you snorted all the drugs you were meant to sell?

Ravi: That is in the past. I wouldn't do that now, with your money. I can assure you, you have my word.

I'm not reassured.

We can order buy up food and cook in unit with others. Men often share, like a partnership. Ravi offered to be my partner. Made him three meals (bacon and eggs, hamburgers and stir-fry).

Me: So what are you making for the rest of the week?

Ravi: Oh, I don't have any money for buy up.

Me: You do have money. Everyone has to work.

Ravi: Well, I need it to buy cigarettes.

Me: Well, I need to get something in exchange for the food I'm buying for you to eat.

Ravi: In exchange, you can have my friendship. (No deal.)

Jason Bird left during the week. Didn't say goodbye to anyone. Didn't want people to know. Something about his sentence brings out the worst in people. He didn't want to get involved in any fights. I know some people may think he should stay in forever but I think he's done his time and I'm glad I met him. I didn't know who he was before but he made me a better person.

Hope I can still make a difference or a change, even a small one. But I'm running out of ideas. Have tried sharing buy up, visitors, teaching English??? Nothing seems to work.

I love you.

Paddy

P.S. Gave in to peer pressure and let Bella go with Tom.

P.P.S. Can't believe Clogs told you I should be on a tighter leash. How much tighter can it get? I'm in jail!

4 January 2014

Beauty,

Thanks for the photos. The kids have grown so much.

Guy here from New York (border security). Was in tight spot (minimum wage) in US and agreed to carry drugs. Listened to conversation with US guy and other experienced border securities.

Inmate: So what route did you take back to Sydney?

American: I flew from Argentina.

Inmate: No one flies straight from Argentina, may as well have had a sign at the airport.

American: Yes, well, I know that now.

Inmate: How much were you carrying?

American: Two grams.

Inmate: That's nothing—

American. Yes, well, I know that now.

Inmate: And how much did you earn?

American: Five thousand dollars.

Inmate: You were the mule, mate. You were the mule.

American: Hindsight is a very valuable thing.

Most people in here are pretty self-controlled but everyone has their moments. Mine occurred a few days ago. Glen (librarian) was getting under my skin and I lost it and called him a spastic. Don't think I'll ever hear the end of it.

Inmate 1: Don't get on Jacob's bad side. He went totally postal.

Inmate 2: Really? What happened?

Inmate 1: Went off his nut at Glen and, brace yourself you won't believe the language that came out of his mouth, couldn't believe it.

Inmate 2: Whaddid he say?

Inmate 1: Called him a spastic.

Inmate 2: Oh, c'mon, taking things too far.

Inmate 1: Control that potty mouth of yours, Jacobs.

Inmate 2: Language, Jacobs, language. We'll have to wash your mouth out with soap.

Received v. sad news today. Bella died. Got hit by a car outside Tom's studio apartment in Bondi. Many inmates more distraught about Bella than finding out about lost appeal, break-up etc. Don't know why they were so desperate for Bella to go when she was such good support for everyone here.

Love you so much,

Paddy

THIRTY-TWO

'Mum, you know Dad?' Lexie asked.

'Yes, I know Dad.'

It was a sunny day late in autumn. Most of the leaves had fallen from the large magnolia tree next to the deck in our backyard. Lexie and I had just finished painting each other's toenails, and were sunning ourselves like the cat she still coveted.

'I can't remember his face. I close my eyes and try to remember . . . but . . . he's like that towel,' Lexie said.

'What towel?' I asked, rubbing a late-blooming magnolia leaf between my fingers. The front was waxy green, and the brown back had the texture of velvet.

'On the pool fence . . . he's fading.'

Five minutes before, Lexie had been singing her rendition of a pop song, exchanging the word *you* for *poo,* and the next she was saying quite possibly the saddest thing I'd ever heard.

Lexie was only six years old and yet she had managed to articulate precisely what I was feeling. When Patrick left, we spoke to him and of him so often, doing our best to include him in our lives. We looked at pictures of him, and I'd blown up a photocopied picture of his head and attached it to an enormous inflatable bat.

The kids had talked to it and played with it until, one afternoon, it snagged on something sharp, and deflated.

There were still pictures of Patrick on the walls and bookshelves. We'd tried to listen to the bedtime stories he'd recorded, but he viewed punctuation as being a matter of personal preference, and charged through books without the necessary pauses. After suffering through several of his recordings we gave up.

We spoke to Patrick for approximately five minutes every afternoon, and saw him once a month when we made the pilgrimage to Mannus, but Lexie was right—he was fading.

It was difficult to say when this had started to happen. It was a slow submersion as he disappeared from the minutiae of our lives. When it became difficult for me to recall his scent, and for Lexie, his features. If I had to pinpoint a time, I would say it happened somewhere between when the appeal was heard, Valentine's Day 2014, and six weeks later, when the judgement was handed down.

So much was riding on the appeal. We had sought advice from a new Senior Counsel, Barnaby, and his junior, Dario. We retained Amar because of his existing knowledge of the case. Barnaby's estimate was a possible reduction in sentence, between six and eighteen months.

We were fortunate that our business continued to be profitable, thanks to James, and to my nephew Dylan, who had started working for us, and that by appealing we wouldn't lose our house or be forced to live below the breadline, unlike so many other women I had met in our situation. James offered to loan us some of the money for the appeal, insisting that we only pay him back when we were able.

The appeal was heard at the New South Wales Supreme Court in Sydney. 'Banco Court,' said the official at the information desk before I'd even asked a question.

'Sorry?'

'You're here to be admitted to the bar?'

'No, I'm here for the Jacob appeal.' I said.

He apologised, and directed James and me up to the thirteenth floor. As I rode the elevator I realised how much my soul was crying out for the eighteen-month reduction. I imagined bundling up the kids in the car and driving straight down to Mannus to bring Paddy home.

Amar was already there, talking to two other men. I recognised one of them, Dario, from his chamber's website, and assumed the other one was Barnaby, the SC. I bounded over to greet them. The barristers turned in to each other and away from me, like human elevator doors. In a panic, Amar stepped forward to separate me from the men. The barristers were like Old Testament gods, not to be approached directly.

We waited for several hours while another matter was heard. It was different from the local or the District Court. Three judges sat at the front of the room and, despite it being the Supreme Court, some things were more informal, almost as if we were privy to their private discussion.

During our proceedings, Patrick's good friend Dave arrived and sat down next to me. 'Sorry. Got a warning about courtroom decorum,' he said. His long hair and colourful shirt made him an unlikely looking law student.

At one point, an issue arose about the number of firearms related to the charges. Patrick was said to be in possession of two firearms, not one. I sat in the front row of the gallery, waiting for someone from our team to object or clarify the point, and not one of our three lawyers said anything or even seemed to have noticed the mistake.

I'd grown more assertive in the past few years and quietly called out, 'Amar, Amar.' At first, he seemed to think it best to ignore me, but then looked around disdainfully before starting to wave his arm, as though he were swatting away a fly.

In the recess, I raised the issue with the team and Dario said, coldly and indifferently, 'It's just another detail.' While it might not have been the very crux of the case, it was not just another detail to us. It was our life, our future. We'd borrowed thousands and thousands of dollars to have the appeal heard in the Supreme Court, we'd sought advice about the best counsel, had meetings and sent and read correspondence, and yet, if I hadn't followed up on this point, it would not have been rectified. I didn't know if the legal team weren't familiar with the fundamental details of the case or if they simply didn't care.

At the end of the proceedings, the barristers deigned to speak to me again. 'It went better than I thought it would,' Barnaby said, his large paunch bursting through his black vest. 'Be quietly optimistic,' he advised, 'but remember that, in there,' pointing to the courtroom we had exited from, 'is the realm of disappointment.'

I was aghast. The realm of disappointment? We had made our decision to appeal based on a letter from Barnaby and Dario that had advised us he had a reasonable expectation of it succeeding. Now, after all the time and energy and cost, he decides to tell me about the realm of fucking disappointment? I was livid, even as I recognised that Barnaby was trying to manage my expectations.

It took me weeks to shake the feeling of unease from the appeal. Then, at 2pm on 23 April 2014, the judgment was handed down. In legal terms, the appeal was a success, as many of the charges were overturned, and the court agreed that the remaining sentences were manifestly excessive and therefore should be reduced. And as I sat in a small room in the Supreme Court filled with hope, I learned that Patrick's sentence had been reduced, but only by six months. Still, six months is six months. It was only when I realised that there were still nine long months to go that he started to quietly slip away.

Unlike Lexie, I could still remember Patrick's face. His dark, almost-black hair and eyes, his high cheekbones, his thick lips, and the crescent-shaped scar just above the middle of his eyes. For me, it was his scent that eluded me. Sometimes I thought I caught a whiff of him and then, almost immediately, it was gone.

To my mind, we become not only the stories we tell ourselves but also the stories we tell each other. When Patrick first went away, everything was so painfully hard and out of kilter, but we changed. Our little family of three had adapted and, ever so slowly, his starring role in our lives diminished.

Most of the kids' stories spilled out spontaneously, rather than in the contrived environment of the recorded phone conversations or the visitation room. Lexie's stories were now about her new best friends—identical twin boys Tate and Curtis.

'Tate's a good friend,' she said at dinner one night. 'Today when we were running, he slowed down, so I could beat him.'

'He does sound like a good friend,' I agreed. But when she was finally granted permission to tell the two boys about Paddy, she was hurt by their response.

'I told them, like, the worst thing that has happened in my entire life and they didn't say anything. And then Tate completely changed the subject.'

Interestingly, the twins' father had the same reaction when I told him before the kids had their first playdate, though their family did welcome Lexie with open arms.

When the kids did share their stories with Patrick, a gap remained. Patrick had never met Tate and Curtis, and they hadn't met him. Patrick rarely came up in their regular conversations anymore, and when he did, the kids regarded him with distant awe, the way they might an elderly relative. At dinner or when visiting friends, the kids liked to tell the same stories over and over again, but after that first Christmas apart, none of the stories involved Patrick.

Around that time one story dominated. We were at a dinner party at my friend Pamela's house when her son Ollie asked why we had decided to send our children to an alternative school. I gave a long, impassioned speech about how it nurtured creativity and imagination, and how, from a very young age, the students come to understand who they are. Then Ollie said, 'So what sort of person are you, Nick? A leader, an explorer, an artist?'

And Nick replied, 'Me, I'm a person who cheats at maths.'

The kids told this story many times, and they told it to Patrick on a visit, and he laughed, but it didn't have the same impact because he wasn't there.

There was no trace of Paddy left in the bedroom I'd shared with him. After the disappointment of the appeal I made some changes. I painted over the original tangerine walls with fresh white paint, bought a new white bed and side tables, and new linen, and covered the wall behind our bed with grey and white birch tree wallpaper. It was so light and I would stay up late reading. Books had always meant a lot to me but since Patrick had gone, books had meant everything. After I made dinner and bathed and read to the kids, I would hole myself up in my beautiful new bedroom. Immersed in someone else's story I no longer had to think about the sadness of mine. Like old and new friends, the words amused and delighted, soothed and counselled me. I was alone but not lonely.

I'd become used to being a single parent. I made all the decisions about where I went and what I did without having to consult with anyone. I could stay at dinner parties until I was ready to leave. No one asked me to turn out the light when I stayed up late reading. I ate lighter meals, of soups and salad and sushi, I could wear my threadbare Cottontail undies every day of the week. I could stack as many decorative cushions on the bed as my heart desired. Then, just when things had settled down, and everything seemed calm and smooth and manageable, they changed again.

'Hey,' Patrick said, when the American-accented recorded message finished.

'Hey.'

'Work release is approved. I'm being transferred to Sydney— Parklea.' His voice charged with excitement.

'When?'

'Tomorrow.'

PART V

'IF YOU WANT TO SEE THE BRAVE,
LOOK AT THOSE WHO CAN FORGIVE.'

Bhagavad Gita

THIRTY-THREE

'The fences are so high,' Nick said, crestfallen. We were standing outside Area 4 of Parklea prison in Sydney, holding a large bag of Patrick's work clothes. It had taken him five days to reach Parklea after setting off from Mannus on the milk run. I'd noticed something different in his voice when he called from Parklea, though he assured me he was fine. 'No green clothes, please, if you can,' he'd asked me.

'Is that the visiting area?' Lexie asked, pointing to the small, square, covered concrete area in front of the main building.

'I don't know, Lex,' I said.

'Hope not,' she said as an extremely tall CO walked out to unlock the gate and escort us inside.

'Shouldn't you be at school?' the CO asked Nick, eyeing him with friendly suspicion.

'I was sick,' Nick said.

'Was?'

'This morning.'

'What was the matter?' the CO asked, genuinely interested.

'Hypochondria,' Nick said, as though he were stating a proper malady.

'You're honest, I'll give you that,' the CO said.

I handed the CO the clothes, and we all stood as he painstakingly recorded every item of clothing, including brand, size and colour. From our vantage point in front of the office, I could see into the main quadrangle. It was brick and concrete and had two storeys; similar in design to the public high school I'd attended. I could see men in green, jogging. Not surprisingly, Patrick was not among them. It was strange, though, knowing that he was only metres away, beyond a wall, but we weren't allowed contact.

In Area 4, Parklea, visits were only held on weekends.

'Excuse me, but is that the visiting area?' Nick asked the CO, pointing to the same covered area Lexie had asked about. It contained a sink, a vending machine, and a small waist-height fence that ran around the perimeter of the area, giving it the appearance of an animal pen.

'Sure is, buddy,' the CO responded.

'Excuse me,' Nick said again. 'Can I ask you another question?'

'You can ask.'

Nick took a moment to decipher his response. 'Will I be able to walk on the grass over there with my dad?'

'Sorry, mate, that's not for visits.'

'Can Dad walk around there other times?' he asked hopefully.

'I thought you said one more question . . .' the CO joked. ''Fraid not, it's out of bounds for everyone.'

'Even you?' Nick asked boldly.

The CO smiled. 'Great kids you've got there,' he said.

'They have their moments,' I replied.

'Can't be easy, what you're doing,' the CO said, as he continued recording the items of clothing.

On the way out of Area 4, I said to the kids, 'I know it's not Mannus, but we won't have to travel, we'll be able to see him every week.'

'I s'pose,' Nick said, unconvinced.

'I don't like it either but maybe we can try and think about it from a different perspective. In one of my favourite books, the main character says he could have fun with his special person even in a Turkish prison.'

'But then we'd have to go all the way to Turkish,' Lexie said, completely missing the point.

'Turkey,' Nick corrected.

'I don't want him to be in a Turkish prison, or any prison. In the book, the man was trying to say to the women he loved that it didn't matter where they were as long as they were together,' I said, unlocking the car. I could tell from Nick and Lexie's expressions that, after traipsing around various prisons, they thought my suggestion was ludicrous.

The following weekend, we joined the long visitor queue outside the fenced perimeter of Area 4. Visits were held in two-hourly blocks at the weekend, from 8.30am to 10.30am or 12.30pm to 2.30pm. We'd booked in for the latter. On the drive over to Parklea, the kids had decidedly changed their tune about the visit. Interestingly, it was not because of my pearls of wisdom or because they wanted to see their father; it was because of the Area 4 vending machine. They'd spent an inordinate amount of time discussing the merits of a Mars Bar versus Cadbury Marvellous Creations.

Visiting a different prison is almost like visiting a new country. Each one has its own rules and procedures. Unlike Mannus, Parklea didn't allow you to take anything in, except for coins for the vending machine, and once the visit started visitors were not allowed to use the toilet. Phones and prescription medication weren't allowed on

the premises and personal items, like wallets and car keys, were
to be placed in lockers on the other side of the fence.

As the line grew longer I noticed we were the only unmarked
ones. Everyone else was covered in colourful, cursive, exotic-looking
tattoos on their arms, necks and legs. We looked like blank pages.

'Maybe we should get tattoos,' I whispered to Lexie.

'Can we? Can we really?' she asked, jumping up and down.

'When you're eighteen. You can get "Mum" on your neck or
the side of your face.'

'As if,' Lexie said, rolling her eyes.

The afternoon was long and hot. The line continued to grow,
snaking over the internal road that led to the main part of the
prison. The kids leaned against me in the heat, until I couldn't
hold their weight any longer.

'Go and read the sign,' I said to Nick, who was now reading
fluently.

He walked down to the gate, skim-read the sign and walked
straight back. 'This jail is so restrictive, you can't even have leaves!'
Nick said at children's volume, a much higher level than required.
As a result, the rest of the line began to titter. Nick looked up at
me quizzically.

'You know the leaf on the sign? It's a marijuana leaf. A type
of drug,' I whispered.

'I didn't know,' Nick said, burning with shame.

'I'm glad you don't know what a marijuana leaf looks like,
you're eight years old!'

At 12.37, seven minutes after the visit was due to start, a round-
bellied CO with a cockney accent approached. 'Didn't you folks
get the message? Visits are cancelled today.'

The mild annoyance I was feeling turned to fury. How can they
do this? I raged inside.

And then I noticed that the CO was unfolding a small card table and an assortment of stationery. It wasn't until he passed a bundle of green visitors' forms through the gate that I realised he wasn't just a CO, he was an aspiring comedian.

We progressed in the queue and, at around 12.50, it was our turn to be processed. The comedian/CO, who was now seated at the table, checked my driver's licence and Medicare card against my form. Then it was time for the contraband spiel: no mobile phones, prescription medication, prohibited weapons of any kind, alcohol, sharp implements, paper money . . . Then I had to place my handbag in a plastic bag, and a different CO scanned us with a hand-held wand.

In the small office across from the visiting area my ID was checked again, and placed in a pigeonhole for easy access during visits. I was given a key for a locker, and everything except a total of twenty dollars in coins had to be locked inside it.

'Dad!' the kids chorused as Patrick emerged at the entrance of the visiting area. We took turns hugging him and then sat around the small table. Nick mumbled a perfunctory greeting and spent the next few minutes rubbernecking the vending machine. Lexie refused to say hello because she hadn't been allowed a chocolate bar, as she hadn't finished her sandwich which had to be left outside.

'How's school?' Patrick asked, with more enthusiasm than the question warranted.

'Good,' Lexie said, without any enthusiasm.

'Not good,' Nick said, craning his head to see past the queue.

'Tell me three things I don't know about your day at school yesterday,' Patrick said, using a technique we'd used in the past to try to get Nick to communicate.

'I didn't go to school yesterday,' Nick said.

'Me neither,' Lexie added.

'Why didn't you go to school?' Patrick asked the kids. And then me, 'Why didn't they go to school?'

'Nick had growing pains in the night, and I was up massaging him and running a bath, and in the morning I was just too exhausted.'

'You need to be tough on them,' Patrick said, and I felt a pang of resentment.

'Can I get a chocolate now?' Nick asked.

'Wait till the line dies down a bit,' Patrick suggested. Nick sighed and Lexie twisted angrily in her seat.

'Have you got any new Pokémon cards?' Patrick asked Nick, holding his hand.

'Not into that anymore,' Nick said, unenthused.

'What about new rocks or fossils for your collection?' Patrick asked.

'Don't collect them anymore.'

'Because Graham said he could take us to that property near Cessnock again . . . the one with all the fossils.'

'Yeah, that'd be good,' Nick said, unconvincingly, before joining the vending machine queue. 'All the good stuff's gone,' he said, having returned. 'There's only Bountys and Picnics, and cans of tuna.'

'There must be something you can have,' I said, heading back with him to the vending machine. We walked past other men, some of them the size of bears. The energy of the place felt menacing and dangerous.

The kids were right; the vending machine was almost empty.

'Must have been cleaned out from this morning's visit,' I said.

'You don't say,' Nick replied, sarcastically—something that was dangerously close to becoming a habit.

'What about chips or a soft drink?' I suggested.

'There's only plain mineral water and salt and vinegar.'

'Well, they're the choices. You can have something here or I can get you something on the way home.'

Nick bought a packet of salt and vinegar chips and a Bounty for Patrick. They were demolished quickly and the conversation stalled. It was not like Lexie to be lost for words but again, in a contrived setting, loaded with so much expectation, she didn't utter a word. When I was on the phone or at a bank counter or speaking to another person, I couldn't get Lexie to stop talking. And here, with her dad, who wanted to hear her talk more than anything else in the world, she was deathly silent.

There were no card games, or pens and paper to play Mr Squiggle or Pictionary, the game the kids had grown so fond of. So we improvised. We played a guessing game by drawing pictures on each other's backs. The kids, who are both very ticklish, warmed to this, and soon enough Lexie was in the mood to talk.

'You know Tate and Curtis from school?' Lexie began.

'Not yet but I'd love to meet them—'

'Well, they're identical, which means exactly the same but that's not actually true—'

Bang! Bang!

Lexie's story was interrupted by the sound of an inmate hitting the table and then yelling. A CO rushed over to discipline him. At the same time a woman wearing a Shine badge accompanied two boys to another table to sit with a brawny man almost entirely covered in tattoos. Paddy's sister Clare had told me about Shine. It offered onsite child minding, a play area, and a place for parents to drop in and unwind.

'You were saying that Tate and Curtis are identical . . .' Patrick said, trying to reignite the conversation, but the moment was gone.

'Why is that woman talking to the wall?' Lexie asked.

'Because Abbass, her husband, broke some rules. He got caught with drugs, so he's not allowed to have face-to-face visits anymore,' Patrick explained. 'He's behind the wall, she's talking to him.'

'Is he in time out,' she said.

'Yeah,' Patrick agreed.

We continued improvising with words games and drawing on each other's backs until we ran out of steam. Nick and Lexie had both become more mature since Patrick had first gone away, and were aware that asking to go or complaining about boredom would hurt his feelings. So, very discreetly, they whispered they wanted to go home.

As 2.30 approached, we said goodbye to Patrick and joined the queue to leave the visitors' area. At first I wondered why the exiting visitors were lining up.

'Jones clear,' a CO called, standing in the doorframe of the adjacent building, his black-latex-gloved hand ready for action.

'Abdulla, clear,' he called, and Abdulla's family exited the visitors' area.

We waited until a CO called, 'Jacobs, clear,' to indicate that he had been searched and we were permitted to leave.

'We should go and check out the kids' play area,' I suggested to Nick and Lexie.

'No offence,' Lexie said, as we walked beyond the car park to the small grassed area where Shine was located, 'but that jail is the worst, most horrible place in the entire world.'

'No, it's the most *boring* place in the history of the world,' Nick weighed in.

'I agree it's not that fun, but I don't think it's the *most* horrible or *most* boring. I reckon there're worse places,' I said.

'Yeah, like what?' Nick said, with the cynicism of an embittered old man.

'What about a volcano, or a snake hole, or a . . .'

'Toilet,' Lexie said. 'Like, actually *inside* the toilet . . .'

'Yeah, we get it,' I replied.

'Orchestra's more boring,' Nick added and I gave him a playful hug.

We walked up onto the balcony of the play area and knocked on the door.

'And who do we have here?' asked a woman, her voice as smooth as caramel. She looked to be in her fifties; her hair was swept back into a large bun.

'This is Nick and Lexie, and I'm Mel.'

'Barb,' she said warmly. 'Let me show you round.' I could immediately tell that Barb didn't have a job, she had a vocation.

The first room had a couch, a TV and a DVD collection, complete with all the necessary cords. There was an excellent variety of books and toys for all ages, and a large cage with brightly coloured budgies. 'And I bet you like drawing,' Barb said to Lexie.

'As a matter of fact, I do love drawing,' Lexie said, taking Barb's hand, as she led us through to the adjoining room. 'I like painting as well, but my favourite thing—' Lexie stopped abruptly, sensing the shift of energy in the room. Inside, were three other children: a young girl, and two boys with long rat's tails. The eldest boy wore old, stained clothes that looked more like rags, and the youngest boy, who, at a guess, would have been two, was wearing only a T-shirt. The three children didn't say anything but they were hostile. Nick and Lexie both tensed with fear, the way I'd seen them do in the presence of aggressive dogs.

'Where's your nappy gone?' Barb said to the youngest boy.

The girl, who was wearing a skimpy purple dress, responded to Barb, with words I could not understand.

'Excuse me for a moment,' Barb said, 'while I get a nappy for the little one.'

As soon as Barb exited the room, the youngest boy gave us the bird, and the eldest ran his finger across his neck, presumably suggesting we were going to die.

We'd been to a maximum-security prison visitation room, in the presence of men convicted of murder, manslaughter and armed robbery. But being in a room with those three small children scared me more than anything else I'd seen. There was a wildness in these children's eyes. Something so volatile and unpredictable. If someone told me they'd been raised by wolves, I would have believed them. Even with the violent energy of the visitors' room, there was a sense of restraint. Whether it was because the men knew the rules and the consequences of breaking them, or whether it was the presence of the guards, I don't know. I shuddered at the horror these kids must have already seen in their short lives.

Nick and Lexie both looked up at me.

'Want to go?' I asked, already knowing the answer.

'Yeah, youse can fuck off,' the older boy said.

I thanked Barb, and we walked out of the centre in silence. It was only later, when we had driven out of the prison gates, into Sentry Drive and onto the M7, that Lexie said, 'Mum, you know how you said that there are worse places than visiting Dad?'

'Yes.'

'That kids' play place is, like, infinity times worse.'

THIRTY-FOUR

Parklea Correctional Centre
5 June 2014

Beauty,

Thanks for work clothes and going to the effort to buy new blue ones. Such a relief not to be in green. Used to be my favourite colour.

Thanks also for the joggers.

Inmate: What brand are they, Jacobs? Your wife get 'em at Foot Locker?

Me: No, Costco—$26.

Inmate: So, it's over?

Me: No, why?

Inmate: Only a woman who doesn't love you would buy shoes like that.

Got back from work release to discover that someone has designed name and logo on the back and sides of joggers. Winners.

Relief to be on work release each day. So grateful to James for organising the warehousing job for me. Coming back at end of the day is hard as men locked up with nothing to do. So much pent-up anger and aggression and nowhere to channel it.

Day 3 of work release, stuff moved to cell with ice addict. Sleep impossible as he leaps around cell like Parkour maniac. Finally stopped moving but noise of him scratching skin is unbearable. Have to leave at 5.45am to catch the first bus to work. Catch two buses and train and same back.

Major problem with me going to work release is my stuff is being taken out of the room. Not able to lock it. Reported to COs but they don't care.

Me: You might not realise but the clothes and food are mine. See, it has Jacobs clearly labelled on it.

Inmate: (laughing) Yeah, we realise, that's why we took it— What are you going to do about it? (laughing even harder)

Have tried to make my letters to you light-hearted but v. hard to find positives about this place. So dispiriting. Privately run. Poor resources. No sporting equipment. No educational programs for people in my section (Area 4). Not a shred of evidence supporting rehabilitation. Can only assume is for profit and not people.

Men who are readers are discouraged about state of books. Approx forty? (Old and uninspiring). Inmate loved High Fidelity, The Fault in our Stars, About a Boy *and esp.* The Book Thief. *Maybe being in here and loving books, it really spoke to him. Said I should read it, but too thick, will have to wait for movie. Inmate put in request for Zusak's other book,* The Message??? *But denied. CO said inmates 'a) aren't interested in books and b) as thick as two bricks'. Can you leave some more books with James when you drop off lunch food? Can take in one book per day (down pants). Inmate can't wait for me to get back. Reads a book a day—more than you. Maybe when I get out you can write a book called* The Book Smuggler!

Meant to be able to cook food we purchase from buy up but no utensils or cookware etc. Sporting equipment/privileges taken away each time someone breaks a rule. Men are so depressed and angry. I understand tough love or zero tolerance, or whatever they like to call it, but there must also be some incentive to do the right thing. Morale so low, surely evidence that it's not working. Their spirits have already been broken. I believe it's why so many of them have turned to drugs. DOC doesn't consider why. Don't look deeper. If they did, might question why they are in so much pain.

Saw Current Affair-*type program on TV about paedophiles that are required to wear ankle bracelets. Show reported ankle device equals paedophile. After program, bus driver on the way to Blacktown station refused to say hello or even look at me. Previously always greeted me. Bracelet visible with shorts. Need to wear shorts because it is so hot lifting furniture in the warehouse.*

I know visitors area is small and boring for kids. Highlight of my week seeing you all. Understand if too hard for kids, though.

Hoped I could make a difference to someone's life in here. Even in just a small way but I haven't managed to do anything. Haven't even made a dent. All I want to do now is survive.

Love,

Paddy

P.S. Put application in for weekend release so everything will be in place for when I'm eligible, last weekend in Nov. Counting down the days. Can you please make sure the pool is good to go? My neck is killing me and can't use Tiger Balm or Deep Heat or anything, floating in the pool always helped.

P.P.S. James told me story of Tom having posted on Facebook wanting someone to deliver a package from Bondi to Darlinghurst —he's a funny one. I believe he wants to turn his life around 100 per cent but don't go picking up any packages from a convicted drug dealer!

THIRTY-FIVE

It'd been nineteen months since Patrick went away. Things had settled down into a routine and I was closer to acceptance than I'd ever been, but events like excursions or children's parties filled me with anxiety. Before he went away, I'd regularly volunteered at school to do reading, and had been on excursions. I still volunteered one afternoon a week but had explained to the kids that, for now, in this season of our lives, I couldn't do any more than that.

Nick had an excursion coming up and he was at me to go. I juggled a few things around at work so I could make it. On the morning of the walk, the large group of students and a handful of parents had gathered at the start of a trail in the national park in Wentworth Falls.

The students were instructed to apply sunscreen before we set off, and while a few students grumbled one pale, freckled-faced boy downright refused. A bout of scuffling followed as the mother, Kerri, attempted to apply sunscreen as her son arched back to avoid it, causing her to trip over a branch.

Kerri looked the way I had felt so many times since having children: exhausted and embarrassed. I loved Nick and Lexie with such passion and ferocity, but at times they felt like emotional vampires, sucking every last bit of energy out of me.

I offered Kerri my hand.

'Not easy, is it?' I said as Kerri wiped her the dirt and sunscreen from her pants.

'No,' she said curtly, 'especially when you're a single parent! You've got no idea.'

I barely knew Kerri, or any of the other parents since I'd stopped doing school pick-ups. Our sons weren't friends and I didn't know the first thing about her life, but it was interesting that she'd made an assumption about the apparent ease of mine.

'Last year and a half's given me a fair idea,' I said. We were at the back of the group, the students listening to a safety talk.

'What do you mean?'

'You haven't heard?'

'Have you split up?' Kerri asked.

I was shocked. All this time, I'd assumed that everyone knew Patrick had gone to prison and, naturally, spent every waking hour talking about us.

'No, but that would be easier to explain,' I said, taking a moment to decide whether or not I should tell her.

'Well, I haven't heard anything.'

'My husband . . . Nick and Lexie's father . . . well, he did something really stupid, to do with prohibited weapons'—no matter how many times I said it, it didn't get any easier—'and . . . he's in prison.'

As I'd come to expect, Kerri winced and then just stood there, stunned, as though I'd slapped her. It was like in one of those movies where a person is frozen in time and everything else moves around them.

'I'm so, so sorry,' she eventually said, grabbing my arm.

'It's okay, not your fault,' I said, feeling even more shame and embarrassment than before I told her. I wondered if she thought Patrick might have hurt someone, so I said, 'Luckily, no one was injured . . . but he broke the law . . .' The group started moving forward but we stayed in our spot as it thinned into a single line.

'I mean, I'm sorry because all this time I've looked at you . . . and it's just that you look so calm . . . so together.'

'Me, together?' What a laugh that was. We started on the trail. Thick spiralled ferns brushed my legs.

'Yeah, I've always thought you were perfect,' she said. All this time I'd been riddled with insecurities about the shame of our situation, worried that other people were judging us, and now someone was telling me my life looked perfect.

'Well, rest assured, it hasn't been easy.'

'Do you need any help? I could take the kids one afternoon . . . or we could meet for coffee?'

'Thank you, that's really nice, but we're good.'

'I still can't believe it!' Kerri said, shaking her head in disbelief. 'I would never have known.'

I realised then that it's true for all of us. We're all icebergs, I remember thinking, so much deeper than what we appear on the surface. I'd looked at other people's lives, thinking that they looked easy or perfect, or simply better than mine. But none of us can possibly know the disappointment, heartbreak or struggle in someone's life unless we share it.

'You know,' Kerri continued, her voice suddenly a whisper, 'my brother went to jail.'

'I'm sorry to hear that—' I said as Nick appeared at my side. 'Nick! Hi, do you want me to walk with you?'

'Nah, I just wanted to make sure you're still here,' he said and ran ahead to his friends.

'It was a long time ago,' Kerri continued. 'Hardly anyone knows.' She'd gone from being snide, to an acquaintance, to sharing her heart with me.

When Patrick first went to prison, I noticed the words 'jail' and 'prison' the way you notice something after it is brought to your attention. One day you'd never even thought about it, and the next, it's everywhere you go: in conversations, books and TV shows. More often than not, the word 'jail' was part of a joke, a punch line. 'Wouldn't want to end up in jail,' I'd heard people say. Or, 'I've gotta see my parole officer,' I'd heard one man joke to another. One night I went to a comedy club with friends and every single act had a prison joke.

For some people, prison is their line in the sand. 'I can cope with pretty much anything else, but prison I could not do,' a former colleague said to me one day about her teenage son's difficult behaviour. And at a kids' birthday party, a mother who'd heard about someone fostering a child whose parent was incarcerated said, 'I mean, what hope does a child have if their father is in jail?' Neither of those people knew about Patrick's situation.

As time passed, and I shared my story with more and more people, some of them also shared their stories with me. About ten others told me they'd had a brother in prison at some point. My hairdresser told me her son had done time after becoming addicted to ice, and an acquaintance told me her husband did weekend detention after he was in a farm accident that resulted in a death. None of us want to come right out and say, 'Nice to meet you, my husband [or my brother or my boyfriend] is in prison,' but when we do tell our stories, we form a connection, a bond.

A woman I'd met at Mannus had told me that after her husband went to prison, she was forced to return to work in an entry-level position in order to support their seven children. Another told me that her side of the family completely turned against her husband, refusing to even shake his hand after he'd been released.

Of all the people who knew about our situation, there was only one who treated me differently because of it. I was at a barbecue in my hometown. All the guests knew about what had happened with Paddy, and when they asked me how I was or how things were going, I told them honestly.

I'd tried to start a conversation with Matthew—someone who'd grown up on the same street as me—and he promptly shut it down. His body language was brusque, and whenever I spoke, he turned away from me or swiftly changed the subject.

'What's up with Matthew?' I asked Mum later at her place.

'Why?' Mum looked uncertain about what to say.

'What?' I asked.

'He . . .' she began and stopped.

'Tell me!' I insisted.

'He told his mum . . . he doesn't want to have anything to do with you anymore,' Mum said, 'because of Patrick.'

'No!' I said in disbelief. 'Really?' Though I hardly saw Matthew anymore, at one point in my life he'd been like a brother to me. His reaction was only one out of so many other generous and kind and graceful ones. And I told myself that it didn't matter. That it didn't hurt. But it did . . . it hurt like hell.

THIRTY-SIX

When I was a university student, a popular piece of graffiti was 'A woman needs a man like a fish needs a bicycle.' At that time of my life, and in the first half of Patrick's second year away, I began to think there was some truth in the phrase. It had come to feel like we had always been a little family of three. I'd settled into work and James continued doing such a fantastic job that he joked I almost had one of those businesses where I go in and pick up the cash. The kids were great, I was happier, and then, virtually overnight, our house began to fall apart. The oven stopped working, the dishwasher made the dishes dirtier than before they went in, the side gate fell off. The pool turned green. Possums moved into the roof and our chicken coop became infested with rats. Even though we living in a house, it began to feel as though we were battling the natural environment. Like it was relentless and impersonal. As soon as one thing was fixed, another broke.

I tried to deal with some things myself. I replaced the screw in the side gate, which lasted, at most, a couple of days. I bought and set traps for the rats, enticing them with peanut butter and bread. I managed to catch two on the first try and then had the unpleasant job of killing them. But my other repair attempts proved unsuccessful, and I finally conceded that I needed someone else to fix things for me. I didn't care who it was, but every single contractor turned out to be a man.

Had Patrick been there, he wouldn't have been able to fix most of the things either, but he would have helped to book and coordinate the jobs. Our friend Simon fixed the side gate; another friend, Rob, replaced the faulty kitchen tap, and the flyscreens that possums had ripped apart; and Dylan, a qualified carpenter, made some repairs. And I was grateful for their help, but when it came to the pool and the oven and the dishwasher, I needed to call the experts. Which was, it seemed, a full-time job in itself.

It was one thing to book in a contractor or a technician and quite another for them to actually turn up. When I described the problem to the pool man, he advised me to turn the pool pump off, and, after a spate of rain and then hot weather, the pool turned into a green swamp. He eventually came and fixed it, and almost as soon as he left, the pool and the vacuum stopped working and I had to call them out again. And, sod's law, when they returned to inspect, the vacuum was working again.

Soon afterwards, a shelf broke, a kitchen drawer got stuck, and a tree fell down in the backyard. Simon and Rob were both away, so I called various handymen. Some never showed, and others quoted but I never heard from them again. Then a friend told me about Hans, a young man who had started his carpentry apprenticeship in Norway before coming out to Australia.

Hans, like most other tradesman I'd encountered, was not interested in small, quirky jobs. So, my friend asked my permission to tell Hans about my situation, in the hope that he'd have some sympathy for me and complete the work. I agreed and Hans came over the following day.

'What'd 'e do?' he asked, his voice muffled by the screw in his mouth.

'Linus didn't tell you?' I asked surprised, as I held his coffee, watching him work on Nick's bedroom shelf.

Hans was now holding several more screws in his mouth and just shook his head. It felt strange, I knew next to nothing about Hans, and yet he knew the beginnings of something so personal about me.

'It's to do with prohibited weapons,' I said. The words no longer carried the sting they first did. I thought that would be the end of Hans's questions, but my answer piqued his curiosity.

'Two years is a long time,' he said.

'Yeah, but you get used to it,' I said, clearing some of Nick's comics from the floor.

Things were quiet for a while as I gave him a hand holding the shelf in place.

'So when you see him . . . when you visit . . . is there a place where you . . . ?'

I knew what Hans was driving at—he, like many other people, wanted to know if we were able to have sex.

'I'm not sure what you mean?' I said, feigning confusion. It was a very audacious question, considering we were strangers. If he wanted to know the answer, at the very least he could say it.

'When you visit, is there a room where you can . . . you know?' Hans, a tall, burly man, who, by the look of his biceps, spent every waking hour at the gym, apparently could not bring himself to say the word 'sex'.

I continued to play dumb, so Hans resorted to the universal language of gesture. There he was, a strapping grown man, moving his index finger in and out of a circle he'd made with his thumb and forefinger.

'I take it you're referring to conjugal visits, sex? Unless that's some weird thing you do in Norway?'

He nodded sheepishly.

'No, we don't,' I said, 'not that it's really any of your business.'

He gave another abashed smile before shaking his head and saying, 'Man, how is he surviving?'

How is *he* surviving, what about me? I thought. 'You're single, aren't you? What do you do?' I asked.

The tables being turned, he wasn't keen to discuss his obviously non-existent sex life either.

Hans was still working when I returned from picking Nick and Lexie up from the bus stop. They wanted to watch him work and loved his 'funny' accent. Inspired by the show *Horrible Histories*, they made up a chant that went along the lines of 'The Viking way, the Viking way, the vicious, vicious Viking way.' Under normal circumstances, I would have told them to stop, but I figured he deserved it.

Hans completed his repairs and the electrician repaired the oven, but the dishwasher and the pool remained unfixed. Then the toilet cistern broke, and that's when I started to really resent the house. It wasn't just the maintenance, which was part and parcel of being a homeowner, it was the memories. The good memories of Patrick being in the house had all but faded away and the bad ones were magnified.

When I had first walked into our house, I'd been taken by the feel of the place. I liked the way the kitchen and dining area opened out onto the backyard. But now, after all that had happened, when I stood in the kitchen I remembered the policemen looking down at me. It was impossible for me to answer the front door without remembering the police standing on the porch. Sometimes, even a knock at the door brought back the feelings of intimidation.

And it wasn't just those places in the house, it felt as though all of the hurt and anger and grief had soaked into the walls. Being anywhere in our house except for the newly renovated bedroom just depressed me.

'Why don't we move?' Patrick suggested one afternoon at Parklea, after I told him how I'd been feeling.

'Maybe, when you get out,' I said, holding his hand. We would have to sell our house to buy something else, and it seemed like an overwhelming task to get our place ready to go on the market and then to move. The kids weren't with us on that visit, and I hardly knew what to do without them there to correct and coax and bribe.

'May as well look,' he said, 'you never know.'

The week after our conversation, as I was about to throw the papers into the recycling bin, the real estate section caught my eye and I flicked through. I wasn't expecting to find anything but there, taking up half a colour page ad, was the house I'd always wanted. It was old but it had good bones, and a separate studio. It was in need of updating but that could wait. I rang the agent and he told me that the contract for the house had been signed that morning. I couldn't believe it. He took my details and said he'd let me know if the sale fell through during the cooling-off period. In an instant, I had gone from absent-mindedly flicking through the real estate section to feeling as though some other buyer had swindled me out of what was rightfully mine.

'It means there's something better out there for you,' my friend Jen said over lunch one day.

'You're right,' I said, but I didn't believe it for a second.

'Picture what you want,' she said. 'Close your eyes and picture it, and it'll come to you.'

Later, when I closed my eyes and thought about what I actually wanted, I couldn't see a roofline, or doors or windows, or a shed, or any particular style of house. All I could see, all I wanted, I was surprised to learn, was somewhere completely surrounded by trees.

Several weeks later, Hamish, a real estate agent, was sitting at my kitchen table. He'd come to appraise our house. On the off chance the other house fell through, we would be ready to put ours on the market.

'Do you have acreage? Anything backing onto bush? Doesn't have to be a house, just something with trees,' I asked.

'Blocks are pretty rare these days, it's mostly built out,' Hamish said.

When he left, I started searching a real estate website. I scrolled down through a number of listings to one I hadn't seen before. It was a block of land in Warrimoo not far from where we lived, and it was listed with the agency Hamish worked for.

I drove straight there. It was located at the end of a cul-de-sac, backing onto the national park which was almost completely covered in trees. Eucalyptus gums, turpentines, banksias, and so many other types that I hadn't yet had the pleasure of acquainting myself with. The block itself was steep, mountain-goat country, but it was beautiful. I drove into the national park and down to a lookout.

There was a large boulder that connected to a big escarpment. The view was magnificent. As far as the eye could see extended a deep valley filled with trees, and a creek that snaked around the bottom of the mountain. I was used to looking up at trees, but standing on the rocky outcrop, I was seeing them from high up.

The way birds do. The canopy was a patchwork of green, as thick and comforting as a blanket.

I thought back to that day at Silverwater, to the moment when we'd all been transfixed by the sky. I'd thought then that the sky was the polar opposite of a prison, but I realised then, in the park, that the sky was only one element of it. It was nature: the dirt beneath my feet, the rocks, the trees, the birds and the bugs. Everything untouched and untamed.

Due to the incline of the block and the fact that services weren't connected, it was reasonably priced—approximately half what our house had been valued at. I called James to ask his advice, and he told me that if I thought it was what Patrick would want, I should make an offer. I did and, later that night, Hamish called to say it had been accepted.

Then, several days later, he called me to tell me that there were several other interested parties, so if I still wanted the property I would not only have to increase my offer but sign the contract immediately. And therein was the problem: Patrick wasn't able to sign the contract straightaway.

I called a solicitor to ask how to proceed. She told me that to secure the property, I would have to sign without a cooling-off period, meaning the purchase was locked in. Until we sold the house, I would need to use the equity we had in it, but if we didn't get the financing for the sale approved, we would stand to lose the deposit.

The real estate office was tiny. It had a large purple feature wall, a table and two round chairs, which Nick and Lexie sat on, eyeing off a large bowl of M&M's.

'Is there somewhere we can talk?' I asked when Hamish appeared in reception.

'It'll have to be here, I'm afraid,' he said.

I looked over at the young receptionist as Hamish thumbed the belt loops on his trousers, hoisting them up to his waist. 'Okay, look, um, I don't know the first thing about you and . . . so I'm going out on a limb here . . . my husband can't sign the contract just yet . . . because . . . well, he's in prison.'

Like every other person I'd told, Hamish recoiled, and the receptionist looked like she'd just witnessed a car accident, but I'd come this far. 'I know I could have lied and told you he's overseas or that he's been deployed with the army, but I wanted to tell you the truth, because it's connected to why I love the property so much.'

'The last couple of years have been really tough . . . and going to see him . . . in there . . . made me realise just how much I love nature . . . I'm guessing from your facial expression you've never been in this situation, and, believe me, I never thought I would be either . . . which is not to say you will,' I added quickly, 'but I'm hoping you can remember what it feels like to be disappointed or to have your world fall apart . . .'

My monologue ran out of steam because of the disturbed look on Hamish's face. I'd obviously made a fool of myself and of him. At least the kids were okay. They were focused on eating as many M&M's as humanly possible.

It's not meant to be, I thought.

'What did he do?' Hamish asked, hoisting up his trousers again. It was a pretty valid question under the circumstances. I imagined he wouldn't call in any favours for a cold-blooded killer or a man who blows up buildings.

'Yeah, sorry, I should have said.' For some inane reason I started thinking about the worst possible thing I could say to Hamish and I started laughing.

'What's so funny?' Hamish asked.

'He killed the last real estate agent who didn't help me!' I said, still laughing.

Hamish laughed nervously until I explained that of course I was joking. He only tortured the agent, I thought of saying, but decided against it.

'Nothing like that,' I said. 'It's . . . it's to do with . . .'

'Paperwork?' he asked.

'Something like that,' I replied. 'Basically, he was . . . an idiot.'

And Hamish laughed enthusiastically, as if recalling a very specific period of idiocy.

THIRTY-SEVEN

'What are you doing tomorrow?' a friend asked at dinner on the eve of Patrick's first day release.

'What do you think she'll be doing,' another friend answered on my behalf. 'Having sex!'

In the week leading up to his 'big day out', it was all my friends could talk about. Many of them had offered to take the kids for the day, or the afternoon, or an hour, until finally my sister-in-law Fiona offered to walk the kids out to the letterbox and back. 'That'll give you enough time, won't it,' she laughed as if it was the funniest thing she'd ever heard.

With the exception of the Norwegian handyman and a few close friends, no one had asked about the conjugal visits, but it's human nature to be curious about such things. And as the day visit drew near, I began to think about it as well. It had not only been so long since we'd been physically intimate, we weren't emotionally intimate either. He told me that he loved me, and he wrote me letters but they were mostly anecdotal or requests for my ever-increasing to-do list.

Because the kids became so distressed after their visits to Parklea I had stopped taking them. Naturally, Patrick missed us but he didn't want to unnecessarily upset the kids and encouraged me to do what I thought best. So, it had been some time since I had seen him. I didn't feel connected to him on any level anymore and the thought of him coming back to the house we had once shared filled me with apprehension.

'Okay, okay, we can cry,' Lexie said. 'You've told us, like, a million times!'

I'd read that it could be very upsetting when day-release visits ended, and I wanted the kids to be prepared. It was six-thirty on Sunday morning, and we were driving to pick up Patrick from Parklea. He had approval to come home for a period of up to twelve hours. I had applied to be his sponsor, which meant that neither of us could leave the house during the visit.

We arrived at the prison, buzzed for the guards, and waited outside the wire fences until a CO escorted us to reception. Patrick was already waiting for us, wearing a blue T-shirt, jeans and his Winners sneakers. I was prepared for emotional turmoil at the end of the day but I hadn't prepared for the sight of him in his pre-prison clothes. It'd been so long since I'd seen him in regular clothes and it made me think about the past, and the usual agonising question of why all this had had to happen, but I was also relieved that he was coming home and that this chapter of our lives was finally coming to an end.

There in Area 4 reception I burst into tears, and now that I'd started crying there was no stopping me.

'Mum, Mum, why are you crying, Mum? He's coming home,' Nick said, confused.

'Sometimes . . . when you're happy,' I said, speaking through the sobs, 'you cry. It's . . . called . . . tears of joy.'

Nick looked unconvinced but the CO, who was polite and respectful and no doubt used to this sort of thing, nodded to indicate that I was telling the truth. I calmed down and signed the day visit forms, agreeing to the following conditions: we were to remain in our home at all times and switch off the internet, and Patrick was not permitted to make any phone calls, commit any crimes, handle money, take drugs, drink alcohol or drive a car, and had to remain connected to the black monitoring box that was to be plugged into the home phone line.

As soon as we walked in the door, the kids were all over Patrick, wanting him to play and share their lives with him. 'Do you want to jump on the trampoline? Can we wrestle? Do you like my drawings? Want to play Minecraft? Can I show you my lip balms?'

'Just hang on,' I said. 'We need to plug the monitoring box in and Dad wants to have breakfast.'

The kids groaned.

'We've got plenty of time. We've got all day,' I said.

I called the monitoring company, advising them that we'd arrived home and reported the box number. Patrick read the instructions on the sheet, unplugged the internet cable and plugged the monitoring box into the phone line, so the company could download the software that connected to his ankle bracelet. The woman on the other end of the line explained that the phone would ring, and she instructed me not to answer it because this was the software downloading.

'Do you mind if I have something to eat?' Patrick asked tentatively, looking at the breakfast food I had laid out on the table. It was as though he were a guest, a stranger in his own house. All through breakfast, while he was devouring smoked salmon and cheese and fresh figs and juice, the shrill sound of the phone continued.

The monitoring company called my mobile to explain they could not get a reading. I rang our telephone provider to turn off call waiting and double-checked that the modem was switched off. For two and a half hours, the home phone continued to ring as they tried unsuccessfully to download the software. By a process of elimination, we realised they couldn't get a signal because of our back-to-base hard-wired alarm. Corrective Services was notified and Patrick was allowed to stay as long as the monitoring company could continue to reach us on the landline.

After breakfast, Patrick played with the kids for several hours. They jumped on the trampoline, played cards and Jenga, and he finally got to see Lexie's extensive lip balm collection as well as the vast array of craft she'd made during his absence. While Patrick played with the kids he was happy and buoyant, but after two solid hours of it he retreated into himself like a turtle into its shell. He became quiet and completely uncommunicative, an outline of his former self.

He wandered around the house, taking it in. I thought about the way everything in your home looks after being away on holidays and wondered what this must feel like for him. He stopped in front of photos and opened drawers to see what was inside. I had lived with him in that house for five years before he had gone away, and yet it felt like he had never been there before.

As Patrick wandered down the hallway, one of the doors slammed shut from the wind and he jumped. And later when I touched him on the elbow from behind, he flinched and said, 'Don't do that.'

We sat down for lunch and Patrick listened to the kids telling him the stories they'd wanted to share with him for so long. He listened but didn't speak.

The home phone rang. It was the monitoring service again. They spoke to me, checked my ID and then spoke with Patrick to check that he was still on the premises. We joined the kids in the living room to watch *The Simpsons*. After a couple of episodes, he led me to the bedroom. He stood just inside the door for a moment, looking at all the changes—the paint, the furniture, the wallpaper and the linen.

'It's nice,' he said.

I felt nervous and vulnerable, like it was our first time. Like he was visiting my bedroom, not the room we'd once shared.

He moved a stray piece of hair out of my eyes and, with the back of his fingers, caressed the side of my face. He moved towards me and kissed me, tenderly, passionately. Our tongues collided as his hands moved down my arms to my fingertips. He kissed me again and lay me down on the bed, propping himself on one elbow beside me. In between kisses, he slowly and expertly began to undo the buttons on the front of my dress, revealing my expensive new lingerie. He unclasped my bra, moving his hands over my body, and resting on the curve of my stomach. His fingers were electric; every part of me felt alive, reminding me what I had missed. Of what it is to touch and to be touched. Soon we were moving and caressing in a way that only lovers who truly know each other can.

And then phone rang.

'Leave it,' Patrick said. In addition to Corrective Services and the monitoring company, friends and family had called to see how he was.

'But what if—' I said and Patrick put his finger to my lips. The phone abruptly stopped ringing.

'Mum, Dad, it's the people from the jail. They said you have to come to the phone right now!' Nick shouted.

We spoke to Corrective Services, answered their questions and tried to resume what we had started. Then, not even five minutes later, the phone rang again. It was Corrective Services, who explained that sometimes people try to pop out immediately following a phone call from the department.

We did eventually make love but, after all the interruptions we weren't able to recapture the level of intimacy we'd had before. Afterwards, Patrick went into a deep sleep and sometime later in the afternoon I had to shake him awake to speak to the monitoring service again. I thought that having rested, he would have been more relaxed; instead, he woke up a completely different person.

I was in the kitchen washing up. Patrick came in and started to stack the dishwasher.

'It's not working,' I said.

'Why not?'

'I don't know. The technician came and said he couldn't find anything wrong with it.'

'It's the filter. You've got to clean the filter regularly,' he snapped and forcibly pulled out the bottom rack to access the filter.

'It's not that.'

He turned around to get some paper towels from the pantry. 'It's a mess, everything could fall out!' he said, angry about the state of the cupboard.

Over afternoon tea he became very agitated. 'The house has gone to rack and ruin,' he announced.

'What?'

'You should have been on top of things.'

'I have been,' I said, wounded.

'The dishwasher's not working, the side gate is broken and the chook cage hasn't been cleaned out since I left.'

'You've been gone for almost two years. It's been cleaned out many times. And the side gate has been fixed twice already,' I said defensively. 'I think the whole thing needs replacing.'

'Well, you need to get on it,' he said coldly.

'I'm aware of that, but during the week when I'd planned to see to it, I was at the hospital with Lexie, and when I wasn't working and looking after the kids, I focused on getting the pool sorted out, because you asked me to make sure it was a priority.' The pool company had finally advised me that the pump was broken, which had, in turn, blown up the solar heating, so I had to manually clean the pool.

'I just expected that things would be in better condition,' he said without apology.

I walked down to the bathroom, closed the door and cried. I had been looking forward to him coming home but he wasn't home. I didn't know who he was anymore. He certainly wasn't himself. It was so out of character for him to get angry. I felt like going for a walk but the terms of his release prevented me from leaving my own house. Patrick's mother had applied to be a sponsor but had not yet been approved.

I splashed water on my face and told myself that maybe it was all due to the anxiety and expectation of the day. It must be worrying knowing that at any time, for any reason, he could be sent back to prison.

Patrick played Lego with the kids, pausing momentarily to snap at me about the pantry again. I bathed the kids and made their dinner for them to have in the car, and at five-thirty, I called the monitoring service, as per procedure, to let them know we would be leaving home in half an hour.

Upon arriving at the prison, I signed the relevant paperwork, and after Patrick had been breathalysed and searched, the kids and I were escorted back outside. As I turned the key in the ignition, I noticed that the car parked next to ours had a sleeping toddler in the back. I've sometimes left my kids in the car when I've run into the petrol station, or when parked outside the bakery at the local shops, but I'd probably draw the line at leaving them in the prison car park, at night.

Patrick continued to come home for his monthly day release visits. Each time, he grew more and more angry. He went from silent to disturbed, and flew into a rage over the smallest things. Finally things deteriorated so much, I couldn't see a future for us.

THIRTY-EIGHT

I was slumped on the couch in Steph's small office, feeling more disappointed and lost than I'd ever been in my life. It was only two months shy of Patrick's release date, and all the effort and the heartache that had been expended seemed to count for nothing.

I'd spent the first part of the session tearfully recalling some of the day visits. This was the first time I had seriously entertained a real kind of split—separate houses, custody arrangements, alternate Christmases with the kids.

'Do you love him?' Steph asked gently.

Days before, my sister, Amy, had asked if I was still *in love* with him, wanting to know if my heart skipped a beat when I saw him. In the very beginning, I'd been in love. I'd spent countless hours day-dreaming about him and practising my new signature.

'I don't know,' I said, tearing small strips from the tissue.

So many different things ran through my mind. We'd been married for sixteen years and we'd been in love, once, but that butterflies-in-your-stomach feeling had gone. Once I'd believed that was because our relationship had deepened into something far richer and more complex. We got married, built a life together, had children, and a house and a mortgage, and while that might not be the stuff of an onscreen love story, it was real life. And much of our life with the children involved tedious and mundane things. Stacking the dishwasher, doing the laundry, picking the kids up, taking them to sport and music. As David Sedaris once wrote about the dearth of films about long-term couples: 'Look, they're opening their electric bill.'

After the stress of the court case and the long hard slog of Patrick in prison, for him to come out and direct all of his anger and blame at me was more than I could bear. It wasn't because I didn't love him anymore; I just didn't think I could do it anymore.

'I think . . .' I started, red-faced and bleary-eyed from all the crying, 'we should get a divorce.'

Steph waited while I blew my nose and started making my way through the box of the tissues.

'It's perfectly understandable for you to feel like that,' she said.

'I didn't think him coming back . . . would be so hard,' I said, looking up again at the drawings.

'You are under an enormous amount of pressure. And the adjustment of someone returning home can be more difficult than the initial period of them going away.' I looked out the window at the date palm tree shading Steph's car. The branches sprang out from the top like leaves from a pineapple. The trunk even had a yellowish tinge and a criss-cross pattern. There was so much shade from such a small thing, I recall thinking.

'I can't give a proper diagnosis without seeing him but from what you're describing . . . it's textbook PTSD—post-traumatic stress disorder. Reacting to loud noises, polarised behaviour, flashbacks. I've worked with a lot of clients suffering from PTSD. I've worked closely with police officers and the transition back into regular life can be very difficult for them. And Patrick's coming from an intense and aggressive environment into a space that hasn't been his home for almost two years and then, unlike other PTSD sufferers, he has to keep returning to the stressful environment, to prison. That can't be easy.'

I thought about what Steph said. It was hard to imagine what Paddy must have been through. In his letters and conversations, he'd always made things sound so funny and light-hearted. He recorded any conversations or characters we knew the writer in me would find interesting. And yet, when he came home, he wasn't the Patrick from the past, or the Patrick in the letters, or the upbeat person from the visits. I didn't know what had happened to him on the inside or who he was anymore.

'You know I've never told you what to do, that's not part of the work we do together. These things are your decisions to make, but I will say this: you are both under a great deal of stress right now, and when things are like that, it's not easy for anyone to make a rational decision,' Steph said. 'It's going to take time for things to settle down, so that you can both make a decision about the future.'

I couldn't see a future. With Patrick or with anyone else. While Patrick had been away, I'd received two propositions. One from a sixty-year-old banker with a toupee. The other from an unemployed man who lived in his parents' garage. It was depressing to know that, as a yellow-eyed, yellow-toothed, wobbly woman, these were now my options. But I didn't care if I lived alone with a hundred cats, I just wanted this to end.

It would have been nice to believe that our love was strong enough to endure anything. But how long did I have to wait? We had already endured so much. The court case, and then the crucible of prison. I'd lost my faith that we could move past this.

'In my experience from counselling many other couples, marriages can endure the worst of storms. I've seen couples overcome affairs and gambling . . . all sorts of issues where trust has been broken.'

I blew my nose again, noisily.

'It takes time for something as complex and intricate as a marriage to be rebuilt.'

I'd never heard the word 'intricate' used to describe marriage before. I recalled an art lesson where the teacher used it to describe the ornate details in period architecture. The kind you see on cathedrals. We had been married for sixteen years. And I know that in itself is not a reason to stay with someone, and nor is having kids together. But they have to count for something.

I thought about how much effort I had spent on renovations or writing stories in order to make them work. And then about how little actual time I had spent on my marriage. I mean, I had stayed, but I'm talking about actual work. Often, it seems marriages are like old buildings left to crumble and corrode until there is no other choice than for them to be condemned. If a marriage is as precious and magnificent as an ornate ancient building, it would take gloved hands, careful strokes and a lot of time to restore it to its former glory.

THIRTY-NINE

'This is the third time they've lost the paperwork,' Patrick said, distraught.

'So you're not coming home?' I asked.

It was the end of November and Patrick was due to come home for a full weekend visit. Not only was it was disappointing for him but so much work had gone into preparing for it. I'd spent the day shopping and cooking and stocking the cupboards because once he came home I wasn't permitted to leave the house. I cleaned the house and the pool, and had a new phone line installed so the monitoring box could be plugged directly into it.

'The COs haven't even submitted it. So many men have missed out on leave because they don't care.'

'Hopefully they can have it approved for next weekend,' I said with forced optimism.

'That's what the COs said but they should try being locked up in here for the weekend . . . worried you're going to get stabbed in your sleep.'

It was the first time he'd alluded to any real danger and it sickened me. His letters had mentioned dark and funny things but they were always part of much bigger gallows-humour stories. He shared them with me because I continually asked him to. He'd been so insistent he was okay, that I didn't think he was in any serious danger.

'Dad's not coming home,' I said to the kids in a conversation that was strangely reminiscent of the one when I'd told them he'd gone to prison. It was another hot afternoon and they were sitting on bar stools.

'But why?' Nick asked, defeated. He hadn't said much about it, so I hadn't realised how much he was counting on the weekend release. 'Dad told me that he was following all the rules and he hasn't done anything wrong.'

He ran outside and started kicking the base of the trampoline so forcibly that the sole of his boot came clean off. Of course, Lexie was far more vocal in her protests, saying that she hated the guards and the jail, and she began, very dramatically, tearing up the drawings she'd done for Patrick.

'You can give them to him next weekend,' I said, trying to stop her but I could have more easily stopped an avalanche.

I couldn't bear the thought of eating the food we had been going to share. Preparations were underway for the Hands, Heart and Feet end-of-year performance, so I boxed up the food and took it to John and Emily.

'It's okay to be sad and angry, you know,' John said, walking us back to our car at the end of our visit.

Nick looked up to me to confirm that was the case. I nodded.

'Sometimes, when things are hard, know what I like to do?' John said.

Nick shook his head.

'Thwacking.'

'What the heck is that?' Lexie asked, and John picked up a large stick and began hitting a nearby tree, the action making a distinct *thwacking* noise. For a few minutes, the kids channelled their pent-up feelings into the whacking and afterwards they were noticeably calmer.

'Can we take the sticks home?' Nick asked.

'I don't see why not,' John said.

And the kids spent the next two days wielding sticks and thwacking. At times, I joined them, and it helped to release the tension. But no matter how many times I hit a tree, I could not stop thinking about Patrick. His words 'stabbed in your sleep' kept haunting me. I had to do everything in my power to help him.

On Monday, at Patrick's request, I wrote to Corrective Services.

To the Commissioner,

I feel compelled to write as my husband Patrick Jacob did not receive approval for his first weekend release on the weekend starting Friday 28th November. His paperwork was initially submitted eight weeks ago. It has now been submitted 3 times to date and he was told that it had been misplaced and couldn't be approved. My husband also told me that some of the guards said, 'How's being polite working out for you Jacobs? See, it doesn't work like that around here.' Another guard also said, 'Good luck with getting out at Christmas.' Family members also wrote to Corrective Services regarding the new award and the collective responses explained that Patrick would be eligible for weekend leave for the last two months of his sentence.

My husband has owned his charges and to my know-ledge has served his time without incident or trouble. His sentence has had an impact on our family and it is increasingly difficult to manage the expectations of our children after he did not receive the weekend leave. He was also told by one of the officers that as a consolation he would be granted work release for Sunday 30th November. This was not granted and subsequently I was not able to visit him in jail either as we were expecting him to be at work and therefore did not book a visit in time.

Prior to my husband's sentence I worked as a freelance writer and journalist. I have received numerous offers to write about my experience in major publications. I have declined all offers out of concern for my husband and respect for the Corrective Services. It is increasingly difficult to maintain any respect when it seems that the employees of the Corrective Services don't seem to respect the dignity of the inmates or their eligibility for leave and visitations.

I am writing this for the sake of my children only. I hope that I can continue to instil in them a respect for authority and procedure. Our children, aged 9 and 6, are scared by the atmosphere at Parklea visit centre. The intimidating appearance of some of the inmates, the nature of the language and the sometimes aggressive nature of the inmates' children has forced us to make the very difficult decision not to take the children to Parklea facility anymore. The website for Corrective Services under family support states: 'Corrective Services NSW recognises that visits to inmates in correctional centres are important to strengthen and maintain family relationships.' I am doing everything within my power to maintain our very strained family relationships and for this reason I implore that the Corrective Services does everything in their power to approve Patrick Jacob's weekend leave for the forthcoming weekend (6th and 7th December) and the following weekends until his release date. This will strengthen our family in this very difficult time as we approach Christmas.

Yours truly,

Melissa Jacob

Several days later, James called. 'It's been approved, I just got the call.'

FORTY

Beauty,

Arrived back from work release, CO's acting weird.

CO: Would you say I've done everything to help you, Jacobs? I've always submitted your forms, wouldn't you say? Remembered your request for your new shoes ... the shoes you're wearing (referring to my Winners).

New cellie explained that some inmates hassled COs on my behalf. Felt bad for me not getting leave because I'm a 'normal'.

Inmate: Is Matthews one or two T's?

CO (Matthews): What are you rabbiting on about, Crosley?

Inmate: Just fact checking for Jacobs. Want to make sure they spell your name right. You know his wife's a journalist?

CO: Yeah and I'm the King of England.

Inmate: You're f$*#ed now! Your name's going to be in the papers. Front page.

The COs told Crosley he was full of it but then googled your name and read some stories. Then, according to Crosley, they ran

274

around like headless chooks, getting paperwork signed and making calls. Crosley said they're really packing it.

With any luck, probably thanks to your stories, I'll be out this weekend.

Love,

Paddy

I'd written for many years but only worked as a proper freelance writer for a few years before Patrick went to prison. After he'd gone away, I'd tried to keep working as a writer, pitching ideas, having stories published, but coordinating interviews, and trying to keep the kids quiet when I was on the phone after my regular work had finished, but it was too much. The final straw came when I'd organised to interview Dr Dan Siegel, a Harvard-educated, *New York Times*-bestselling author, and expert in the field of interpersonal neurobiology. I had been commissioned to write an article about helicopter parenting, and was particularly interested in Dr Siegel's research on the way stimulating emotions causes growth in the integrative fibres of the brain. I'd talked to Nick and Lexie about how the more they learn, intellectually and emotionally, the bigger the bushes in their brain will become.

'What I don't understand,' Lexie said, rubbing her chin, 'is if all these people are getting giant bushes in the front of their brain, why don't you see people with enormous foreheads?'

I had chased and chased to get the interview, and was only allowed five minutes, Saturday morning, our time. The kids knew how important the interview was, and I told them not to come in unless the house was on fire. During this time Lexie interrupted me twice, first to ask if she could have a biscuit, and second to ask if she could have a birthday sleepover. To which I replied, 'Your birthday is in March, four months away!'

I felt then like I was on a stretching rack—being pulled beyond what I could bear. So I decided to stop chasing other people's stories. My own story had become all-consuming and I had no time to document anybody else's.

FORTY-ONE

'It's over, it's over,' said Patrick, rocking backwards and forwards and repeatedly striking himself in the head. It was Friday evening and we'd just arrived home for the weekend visit to discover that the newly installed phone line was dead.

'What's wrong with Dad?' Nick asked, distressed.

'You need to calm down, you're scaring the kids,' I said.

He didn't stop. He moved and stood near the glass sliding doors and continued hitting himself. Nick looked back and forth from Patrick to me.

'He's worried he might have to go back to Parklea because the phone line isn't working,' I said, trying to speak as slowly and calmly as possible. 'I need you and Lexie to go and watch TV, so we can get this sorted out.' I started dialling the number for the monitoring service.

'Who wants to play Old Maid?' Lexie asked earnestly whe she came into the room.

The monitoring company gave us forty-five minutes to resolve the issue. The phones had been an ongoing saga. The alarm had been disconnected but to ensure there weren't anymore problems I had a second line installed, during which the original line was disconnected. It took our service provider weeks to repair it and now the second line was not connected. Corrective Services weren't permitted to connect to the original line because it wasn't on the weekend-leave paperwork. I called a local electrician who'd done some work for us in the past, explained the situation, and begged him to come over. He did and, a few minutes before the deadline, reconnected the line. But, as the night wore on, I began to wish Patrick had been sent back to Parklea.

'Why aren't you using the dishwasher?' Patrick asked as I washed the dinner plates.

'It's not working.'

'I pulled out the filter last time,' he said, slamming open the dishwasher drawer.

'Yes, but it's still—'

'There's a part missing . . . where is it?' he barked.

In all the time I'd known Patrick before he went to prison, I'd always been the fiery one. I could count on one hand the amount of times he'd lost his temper. Now he was angry all the time.

'Where is it?' he demanded. 'Where is it? Where is it?'

Patrick's litany of complaints continued the following day. Chief among them was the dishwasher but he also had strong feelings about the kids having too many days off school, the need for neater drawers, and wanted to know why I didn't have an inventory of all food items so that we never ran out. For most of the day, I bit my tongue, putting it all down to PTSD. In the late afternoon, things escalated and I couldn't hold back anymore.

As I put the lunch things into the fridge, I realised I hadn't given Lexie her antibiotics for her middle ear infection. I put the dosage into the syringe and called her. Patrick had come inside and was sitting at the dining table.

'You claim to be so busy and you forgot her antibiotics. What's more important than the children's health?' he asked.

I was gutted. The Patrick I knew wasn't malicious.

'I paid a babysitter to be with Nick while I was at the hospital with Lexie until two in the morning, so don't say I don't care about the children's health!' I filled the kettle with water to make tea. 'Why didn't you take her to the hospital? Oh, that's right,' I said, 'because you weren't here.' It was a low blow but it was how I felt. 'And if you're so concerned about the bloody antibiotics, you could have given them to her. For two years, everything has been on my shoulders.'

'Don't tell me about two years. Try being in prison for two years.'

'I've done everything . . . everything while you've been in there,' I said, my voice breaking. I was crying out for a shred of validation or insight.

'You haven't done the dishwasher!' was all he said.

'It's on the list,' I replied, 'my very long list.'

'Every chance you get you have a little dig, don't you? Your "very long list!"' he mimicked. I was standing in the kitchen, leaning against the bench. It was as though all the events of the past four years were weighing on me, and I just felt tired. When would this ever end?

'You're always complaining. Every visit, you'd always find something to complain about,' he continued, rising to his feet.

'I think, under the circumstances, I have every right to complain now and then.'

'Now and then,' he scoffed. The kettle was a stovetop variety and took a long time to boil. I was surprised Patrick hadn't complained about that as well because he'd always hated that kettle. I usually didn't mind the time it took, as I loved the shape, the colour and

the sound of it. But now I couldn't wait any longer. I poured myself
a glass of red wine instead. It wasn't even five o'clock.

'What do I need to do for you? Corrective Services is happy,
parole is happy, the only one who's not happy is you,' he said. And
he stopped, as if to harness all the anger and hatred and bitterness
that was inside him: 'Haven't I suffered enough?'

'We've all suffered,' I spat.

'Suffered?' he scoffed. 'You haven't been in prison.'

'Yes, because I didn't do anything wrong! You did. You broke
the law. You tore our family apart. You!'

I was enraged. The one person who should have been able
to empathise with my situation couldn't even give me a speck of
understanding. Strangers had more empathy than he did. I wanted
to go. Get out of the house. Go for a walk or a run, let off steam.
But, as his sponsor for weekend release, I wasn't even allowed to
leave the perimeter of our yard.

I stormed outside and sat on the edge of the pool. The evening
was hot and I dangled my legs in the water. I didn't know if I loved
him or hated him. Thoughts darted at me from all directions.
I gulped the wine, kicking the water with my feet so it shot up
into the air.

A few people had said to me that they wouldn't stand by their
partner if they went to prison, but I'd stood by him. I had bent
over backwards supporting him through the court case and prison,
doing errands for him, and for other people he'd met because he'd
asked me to. If anyone had a more bizarre to-do list than I did,
I would like to see it.

I had sacrificed so much for him, for our family. My life had
been put on hold. My writing career, my freedom. Like this is what
I wanted for my life? I used to be fit, I used to be healthy. Keith

Richards is a picture of health compared with what I see staring back at me in the mirror these days, I thought.

Patrick had broken the law and there had to be consequences. I accepted that but what does it say about the prison system if he was now more messed up and aggressive than before he went in?

'Why? Why? Why?' I cried out. I hastily poured myself another glass of wine from the bottle I'd had the foresight to bring with me. Some of it spilled into the pool. It looked like blood. I'm not sure if it was the red-hued water or the anger that pulsed through me, but I thought that I could understand how people came to kill their spouses. And if it weren't for the fact that Nick and Lexie's remaining parent would be in prison, I might have.

I wished I'd never met him. But then again . . . I wouldn't have Nick and Lexie. Maybe I could have done it Lexie-style. Met him, had the kids and then got rid of him.

But the thought of him dying or leaving didn't bring me the comfort I craved. It just intensified the pain I was already feeling. And what saddened me more than anything else was that it had come to this. After all this time, and energy and effort, and after all these years, our marriage was crumbling right before our eyes.

I needed to talk to someone. I called our long-time friend Dave. He had known Patrick longer than I had, and had regularly been to court and visited him in prison, and often called me to see how I was going.

'He loves you passionately,' Dave insisted, after I told him about Paddy's behaviour towards me. He had such a way with words, and I reflected that one day he would make an excellent lawyer, or a poet. I often thought that he looked and sounded like a poet, with his flowing golden locks and dapper clothing.

'He has a strange way of showing it,' I said.

'He's a doer, a provider. That's how he shows love, you know that, Mel.'

'Yes, I s'pose,' I said, sniffling into the phone.

'Not being able to do that for you for so long, and even now not being able to handle money or use the phone . . . He's had no control over anything for so long and being so close to the end . . . it's tearing him apart. Providing for you has to count for something, I'm absolutely useless at that, ask Ange.' As a part-time law student, Dave also had a poet's income.

Dave was right. Patrick was a great provider and he loved doing things for me. On every day release, he had replaced spare keys, and refilled water bottles and ice cube trays, and recharged my phone. After one day-release visit I'd remarked to Amy, 'Patrick makes my life so much easier.' And she had said, 'That's the most ironic thing I've ever heard.'

'Are you still there?' Dave asked.

'Yeah, sorry . . .'

'If I may be so bold . . . Patrick has experienced some things and seen some things he thought best not to tell you.'

'What things?'

'I don't think anything happened, as such, but I know he wanted to spare you the details of some incidents, so as not to worry you. People think love is all about being gushing and impulsive, but restraint is also intrinsic to love.'

Dave's words gave me pause. I could see how Patrick might have thought that sparing me the details was noble. But he was wrong. I wasn't some pathetic nineteenth-century woman who fainted at the drop of a hat. I was strong. I was brave. And I could handle whatever it was he was afraid of telling me.

I found Patrick sitting on the floor of our darkened bedroom.

'What happened to you?' I asked.

'Nothing's happened.'

'I don't mean now . . . I mean inside, in prison.'

He didn't respond. He continued sitting there, looking at the wall, which was weird enough in itself. I moved towards him and he lowered his head.

'I need you to talk to me. If we're going to get through this, you need to tell me what happened.' I put my arm on his shoulder and he flinched.

'I don't know where to start.'

'Start anywhere. Start at the beginning, the end. I don't care, but don't shut me out.'

He averted his gaze from mine and, this time, stared at the ceiling.

'You don't want to hear about it.'

'I do want to hear about it—'

'You don't want—'

'I do—'

'You don't want to hear that an inmate smuggled a pen into the milk truck in case he felt like stabbing someone, or that another one hacksawed through a pregnant woman's neck, or that a man poured petrol on his wife and set her alight.'

'I didn't know . . .' I said, starting to cry. 'I'm sorry,' I continued, moving onto my knees, so I was next to him. I tried to put my arms around him but he moved away. His body was as rigid as steel.

'Or that on the way back to Sydney, in Bathurst, they put me in maxo because there was no other room. I walked out into the big triangular-shaped yard, trying to mind my own business . . . and a group of six guys surrounded me, somehow they'd found each other . . . they were talking about all the women they'd raped . . . pulling their hair . . . seeing if they cry or cower . . . the things they've done . . .' he said, his voice trembling.

'I'm sor—'

He cut me off. 'One of them moved in real close. He had brown, crooked teeth . . . all nicotine and hate . . . and he said, "How many have you done? How many have you raped?" He was smiling. And you know what I said?'

Now his voice broke completely and I was bawling too.

'Because I thought they were going to bash me, I said, "They haven't caught me for any yet!" And you know what those . . . those animals did? They cheered and high-fived because they thought I was one of them . . . I know what I did was wrong, but very soon they're going to be out . . . and walking around with you and Lexie . . . just looking for . . .' He began to cry properly now. 'And I know you don't want to hear it, because I heard it and I can't get it out of my fucking mind.'

Patrick was slumped on the floor, broken and damaged. The very lowest point of his life. I'd been so desperate for him to understand what I'd been through, when I had no idea what he'd been up against every day. It occurred to me that our experiences had been the polar opposite: I'd seen the very best of humanity and Patrick had seen the worst.

I put my arms around him and held him. He didn't hug me back, or lean into me, or rest his head on my shoulder. But I held him anyway. I held him tight. 'We will get through this. We will get through this,' I said.

And I knew then, instinctively, intuitively, what love is. It's the greatest contradiction of all. It's the ultimate surrender and the toughest battle. And I was prepared to fight for us.

FORTY-TWO

My great epiphany about love didn't make life any easier. Before the year was out, a bushfire tore through the land the agent had helped us buy. I drove straight there. Fire trucks were sandwiched along the street and a helicopter was releasing large buckets of water onto the flames.

It was devastating. Once magnificent scribbly gums felled, charred or scorched by fire. The dense green bushes and scrub now bare and black. Not all the trees were gone, but those that remained were disfigured. One enormous boughless trunk lay on its side, the coals at one end red with heat, like a gigantic matchstick. Even the agent's sign had melted.

'How lucky are you?' John said on the phone later.

'Lucky?'

'It's cleared the land. A lot of trees need fire to regenerate, it releases the seeds. The Aborigines understood this.'

In the week that followed, I walked in places and on paths I had not been able to access before. Though it was black it was remarkable to actually see the lay of the land. The centre of the block previously appeared to be just a steep, bushy slope but now a flattish, stage-like area flanked by an arc of boulders had emerged.

As I stood motionless, awed by what had been revealed, I thought about the way the fire had exposed the shape of the land, perhaps the way suffering exposes us. I thought about what John told me about regeneration. I had stayed with Patrick but I had been cold. I had been distant. And I knew then that for anything to grow between us, I would have to clear everything else away. I would have to forgive him.

There was a month to go.

'The time will fly by,' everyone said. But it didn't. Not for me. It was the final stretch but, as with most things, the last part was the hardest.

Patrick was still returning home at weekends in the clutches of PTSD. He raged and flinched, and retreated into himself; so much so it seemed like he had completely disappeared.

Finally, 28 January 2015, the date of Patrick's release, was upon us. It was also the day that Nick and Lexie started back at school. So Patrick's mother and his sister Clare picked him up, and met me in Springwood, halfway between our house and the school. I cried when I saw Patrick walking along the street in his blue jeans, blue shirt and his terrible haircut.

'It's over,' he said, holding his body close to mine. 'It's finally over.'

He was out. He was free. We had survived.

And I had been brave, I had been strong, but not in the way I'd always considered strong to be. In the past, I'd equated strength with being tough. Like an emotional armour, impenetrable and unyielding. But if the past four years had taught me anything, it was that strength is the opposite of that. It's having the courage to be vulnerable enough to tell the truth. To share our flaws, the very things that make us who we are.

'Dad, Dad!' the kids shouted when we arrived at the school, and leaped into Patrick's arms like circus performers. Without a hint of shame or inhibition, they kissed his face, felt his whiskers, and squeezed his arms and his chest as though they were checking if it were really, truly him.

Patrick had missed Lexie's candle walk, the school ritual in which parents walk with the students to mark their journey from kindergarten to Year One in the main part of the school. It was recess by the time we arrived at the school and all the other parents had already gone.

We stayed for the student assembly, Patrick and I sitting on the plastic chairs behind the students. Nick and Lexie might as well have sat facing the back wall, with all the time they spent looking around and beaming at Patrick. After the assembly, Lexie ran into Patrick's arms again and Nick hung back. He was torn. I could see that he wanted to go Patrick, but he was older now, and he had a reputation to uphold.

'Mum, Dad, are you going now?' Nick asked.

'Soon,' I said.

''Cause there's no other parents here,' he said, 'so it's a bit weird.'

At home that afternoon, Nick launched himself at Patrick. He wrapped his arms around Paddy's legs, pressing his face into his jeans as if he wanted to savour the moment. And, after he did let go, and for the rest of the afternoon it was impossible for him to be near him without touching him.

'I'm sitting next to Dad,' Nick said to Lexie, who had positioned herself so close to Patrick that she was virtually sitting on his lap.

'I am, I was here first!' Lexie insisted.

'You can both sit next to him,' I said, and we moved another setting across our long antique table. It was our first proper meal together as a family and Nick, Patrick and Lexie sat on one side of the table and I on the other.

We gave thanks for Patrick being returned to us safely, for our family and for the miracle of Patrick learning to cook. For two years we had longed to have a meal together without the anxiety of the guards or the monitoring box and now we were finally all together none of us knew what to say. Eventually Nick said, 'You should learn to cook like this, Mum,' referring to the dish that Patrick had made—Five Spice Chicken á la Zhao.

'Yeah, it's really good,' Lexie agreed. Then once again the conversation stopped. The only constant in the meal was the smile on Nick and Lexie's faces.

After dinner Patrick read to Nick and Lexie in our bed before the kids retired to their own rooms. Patrick had promised Lexie he would stay with her until she fell asleep. And when I walked up to the bedrooms after tidying the kitchen I saw her sleeping on his chest, moving with the rise and fall of his breathing, just as she had done as a baby.

When I went in to say goodnight to Nick I noticed his eyes were wet with tears.

'You okay?' I asked.

'Tears of joy, Mum, tears of joy,' he said smiling and hugging my side. And I knew then that he was more than okay. He had begun to understand the great paradox of being human.

FORTY-THREE

In the weeks that followed Patrick's release Nick and Lexie were smitten. Their absent hero had returned and he could do no wrong. According to them, he was more fun than me, told better jokes, and enjoyed playing with them more. Perhaps it was true. Patrick didn't return to work for three months and made up for the lost time taking the kids camping, abseiling, horse riding, fishing and surfing.

Patrick began seeing a psychologist to unburden himself of things he had seen and heard in prison. While this certainly helped, the thing that brought the most healing was exploring our new parcel of land in Warrimoo, learning that it is an Aboriginal word meaning 'place of the eagle.' As a family we walked trails, discovered caves and rock formations, and built and stoked many fires. And one overcast Sunday morning, we witnessed the most profound and humbling thing: tiny green shoots emerging from the blackened ground. Signs of new life.

And so too our new life began.

With each day that Patrick spent steeped in the family unit and in nature, he began to shed the hardness of his experience. And ever so slowly he softened until I glimpsed the kind and gentle man I had fallen for so many years ago.

In May, Patrick returned to work on a part-time basis, relieving me of the business and home duties and allowing me to fully immerse myself in writing. I abandoned the novel I had been working on, deciding instead to write about our lives since Patrick's arrest. It didn't take Paddy long to remember, in his new role as house-husband, that the pace on the outside is far more hectic than what he had become accustomed to in prison. He juggled part-time work, laundry, cooking, cleaning, school excursions and music lessons, and the endless thankless tasks required of parents.

After one of Lexie's characteristic outbursts Patrick said, 'Now Lexie, I think there needs to be an apology.' To which she replied, 'Yes, apology accepted,' leaving him flabbergasted.

Nick continued to be full of surprises. He continued African drumming, earning a small-fortune from busking. One morning, after receiving a text pic from another school mum, we learned of his other talent. 'How long have you been playing the violin?' I asked when he got home from school. 'About two years,' he said casually.

We learned that sometimes things are better left unsaid. When Patrick went for his first post-prison haircut, the hairdresser asked, 'Who on earth cut your hair? You let a friend, who's not even qualified, cut your hair? Why didn't you just go to the hairdresser?'

But everything else required many words or explanation. And so we continued talking about the experience, exploring new and interesting conversational terrains about parole and what it means to have your passport confiscated. Patrick finally met Nick and Lexie's friends and our new friends John and Emily, and was also surprised they are not African like he had imagined them to be.

Cracks began to appear in the perfect-pedestalled image of Patrick that the kids had held onto while he was away. His return humanised him. And it was a crushing and valuable lesson for them, as they learned that their father was not as indefatigable and fun as their imaginations and memories had led them to believe.

Time passed. We sold our house and moved into a rental property in Springwood, further up the mountains, a beautiful part of the world that not only backed onto bush, but was also home to a family of Tawny Frogmouths and one friendly wallaby. We have plans to build on our land but first we need to learn how to live together again. Lexie finally got a kitten named Mittens, who's widely regarded as the most wayward member of our family.

Patrick and I continued our friendship with Zhao and with Tom. I helped Zhao write a cover letter for a position, outlining his knowledge of financial transactions and explaining that his jail time had given him insight into the more complicated business of understanding human behaviour. Tom has promised to catch up but hasn't yet been able to find the time working two jobs that pay award-wage.

And we did eventually get to the beach.

It was late afternoon. The kids were kayaking from one side of Currarong creek to the other. When they reached the other side, Nick blocked Lexie's kayak. She disembarked, throwing a handful of sand at his legs.

'Mum, Dad! Lexie's throwing sand!' Nick yelled.

'"Tell it to the judge!"' she said, laughing and throwing another handful.

As I sat looking out on the shimmering expanse of water of Warrain Beach, Jervis Bay, perfectly framed by the sandbank to our left and the cliffs to our right, I thought about all that had transpired in our lives.

We are not pieces of puzzle, as I had once thought. We are people. Imperfect and inconstant—ever-changing people.

I would never know the answer to the question that tormented me. Why Patrick chose to do what he did. I also didn't know what triumphs or disappointments lay ahead of us. None of us do.

But I knew with all my heart that I loved him. I ran my hand down Paddy's arm, slipping my hand into his, and he didn't flinch.

I cast the 'why' into the water.

It just is.

It just was.

ACKNOWLEDGEMENTS

Years ago I recall reading an article in which Nick Hornby said words to the effect: 'People think novels slip out. They don't. You have to push them out.' This stayed with me, although I never understood the full extent of his meaning until I wrote my own book. So thank you to all the people who helped me birth this one (there were many stitches!).

For my mother, Lorraine, who instilled in me a love of books and learning and showed me what it is to live a rich creative life. For my father, Gary, the most quick-witted person I know. Thanks for passing on your sense of humour, creativity and love of good music. For Rosemary, for your grace and undying support. John, for your dedication in travelling such long distances in coming to every single court mention. And to Angie, Donna, Brendan (aka James), Louisa, Roseanne, Dave, Bernie, Doug, Neena, Grant, Mary, Dan, Ben, Kieran, Brenda, Michelle and Sandra. I am so fortunate to have a family who not only supported me while Patrick was incarcerated, but graciously supported my decision to write, not only about my life but theirs as well.

When you go through a dark period your true friends become incandescent. Thank you Frieda, Bec, Pamela, Niki, Anthony, Winton, Ruth, Mon, Beau, Ange, Simon, Kylie, Dave, Jay, Susan, Fiona, Emma, Graham, Maggie and Milena and Julianne.

Thanks to John and Emily from Hands, Heart and Feet. The Blue Mountains is so very blessed to have a group that connects people in such an intimate way. Students should be able to claim Medicare rebates for the medicinal service you provide to our community.

For those who read early drafts or fragments and/or gave advice: The Word by Word writers' group of Jen Kingsford, Arna Radovich, Shae Blizzard and Lisa Fleetwood. Thank you for your ongoing critiques and having the courage to tell me when I got it wrong. To Therese Becker, Wyndham Lewis (why you aren't a household name is one of the great mysteries of the world), Markus Zusak, Kaori Shimmyo-Goers, Rebecca Evers, Kylie and Simon McCoy, Tim Elliott, Benjamin Law, Anna Funder, Kylie Fornasier and Liam Pieper.

Thank you to the Allen & Unwin team. No doubt, the chap with the delightful English accent, Tom Gilliat, has something to do with their professional, attentive and collaborative approach to making books. To Christa Munns for your unflappable demeanour, meticulousness and for being my Clara. To freelance editor Sarina Rowell for your unerring eye for detail. And thanks to designer Josh Durham for your brilliant mind.

Thanks also to Ben Naparstek who published my work in the *Good Weekend* and first introduced the idea of writing about this experience. To Danielle Teustch/sensei who taught me how to craft a story. To Tim Elliott, thank you for your inspiring email encouraging me to keep writing, and for introducing me to Richard Walsh, who is not only publishing expert but also a trusted friend.

To all the writers whose words have moved, wooed, consoled and humbled me: Judy Blume, David Sedaris, Nick Hornby, John Green, Rainbow Rowell, Cheryl Strayed, Elizabeth Gilbert, Brene Brown, Liane Moriarty, Marieke Hardy, Magda Szubanski, Lena Dunham, Markus Zusak, Robyn Davidson, George Saunders, Steven Pressfield, Augusten Burroughs, Charlotte Wood, Jennifer Egan, Mandy Sayer, Tim Elliott, Trent Dalton and Benjamin Law, just to name a few.

To the staff and wider community at the Blue Mountains Steiner School. Thank you for holding Nick and Lexie so closely and tenderly during this time. There is much truth in the phrase that it takes a village to raise a child.

For my intelligent, thoughtful and witty son, Nick, and my sassy little dynamo of a daughter, Lexie, I am ever so proud of the way you have grown from this experience and I am honoured to have glimpsed some of the characteristics you will one day fully embody as adults.

And for Patrick, my imperfectly perfect husband, best friend and endless source of material. I hope you know I forgive you—this time from the heart.